L. A. Alford

The Mystic Numbers of the Word

L. A. Alford

**The Mystic Numbers of the Word**

ISBN/EAN: 9783337375393

Printed in Europe, USA, Canada, Australia, Japan

Cover: Foto ©Lupo / pixelio.de

More available books at **www.hansebooks.com**

THE

# MYSTIC NUMBERS

OF THE

# WORD:

OR,

FIVE HUNDRED IMPORTANT THEOLOGICAL AND
SCIENTIFIC QUESTIONS ANSWERED;

ALSO,

THE EXISTENCE OF THE MYSTIC NUMBERS,
AS REVEALED IN THE SCIENCES OF GEOLOGY, BOTANY,
CHEMISTRY, AND ANTHROPOLOGY.

BY

REV. L. A. ALFORD, D. D., LL.D.,

*Author of "The Great Atonement Illustrated."*

---

"Understandest thou what thou Readest?"—PHILIP.

---

LOGANSPORT, IND.:
PUBLISHED BY L. A. ALFORD & SON.
1870.

# INSCRIBED.

To Prof. J. Buchanan, M. D., President of the University of Pennsylvania; Rev. H. G. Weston, D. D., President of the Crozer Theological Institute, Chester, Pa.; and to the Board of Regents of the American University, Philadelphia, Pa., this work is most respectfully dedicated.

The author would also recognize his indebtedness to the Rev. S. Tucker, D. D., and Hon. H. P. Biddle, of Logansport: Rev. H. Smith, Indianapolis; Rev. L. Church and Dr. R. C. Blackall, Chicago, Ill.; Rev. F. Remmington, Cleveland, O.; Rev. T. Allen, Dayton, O.; Rev. J. B. Olcott, Cincinnati, O.; and Rev. Dr. Rowden, for kind sympathy and words of cheer.

To the best of his ability, he has desired to answer, in an easy and familiar manner, and in the shortest possible compass of language, the many perplexing questions that arise in Sabbath Schools, Bible-Classes, Pulpit Discourses, and in Science; and to so blend and intertwine the whole around the golden-threaded Seven as to obviously show its occult nature. To secure this end, the above brethren have lent a helping hand, and to their memory is this work inscribed by the

AUTHOR.

# INTRODUCTION.

That the Mystic Numbers of the Holy Bible have an *allusion* few will deny, but to what they allude is a question that has taxed the minds of the greatest Scholars, Theologians, and Geologists from the remotest records of history to the present time.

Upon the supposition that the number seven referred to *time*, and that the seven days in the week corresponded to seven thousand years, and that, as in six days God made the heavens and the earth, and rested on the seventh, so six thousand years should complete the probation of man, and on the seventh, the Millennial glory *must* commence, all the delusions of 1843 and subsequent periods have had their origin.

Notwithstanding this error in reference to the second coming of our Saviour and the close of time, the Mystic Numbers remain; their history commences with Creation and follows through every dispensation and administration to the close of the Sacred history—from Genesis to Revelation. In this discussion we will endeavor to show that the number seven does not allude to time, or its duration, but still it has an allusion.

The Mystic Number Seven, by its strange relations to matter and to man, has led to the wildest speculations and the most astonishing theological absurdities. PRICHARD, perhaps the greatest writer on ethnology, gathers all his conclusions from the mystical seven. He thus analytically divides the human skull, and draws his conclusions of races therefrom, viz.: First, the Iranian, from Iran, the primeval Persian or Arian race, embracing the Caucasian, with portions of the Asiatic and African nations. Second, the Turanian or Mongolian. Third, the American, including the Esquimaux. Fourth, the Hottentot and Bushman. Fifth, the Negro. Sixth, the Papuan, or wooly-haired Polynesian. And, seventh, the Australian.

Thus the different races have been distinguished by the formation of the cranium to seven different molds.

The earth, by Mr. Hugh Miller, has been geologically divided into seven different strata, and it is a fact worthy of notice, that there are seven channels to the intellectual mind, viz.: Two nostrils, two eyes, two ears, and the organs of speech.

Science, Nature, Man, is, indeed, robed in the Mystic Numbers of the Word.

# CONTENTS.

### CHAPTER I.
Theology—The Seven Attributes of God—Creation.................. 9

### CHAPTER II.
The Six Days' Work Continued—Seven Properties of the Atmosphere—Clouds—Tones of Music............................. 24

### CHAPTER III.
The Third Day's Work—Holiness the Creator—The Shrub—The Seven Properties of the Tree—Of Water........................... 33

### CHAPTER IV.
The Sun—Truth's Work—The Centrifugal and Centripetal Forces. 39

### CHAPTER V.
Animal Life in the Sea—Life's Work—The Fowls of Heaven...... 43

### CHAPTER VI.
Creeping Things—Beasts—Mercy's Work—Love—Man............. 47

### CHAPTER VII.
Attributes Given to Man—A Moral Being—Their Connection to the Senses....................................................... 57

### CHAPTER VIII.
Law of Life—Murder—Senses Totally Depraved—Attributes Accessible to the Spirit................................................ 62

### CHAPTER IX.
Plan of Redemption—New Birth—The Holy Spirit.................. 70

### CHAPTER X.
Man Before the Fall—Powers—Dominion............................. 85

## CONTENTS.

### CHAPTER XI.
First Dispensation—Man's Work—Cain's Wife—Relics of the First Dispensation.................................................. 90

### CHAPTER XII.
Thebes—El Kanark—Eden—Marriage—Relics of Man............ 109

### CHAPTER XIII.
God's Purpose of Grace—Covenant—The Parties—Garden of Eden Planted—Why?................................................ 134

### CHAPTER XIV.
Second Dispensation—Sons of God—Book of Revelation............ 143

### CHAPTER XV.
Covenant with Noah—Book of Job—The Two Witnesses—Babylon the Great—Vials of Wrath—The Great Battle................ 171

### CHAPTER XVI.
Duration of the Battle of Babylon—Its Fall—The Ark—Noah's Depravity—Effect of Strong Drink................................ 196

### CHAPTER XVII.
Moral Law—Decalogue—Ceremonial Law—Polygamy................ 226

### CHAPTER XVIII.
Change of Dispensation—Christ—Three Witnesses—Election.... 250

### CHAPTER XIX.
One Mediator—Satan's Work Destroyed—Lord's Supper............ 271

### CHAPTER XX.
Seven Primitive Elements—Crystallography—Elements and Attributes—Seven Liberal Arts and Sciences...................... 297

### CHAPTER XXI.
Anthropology—Man's Will—Life—Death—Resurrection............ 317

### CHAPTER XXII.
Channels of Glory—The Two Memories—Repentance—Faith...... 334

### CHAPTER XXIII.
Geology—Adam in Eden—How Long—Portals of Glory—Inosculation of Attributes and Senses—Millennium—Acceptance of the Saints in Glory—Recognition................................ 365

THE

# MYSTIC NUMBERS OF THE WORD.

## PART I—CREATION.

### CHAPTER I.

WHAT IS THEOLOGY?—HOW DIVIDED?—WHAT ARE ATTRIBUTES?—WHO MADE THE WORLD?—HOW?—THREE IN ONE—IS GOD DIVISIBLE?—THE SEVEN SPIRITS OF GOD—THEIR WORK—THE LENGTH OF THE DAYS OF CREATION—EACH ATTRIBUTE IN ITS SEPARATE WORK—THE SEVEN COLORS OF LIGHT—HOW MANY KINDS OF LIGHT?—HOW ARE ATTRIBUTES DISTINGUISHED?—LIGHT SELF-PROGRESSIVE—THE SUN'S LIGHT.

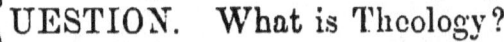

QUESTION. What is Theology?
*Ans.* Divinity. The unfolding of the Creator in his works, character, and attributes.
*Q.* What are His works?
*A.* The world and its surroundings—the sun, moon, and stars, and Man, the governor of all living creatures, and the grand object of God's special care.

*Q.* How is Theology divided?

*A.* Into *revealed* and *unrevealed;* or into *natural* and *revealed* theology.

*Q.* What is natural theology?

*A.* Natural theology pertains to the probable cause of all that we behold—the Author or Maker, as only known by the majesty, grandeur, and power revealed in the motions of the heavenly bodies, and in the conceptions and aspirations of our intellectual powers.

*Q.* What is revealed theology?

*A.* The Holy Scriptures, wherein God's person and attributes are unfolded.

*Q.* What are attributes?

*A.* They are acting mental properties, upon which the conception of a moral action is predicated.

*Q.* Who made the world?

*A.* God.

*Q.* How?

*A.* Not by an agency, nor by any delegated power, but by himself alone.

*Q.* How does revealed theology represent him to us?

*A.* By the association of the Father, the Son, and the Holy Ghost, or Holy Spirit.

*Q.* How can we comprehend three in one— only one, yet three?

*A.* By every pebble on the sea-shore, by every rock on the mountain side, and by every orb in the expanse of heaven; each and all inhere in the Mystical Number *three*, and in their entities unfold to man the unity of Deity.

*Q.* How so?

*A.* The rock is a triplicity, three in one, and yet but one, there being in its composition *substance, cohesion,* and *gravity.* These are easily comprehended by the human mind, and as no substance can be devoid, or divested of these properties, no one need doubt their application to Jehovah, who said: "Let *us* make man."

*Q.* Is God divisible? can He be divided?

*A.* Not in entity, but by association He is infinitely so. He can personify whatever he chooses, and His Creative Spirit pervades all His works, and superintends all the vast surroundings of His Throne. His works, as revealed to us, show Him in His triplicity. *First*, as the infinite center and stability of all things visible and invisible, the pillar of eternal strength, the unchanging God; *Secondly*, as the Creator of all things; and, *Thirdly*, as the Redeemer of a sin-ruined world.

*Q.* Who of the Three, that bear record in heaven, made the world and its surroundings?

*A.* The Holy Spirit, or the Seven Spirits, or attributes of God.

*Q.* What are these Seven Eyes—these Seven Spirits — these Seven attributes — the Holy Ghost?

*A.* They are *Light, Life, Holiness, Justice, Mercy, Truth,* and *Love.*

Or, as arranged in their creative work, are *Light, Justice, Holiness, Truth, Life, Mercy,* and *Love*—the "Seven Spirits of God."

*Q.* How do we understand that the Spirit of God made the world and its forces?

*A.* By revealed theology. Gen. i: 2: "And the Spirit of God moved upon the face of the waters."

If then the Spirit of God, which is the Holy Spirit, displaced the vapor of the chaotic world and began its present arrangement, with a design to adapt it to the uses of man, we see no good reason to doubt that the Holy Spirit continued the work and finished it.

We find that the Holy Spirit became the reprover of the world immediately after the fall of man, for God declares: "My Spirit shall not always *strive* with man."

Thence we learn that God's Spirit not only made the world, but became the moral luminary to all responsible creatures, and began its work, or revealed its work, of striving with man, as recorded in Gen. vi: 3.

Here we have the first and second reference to the Spirit of God. One in Creation, the other in Redemption: the first shows the Spirit's power in fashioning the earth *for* man; the second reveals the Spirit, as a reprover of the world, *in* man.

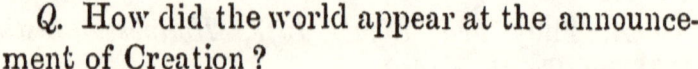
*Q.* How did the world appear at the announcement of Creation?

*A.* Chaotic—without form and void; perhaps surrounded by vapor, or covered with water.

*Q.* What was the personified nature of the first attribute, or Spirit of God, revealed in Creation?

*A.* Light. His work was to create light for all coming ages, and to so arrange that light, that the seven colors should be embraced in its matter, and that the flames of light thus created should be self-luminous and perpetual.

Thus the light created is supposed to be incandescent burning hydrogen in its essence, yet tempered by the atmosphere to the wants of those for whom the light was made. "And God said, Let there be light, and there was light."

The London Astronomer, in examining some of the photographs, taken by Dr. Zollner during the great eclipse, representing the "colored prominences" in the solar atmosphere, thus records his amazement:

"Here," he says, "is a vast cone-shaped flame, with a mushroom-shaped head of enormous proportions, the whole object standing 16,000 or 17,000 miles from the sun's surface. In the cone figure we see the uprush of lately imprisoned gases, in the outspreading head the sudden diminution of pressure as these gases reach the rarer upper atmosphere. But turn from this object to a series of six pictures placed beside it, and we see the solar forces in action. First, there is a vast flame, some 18,000 miles high, bowed toward the right, as though some fierce wind were blowing upon it. It extends in this direction some four or five thousand miles. The next picture represents the same object ten minutes later. The figure of the prominence has wholly changed. It is now a globe-shaped mass, standing on a narrow stalk of light above a row of flame hillocks. It is bowed toward the left, so that in those short minutes the whole mass of the flames has swept thousands of miles away from its former position. Only two minutes later, and again a complete change of appearance. The stalk and the flame hillocks have vanished, and the globe-shaped mass has become elongated. Three minutes later, the shape of the prominence has altered so completely that one can hardly recognize it for the same. The star is again visible, but the upper mass is bowed down on the right, so that the whole figure resembles a gigantic A, without the cross bar, and with the down stroke abnormally thick. This great A is some twenty thousand miles in height, and the whole mass of our earth might be bowled between its legs without touching them! Four minutes pass, and again the figure has changed. The flame hillocks re-appear, the down stroke of the A begins to raise itself from the sun's surface. Lastly, after yet another interval of four minutes, the figure of the prominence has lost all resemblance to an A, and may now be likened to a camel's head looking toward the right. The whole series of changes has occupied but twenty-three minutes, yet the flame exceeded our earth in volume tenfold at the least."

The same writer begs those who consider this subject to bear in mind the enormous size of the sun; so great, that if he were represented by a globe two feet in diameter, the earth would appear no larger than a cherry stone.

*Q.* Do we understand the days of Creation to each have been of twenty-four hours' duration, or periods of time?

*A.* Periods, or epochs of time.

*Q.* How many years constituted a cycle of Creation—a period—a day?

*A.* Probably a thousand years.

*Q.* Why so?

*A.* Because it would have taken that length of time for light to be transmitted to all the orbs and worlds in the expanse of the solar system, and reveal them on earth, even allowing light to travel with its almost incomprehensible velocity.

*Q.* How did the attribute, Light, accomplish this object?

*A.* By forming an imponderable body of a radiating quality, and suspending the same in mid-heaven, till other attributes had finished their work.

*Q.* Could an attribute of God create matter?

*A.* The matter of the earth was already in existence, and called chaotic in its relation to the wants of a being shortly to be created.

*Q.* But how could an attribute form *light, air, fire,* or *water* ?

*A.* Just as easy as the sense of sight can measure distances. We need not pace off the number of steps from one object to another before we can tell the distance, for we measure it by the eye; hence the eye can measure heights, the size of substances, and distances. Is not this, then, as strange as that an attribute of God should arrange the light for the eye, so that it could be in possession of a power without which the eye would be useless?

The sense of sight is also a property of the body, and an attribute is a property of Deity; then what the eye does the man does, and what an attribute of God does is done by His sovereign will.

*Q.* Was this attribute conducive only in bringing to view earthly and heavenly objects, or did it occupy a higher and nobler position, bringing to view the ever-blessed God?

*A.* It is an attribute of God, hence it is no delegated power, but is God; therefore it brings Him to our comprehension.

*Q.* How many kinds of light are there in the natural world?

*A.* Seven. This mystical number reveals itself in the Creative work of all the attributes, and indeed tends to the solution of the otherwise hidden problems of Theology by its intrinsic qualities.

It gives, in its peerless rays, the seven prismatic colors, viz: Violet, Indigo, Blue, Green, Yellow, Orange, and Red. Each of these again exhibit seven varieties, which, in respect to their gradations, are entirely equal and alike.

Still farther, the objects from which positive and reflective light appear, are also read by the septenary number, which are, Positive, or solar light; Reflex, or borrowed light; Electric, or polar light; Combustion, or fire light; Decomposition light, as seen in decayed or rotten wood; Chemical light, or phosphoretic; and Living light, as seen in the fire-fly or glow-worm. Thus we readily discover the wonderful harmony in God's creative works, even by the power of a single attribute; and indeed when the works of all his attributes reveal themselves to our astonished vision, we shall more clearly understand this fact, that all the works of God are perfect harmonies, as are seen in the intermingling of the rays of the rainbow or in the perfect harmony of the colors upon the grasses, and upon the feathered songsters, and upon the fishes, and upon the beasts.

*Q.* Are all the attributes of God complete harmonies?

*A.* They are transcendently so. Light is not in any way antagonistical to Life; but Life is aided by it, uses it, and could not perform the offices assigned to it unless it had this power by which it is illuminated.

Light and Life are in perfect harmony with Holiness; and Life, Light, and Holiness, are in perfect unison with Justice, with Truth, with Love, and Mercy.

So all these attributes harmonize together, aiding, assisting, and helping each other, and can not act in contradistinction or in opposition.

These are the *Primitive Attributes*, all others that we call attributes are only derivatives. From *Light* comes Knowledge, Intelligence, Perception, etc. From *Life* comes Power, Majesty, Purpose. From *Love* comes Affection, Tenderness, Peace, Joy, Hope. From *Mercy* comes Compassion, Pity, Forbearance, Long Suffering, Faith, Charity. From *Justice* comes Equity, Honor, and Righteousness. From *Holiness* comes Innocence, Purity, Piety. From *Truth* comes Decision, Infallibility, Unchangeableness, Authority.

All these attributes combined is Wisdom.

*Q.* With what does the attribute, Light, most harmonize?

*A.* With Justice.

*Q.* Why with Justice?

*A.* Because the attribute, Justice, made the firmament and adjusted it to the rays of light.

*Q.* Did the sun at first become the source of light?

*A.* It does not so appear, for the fourth attribute established the sun, and moon, and stars, as the bearers of Light.

*Q.* Are celestial bodies illuminated by the same attribute as are bodies terrestrial?

*A.* Most assuredly. God is the author of all light, and bestows it alike throughout all the realms of boundless space, as the Apostle hath said: "There are celestial bodies, and bodies terrestrial; the glory of the celestial is one, and the glory of the terrestrial is another." So it may be said of the light that illuminates the unseen worlds: its glory here may differ from the glory of the Celestial City, still the same attribute shines at the throne of God as the created light shines upon the world.

*Q.* Why did Jehovah pronounce the work of each day "good" at the close of its labors?

*A.* Because the harmonies of each day's labor must be recognized before the innumerable hosts of heaven.

*Q.* How are attributes distinguished from powers, faculties, or passions?

*A.* By being self-progressive and reproducing.

*Q.* Is wisdom, then, an attribute of God?

*A.* It is not; because it is the decision or resultant of all the attributes, and is infallible.

*Wisdom* could not exist were it not that each attribute of God concurs in all decisions. To illustrate: if we were called upon to decide a certain case, in which human life was concerned, it would become importantly necessary, in giving a wise decision, that we should understand the nature of the crime from every possible stand-point, lest we should be guilty of too much leniency or severity. In order to do this we must have mercy, tempered with justice, that we by our decisions show our wisdom. How much more of Deity, in whose hand is the sword or the pardon, the death or the life of the soul, the day of eternal glory or the night of eternal despair.

Wisdom, then, must be the embodiment of all God's attributes, and not in itself, a single point of observation, as it requires the active testimony of Light, Life, Holiness, Justice, Mercy, Love, and Truth to establish infinite and infallible wisdom. Hence the wisdom of God can not be an attribute, but a decision from them all.

*Q.* Is not the action of a single attribute of God infallible?

Certainly, in its single capacity, but it would not do to say that Light is an infallible attribute of Justice, but both are perfect in themselves. *Wisdom*, being the decision of all the attributes, can not be self-progressive or reproducing. The wise man hath said: "Wisdom hath builded her house, she hath hewn out her seven pillars." Prov. ix: 1. Then the building of God's wisdom is surrounded by the seven pillars of God's eternal attributes.

*Q.* Is not *power*, then, an attribute of God?

*A.* By no means, for life is the grand center of voluntary power, neither could power produce power, nor is power self-progressive.

Let us illustrate the idea of *power* being an attribute. Here is a powerful engine, it has great power; then, if the logic of power being an attribute is correct, it has a *great attribute*. But was it not the attribute, Life, that gave power to the engine? Did not the living man give it its form, condense its steam, apply the machinery, as well as make the engine entire? If this be true, power is not an attribute, but simply the result of an attribute—the work of a man.

So in God's economy, nothing has voluntary power but that in which He has placed the attribute, Life; and to the Life of God is alone due the honor of infinite Power.

*Knowledge*, also, being derived from the attributes, can not become an attribute, more than the power of the engine becomes an attribute, because the machine was the work of a man.

Knowledge is the summing up of the testimony; wisdom, the justness and necessity of the decision.

*Q.* Is Light self-progressive?

*A.* Certainly; because it is not only inexhaustive, but eternal. The French party, who made many discoveries at the time of the great eclipse, August 18, 1868, under the guidance of the great astronomer, Sir M. Jassen, made the following report in reference to light: "The first glance of the red flames, through the Spectroscope, showed that when their light was analyzed by the prism, instead of forming a continuous series of the seven prismatic colors, with which all are so familiar, it formed only a collection of bright lines, separated by wide, dark spaces. The question was settled. The flames were *self-luminous* and gaseous." If self-luminous, they must be self-progressive. So that when the sun, and the moon, and the stars are rendered opaque by the withdrawal of the light now surrounding the sun as a wave-dashing ocean, many thousand miles in depth, the self-progressive and incomprehensible volume of light will not diminish in brilliancy, for "God is Light, and in Him is no darkness at all."

Prof. M. Jassen remarks: "The entire sun is surrounded by an atmosphere of incandescent hydrogen, a thousand miles deep; the flames are elevated portions of this atmosphere, an ocean of fire, with waves many thousand miles in height." In beholding this light the Apostle remarked: "Our God is a consuming fire."

*Q.* What brought out the attributes of Deity in the development of their excellence?

*A.* The plan of human redemption, through which God designed to unfold to all sentient intelligences, and through the vast cycles of eternity, the excellences of His incomprehensible nature, that He might be the Supreme object of Love.

*Q.* Had the attribute, Light, any thing to do with the plan of redemption?

*A.* Every thing. The world was only illuminated by a substance of imponderable burning hydrogen, in the infinitely heated, incandescent state; while the attribute itself, incomprehensibly more brilliant, became the moral luminary of the world, and now "lighteth every man that cometh into the world."

By this light of the attribute only we get our impress of the Eternal God, "for no man can see God and live." This attribute, then, diminishes the overwhelming brilliancy of the throne of God by its reflex light, as taken from the plan of redemption, till we can say in the simplicity of a child: "Our Father, who art in heaven."

*Q.* How does light reproduce light?

*A.* By reflection. The light of the attribute of God upon the human soul dissipates the darkness, and brings "life and immortality to light," and this reflex light in the soul mirrors itself in the soul of another, till it can truly be said of the Church of God: "Ye are the light of the world."

## CHAPTER II.

THE WORK OF THE ATTRIBUTE, JUSTICE—THE FORMATION OF THE ATMOSPHERE—THE WATER—THE CLOUDS—THE SEVEN PROPERTIES OF THE ATMOSPHERE—THE SEVEN HARMONIOUS ATTRIBUTES—THE SEVEN TONES IN MUSIC—THE LANGUAGE OF MUSIC—MAN'S SEVEN ATTRIBUTES — INSTRUMENTAL MUSIC — THE HEIGHT OF THE ATMOSPHERE—SEVEN KINDS OF CLOUDS—THE VASTNESS OF THIS DAY'S WORK.

QUESTION. What Attribute performed the second day's labor in the process of Creation?

*Ans.* Justice.

*Q.* Why was he the second day's laborer?

*A.* Because, to construct the Atmosphere in perfect adaptation to the wants of man—to balance the clouds in mid-heaven—to vitalize the waters in all their relations to animated life—to give the life power to all waters, both fresh and salt; and in all this labor harmonize every department with the attribute, Light, required one of the

(24)

noblest as well as one of the most perfect attributes of God.

*Q.* How did Justice arrange the firmament?

*A.* By condensing the mist, and gathering it into a mysterious vessel, called the cloud; and causing this to ride upon the atmosphere, carrying its millions of tons of water, and gently distributing the same upon the earth, to prepare the aerial ocean for the rays of light, to adapt it to all the variety of colors, and to give to the atmosphere the undulating harmony of sound.

*Q.* But do we not read that Christ made all things "visible and invisible, and that by Him all things consist?"

*A.* Most assuredly, and this is just what we are proving beyond a doubt, for by "faith the worlds were made." "By the word of the Lord were the heavens made and all the host of them by the breath of his mouth." Ps. xxxiii: 6. Hence we see that God made the heavens and the earth; the "*breath*" (mind) " of the Lord made the host of them;" and the Eternal Archetype - the Mediator—made the heavens. So we see that the Seven Attributes, or Spirits of God, *is* God; the Archetypal Jehovah is God; and the Eternal, "I Am that I Am," is God; and these are the only one living and true God.

*Q.* What are the properties of the atmosphere?

*A.* The atmosphere also embraces the Septenary number, and is composed of Nitrogen,

Oxygen, Carbon, Hydrogen, Electricity, Impenetrability, and Density—Seven. It is also susceptible of seven other divisions, viz: Refractibility, Ponderability, Compressibility, Dilatability, Decomposition, and the agent of Combustion, and of the Harmonies of Sound.

*Q.* To what does all this mystical Seven allude?

*A.* To the Holy Spirit—the Seven Spirits of God—the Comforter—the attributes, who made, or fashioned, the earth for the abode of *man*, the climax of the Creation of God.

*Q.* How are the harmonies of Music explained?

*A.* By the Seven Attributes. These are harmonies in the mind of Deity, and in all their associations are harmonies in Creation; and as there can be but seven tones in music, so there can be but seven attributes of the Spirit.

*Q.* What special harmonies do we see in the attributes?

*A.* The most beautiful that the human mind can conceive. Here is Love and Mercy; what can harmonize better? Not even a fifth can have a sweeter tone or a more perfect harmony. Holiness and Justice are also perfect harmonies, as are also Light and Life. And, that man might freely converse with his Creator, it became necessary that the atmosphere should accord to these attributes, that music might become praise and devotion, and thus be accepted of God.

Here is an object that is surprisingly lovely: now, if that lovely creature should be destitute of the attribute, Mercy; had no compassion, no forbearance, no sympathy, its loveliness would deteriorate just in proportion to its want of the outflowing streams originating in the fountain of Mercy. The harmonics of these two attributes are so interchangeable that we say, that that which is lovely is also merciful, and that which is merciful is also lovely.

So we may say of Holiness and Justice; they perfectly intermingle with each other, and can never create a discord, for they are indissolubly united.

*Q.* Then the laws that govern vocal and instrumental sound are unalterably fixed in the formation of the atmosphere?

*A.* So it would appear from the fact that wherever the atmosphere exists the harmonies of sound also exist, and move its properties in every possible direction, conveying a pleasurable sensation wherever the affinities of sound are harmonized, or where tones in harmony are uttered.

*Q.* Is every tone in music, then, a harmony?

*A.* Not if isolated and alone, but when simultaneously sounded with certain other tones, they are unalterably so.

*Q.* Then all concords are the result of these harmonies?

*A.* Perfectly so, for in the scale of music there

are five full tones, and two semi-tones, or half tones; so in the attributes there are those that are easily separated by the natural mind, as Holiness and Truth, which can readily be understood in their separate capacity; but when we attempt to disengage Mercy and Love, we find a connection not unlike a semi-tone; and so on in all their relations; and when some skillful lover of the art of Music shall examine this subject in this light, his investigations will abundantly establish this theory.

*Q.* How could this peculiar relation of the atmosphere to the seven tones in music be developed?

*A.* Only by the creation of Man, in whom are all the attributes essential to its development.

*Q.* Then the harmonies of sound extend from heaven to earth, and thereby cause our songs of praise to be heard in heaven above?

*A.* So it would appear when our natures are restored by the operation of the Holy Spirit, for it is equally true that we can not sing to the praise of God without the "Spirit helpeth our infirmities," as it is true that we can not pray as we ought. The polyphony of the attributes is the cause of the polyphony of sound, and, like a stringed musical instrument, whose strings are in harmony with five thousand other instruments of similar kind, the operator need only cause one single string to vibrate, and the whole five thousand will vibrate with it; so the operator, which is the Seven Spirits of God, need only touch the harmonious chord in the human soul to create praise in heaven. The Apostle even declares that "our conversation is in heaven," and surely our prayers could never be answered if not heard in heaven.

*Q.* Is the language of music, then, a universal language that can not be altered or changed?

*A.* Emphatically so; and to meet all its various harmonies, God has been pleased to incorporate in our spiritual natures the divisible seven, so that we can divide ourselves into seven parts, that is, we can understandingly play five parts, keep the time or fill the bellows with the foot, and sing a part of the music or the words of the hymn or song; but we can not go beyond the number seven.

The power of this mystical number, in its divisibility, is more clearly seen in our relation to music than in any other relation. A man may so school himself as to carry on a conversation with another party and write a letter at the same time, but could not write letters with even both hands at the same time and converse; but he can play five parts on a musical instrument and converse quite understandingly at the same time, only because of the attributes.

*Q.* What relation do the rays of light sustain to the atmosphere?

*A.* Many and wonderful. All illumination, all the vivifying and vitalizing influence of heat, all reflex light by which the shades of darkness are made pleasing as they open to our gaze the innumerable host of the planetary world, and thus teach man the power of the ever-living God.

*Q.* What relation does the atmosphere sustain to animal life?

*A.* In a mysterious manner, part of this unseen element attaches to the venous current at respiration, and thus vitalizes the blood, without which the body would soon cease to live. Heat and cold do not change its properties, so that human life is sustained by it in polar regions as well as under a vertical sun.

*Q.* To what height does the atmosphere, or the aerial ocean, extend?

*A.* Supposed to be from thirty-five to forty-five miles, seven hundred and seventy cubic feet of which is equal in gravity to one cubic foot of water.

*Q.* What farther work had Justice to do than to arrange the firmament?

*A.* The Sacred historian declares that "God made the firmament and divided the waters which were under the firmament from the waters that were above the firmament; and it was so. And God called the firmament heaven. And the evening and the morning were the second day." Gen. i: 6–8.

It would appear, then, that the attribute, Justice, had finished his work when the ocean of air had received all its qualities and entities, and the clouds had been commissioned to carry their ponderous load of waters and gently distribute them over the earth.

Even the clouds that ride upon the atmosphere are known by the septenary number, as seen in the names they bear.

In meteorology one of the four fundamental clouds is called Cirrus, from its fibrous appearance resembling carded wool. The *second*, from its structure in convex masses, piled one upon another, is called Cumulus.

The *third* kind of cloud, from its uniformity in being spread over the sky, is called the Stratus; then again the *fourth* peculiar kind of cloud, from its bearing the rain, is called the Nimbus; the *fifth*, being a mingling of the two, is called the Cirro-Cumulus; the *sixth*, the Cirro-Stratus, and the *seventh* the Cumulus-Stratus.

Thus the clouds even inhere in the Mystic Numbers of the Word.

-*Q*. Why was the firmament called heaven?

*A*. Because through this vast surrounding the eye can trace the Comet till it is lost in illimitable space; and on the confines of which the Eternal Jehovah meets and converses with His creatures; and as the Spirit of God becomes the telegraphic operator through the skies, heaven is thus approachable, and this space is called heaven.

*Q*. Was not the work of Justice, then, a vastly great achievement?

*A.* Wonderfully so, for this ocean of air completely surrounded the entire earth, and was in its oceans, its seas, and its rivers; in its deep recesses, its mountains and its hills; and by introducing into it disturbing elements, or by heat and cold producing a motion of its volume, or an irritability, its entire force rolled on in wave-like grandeur, propelling the clouds to their destination, freighted with health, vigor, and delight.

Thus the second day's work was finished, and Justice had so perfectly mingled the substances of this unseen, transparent fluid, that animal life could be sustained by it in every land and clime; though the least alteration in its component parts would have resulted in the destruction of the whole creation. But his work also had to do with the moral culture of sentient intelligences, and of the plan of redemption, of which he bore a conspicuous and glorious part. For God is just in all His works, and justice proceeds from God.

## CHAPTER III.

The Work of the Attribute, Holiness—How the Work was Accomplished—The Seven Properties of the Tree—The Extent of the Work—Varieties, Colors, Medicinal Qualities—The Time Required—The Seven Properties of Water—The Distinction between Beasts and Trees.

QUESTION. What attribute immediately connected with Justice in the work of fashioning this earth for man?

*Ans.* Holiness.

*Q.* To what did he direct the labors of the third day?

*A.* First to the waters: "And God said, Let the waters under the heaven be gathered together unto one place, and let the dry land appear; and it was so."

*Q.* Why was this the work of Justice?

*A.* Because Holiness and Justice are perfect harmonies, and as animal life was to be sustained by the respiration of the atmosphere, so animal life must be sustained by the inhalation of water; each element partaking in common affinity of the same properties, though differently compounded; as also in the attributes: that which is holy is also just, yet the attributes unfold in themselves different developments.

*Q.* How was this work accomplished?

*A.* By rolling the atoms together and heaping them up in the convex ocean, leaving the mountains and the dry land.

*Q.* Was this *all* the work performed by the attribute, Holiness?

*A.* By no means. Holiness fashioned all the trees, plants, flowers, and grasses throughout the entire globe.

The learned Dr. J. P. Thompson, L L. D., in his work on *"Man in Genesis and in Geology,"* thus remarks, in solving the problem of the growth of plants and trees before the sun had shone upon the earth. He says: "It has been objected to this narrative, that the sun, moon, and stars did not appear until the fourth day, whereas the growth of vegetation requires the action of light, and the light of certain stars requires to travel for ages before reaching an observer on the earth, and therefore there must have been light from the heavenly bodies during the period of vegetable growth described as the third day, and the stars must have existed for ages before, in order that their light might at this time have become visible. But there is in all this no conflict with the account in Genesis if we remember that the language of this narrative is popular and not scientific."

But suppose we could not remember this contradiction, we should then be obliged to understand it in the order of science, and then, by having the key—the mystical number seven—to help us out of the dilemma, we should see no contradiction or ambiguity in reference to vegetation, on the third day at all. No "London Fog," no popular narrative, in opposition to science.

*Q.* For what purpose were these created?

*A.* To be for food to sustain animal life, to beautify and adorn nature, and that the aroma from earth's flower garden might call forth praise to the great Author.

*Q.* Is the mystical seven seen in the plant, the shrub, or the tree?

*A.* Most perfectly; there being *seven*, and only seven properties in the plant, shrub, or tree essential to its life and perfect development.

These are, *first*, the Woody part or substance; *second*, the Sap or circulating medium; *third*, the Bark or covering; *fourth*, the Leaves or foliage; *fifth*, the Flowers or blossoms; *sixth*, the Kernel or reproducing seed; and *seventh*, the Life. Remove from the tree any of these, and its decay, or its deformity, will be apparent.

*Q.* Did the work of Holiness extend over all the earth?

*A.* As widely as did the atmosphere, for the

vegetable kingdom is universal from shore to shore—on every island, continent, mountain, or valley; even the perpetual snows of Greenland fail to arrest vegetation in some of its forms; but the vegetable kingdom can no more do without air than without earth, so perfect are the harmonies of Creation; and here it might be best to look again at the seven colors of light, the seven properties of the atmosphere, and the seven substances of the tree, in order to grasp the idea expressed by the semi-god, or mythological Greek oracle, *Silenus*, "that the mystical number seven tendeth to the accomplishment of all things."

Hence the work of the third day embraced in its detail the vastness of every spire of grass, flower, fern, herb, shrub, or tree, that earth ever has, or ever will produce, with the almost numberless varieties, colors, formations, and medical properties that we everywhere behold; and then we can have but a scanty conception of the labor of the third day.

*Q.* For what purpose were these varieties created?

*A.* For man, who was not yet created, and under whose superintendence the vast surroundings of earth were to be committed, that he might admire and adore the great Creator, while from the foliage and germinating kernel he and millions on millions of animated life might feast and enjoy the beauty, luxury, and bounty of the beneficent Creator.

*Q.* Did the forest trees reach their maturity before the close of this day's labor?

*A.* It would so appear from reading the brief record: "And the earth brought forth grass, and herb yielding seed after his kind, and the tree yielding fruit, whose seed was in itself upon the earth, and it was so. And the evening and the morning were the third day." Gen. i: 11–13.

*Q.* What length of time would this have required?

*A.* Probably a thousand years, or "one day with the Lord."

*Q.* Are the harmonies of this day's work interchangeable with the labors of former days?

*A.* Beautifully so. The element of water being the most abundant, except the atmosphere, of any of the elements, is also represented by the septenary number.

The properties of common spring water (see Enc. Am., vol. 3) are seven, viz.: Oxygen, Hydrogen, Carbonate of Lime, Muriate of Lime, Muriate of Soda, Magnesia, and Sulphate of Potash. Not until the element of water, by the agitation of the aerial forces rolls its volume mountain high, purifying alike itself and the air, and at the same time filling the clouds with mist and rain, by which vegetation is nourished and its full development accomplished, can we clearly see the harmonies of Creation.

*Q.* What is the grand distinction between the life of a tree and that of an animal?

*A.* The senses. The tree neither tastes, smells, sees, hears, or feels in any manner common to the animal kingdom, consequently the tree is impassible—not subject to pain—and can not writhe in agony, even though rent asunder.

# CHAPTER IV.

The Fourth Day of Creation—Truth's Work—The Sun the Grand Time-piece—The Element of Light—The Solar System—The Sun as an Opaque Body not Made During the Days of Creation—The Seven Stars—The Seven Phases of the Moon.

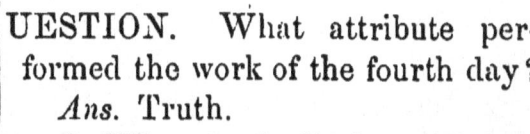

QUESTION. What attribute performed the work of the fourth day?

*Ans.* Truth.

*Q.* What work did he perform?

*A.* He applied the light that till now appeared as a meteor, to the Sun; and enveloped that opaque body with this brilliant, gaseous hydrogen as an atmosphere of overpowering splendor, removing it from the position it occupied during the first three days, but not changing its action or entity.

*Q.* Why was this the work of Truth?

*A.* Because this grand time-piece must be fixed upon an unalterable basis, for the truth of God is pledged in the arrangement.

We thus read: "And God said, Let there be lights in the firmament of the heaven, to divide the day from the night, and let them be for signs, and for seasons, and for days, and for years. And God made two great lights (light bearers), the greater light to rule the day and the lesser light to rule the night; and he made the stars also."

*Q.* Did not the sun shine till then?

*A.* We have no such record. To arrange the wonderful machinery of the illuminating element in a positive and unalterable position, so that through all coming ages till the close of time the astronomer could securely rely upon its unchangeableness, and this, beyond the possibility of a doubt, required the Truth of God to establish.

*Q.* How did the work of this attribute harmonize with the labor of the preceding attribute?

*A.* Admirably. The refreshing dews of the night season were no less necessary to the growth of the plant and the flower, than were the rays of the noon-day sun; nor was nature's hour of sweet repose less needful for *man*, who was soon to be created, and for whom all other things were made, than the tints of the morn, the glory of the noon-day, or the golden hues of the evening. Light and darkness, sun and shade, are in perfect harmony with the perfection of the vegetable kingdom, and their consecutive recurrence is positively essential to vegetation.

*Q.* Was this all the work that the attribute, Truth, performed?

*A.* By no means. This attribute fixed the laws of gravity, balanced the ponderous orbs in the vastness of the ethereal arch, gave them their bounds, and then illuminated them by the reflected rays of the grand center of the solar system. Millions upon millions of shining, twinkling stars cast their borrowed rays of light upon the earth, while upon a more general survey, the mechanism of their surroundings, is incomprehensible.

*Q.* Why was it necessary to transfer this imponderable agent to the sun, and locate it there?

*A.* Because the sun, by the laws of gravity, became the unalterable center.

*Q.* Did not these laws exist before the fourth day's labor?

*A.* They may have existed, but were not till then revealed.

*Q.* Did not the sun exist before the earth was fashioned?

*A.* No. The sun was no sun at all till the light was given to it. It may, or it may not, have existed from eternity in its chaotic state, but until it became enveloped in light, it was nothing but a dark world—an opaque body.

*Q.* Then we do not understand that the substance of the sun, moon, and stars, was made during the fourth day's labor?

*A.* By no means; nor have we any account of

the time in eternity when even the earth's azoic properties were made. Our history of the creation is only a history of the formation of earth to the abode of *man*, and for all the subordinate creatures to be made for him, that, like him, were to be formed out of the earth.

*Q.* Why must Truth arrange this work?

*A.* That God's unchangeableness might be seen in His works. In the labor of this attribute the mystical number seven is also apparent. The rising of Pleides, or the seven stars, have been held as a sacred time-piece in the guaranty of safety to all water crafts, by their occult virtue, from time immemorial. The seven phases of the moon has been equally ancient and traditional, as well as accurate, according to the laws of science.

But, above all, this attribute, like all other attributes of God, has to do with the moral government of the universe, and God's character is predicated upon the fulfillment of His eternal Truth.

## CHAPTER V.

LIFE—ITS WORK—THE FISHES AND FOWLS—ANIMALS POSSESS NONE OF THE ATTRIBUTES OF MAN—THE VASTNESS OF THIS DAY'S WORK.

QUESTION. What attribute performed the labor of the fifth day?
*Ans.* The attribute, Life.
*Q.* Why?
*A.* From the vastness of the animal kingdom it became necessary to divide their creation into two days' labor. The life of fowls and fishes being but a small advance above the plant, or the zoophyte, their creation became the work of this attribute.

*Q.* Why was not man created on the fifth day as well as the birds and fishes?

*A.* Because a single attribute could not fashion a being who was to possess all the attributes, nor was it necessary to create man, till God had prepared a work for him to do.

*Q.* Do not the animal kingdom possess some of the attributes common to man?

*A.* None. They possess the five senses common to man, but none of the attributes; for if they had been so organized they must, like him, be subject to moral law.

*Q.* In what did the work of Life consist?

*A.* First, in filling up the seas, the oceans, and the rivers with the teeming millions of animated life; and, secondly, to fill the air and make it vocal with the almost innumerable host of the feathered songsters. We thus read in the Holy Scriptures: "And God said, let the waters bring forth abundantly the moving creature that hath life, and fowl that may fly above the earth in the open firmament of heaven. And God created great whales, and every living creature that moveth, which the waters brought forth abundantly after their kind, and God saw that it was good. And God blessed them, saying, be fruitful and multiply, and fill the waters in the seas, and let the fowl multiply in the earth. And the evening and the morning were the fifth day." Gen. i: 20–3.

*Q.* This was undoubtedly a great day's work?

*A.* Remarkably so, as it embraced the world of waters, and the aerial ocean that surrounds the earth and waters.

*Q.* In what was the labors of this day the most remarkable?

*A.* In the variety of formations that every-where attract attention, whether it be the *animalculæ*, whose form and shape can only be seen through the powerful microscope—the coral marine zoophyte or polypary, whose animated form becomes as hard as a stone when removed from the water—the fishes with their million sizes, formations, and species, or the monster "leviathans" of the deep, whose fame challenged the credulity of Job; each and all this vast multitude, form a history so marvelously great, that no human mind can fully comprehend its wonders or its work.

Then, again, the remarkable variety of the "fowls that fly in the firmament above the earth," their plumage and their music, their beautiful colors, so bright, so perfect, so exactly in unison with every other bird or fowl of the same specie, the perfect lines of black and white, of red and green, which unite in the fullness of their perfect colors, their lofty and rapid flight through the aerial ocean, places them among the wonderful things of God.

*Q.* Why did not the attribute, Life, create the beasts and creeping things as well as the fowls and fishes?

*A.* Because the work of Creation progresses step by step in the scale of being as it does in the various strata of which the earth is composed. From the life of the zoophyte to the mollusca is but the smallest advance in the scale, and so on consecutively in all their gradations onward and upward, till the noblest of them all is created. Not that it is less needful in the vast chain of being that fishes be formed than beasts, nor again, that it required less skill, but God, in His infinite wisdom, chose to divide the fifth and sixth day's work of Creation by forming the animals that move through and live in the two elements (air and water) on the fifth day. And, again, the vastness of the fifth day's work related to two elements, one (the water) covering three-fifths of the earth; the other (the air) surrounding the whole world. To fill all this vast portion of Creation with teeming life, and fix the bounds of their habitation, required the entheal attribute, Life, the entire period or cycle allotted to it, and so the day closed; for the evening and the morning were the fifth day, and Life could do no more.

## CHAPTER VI.

Mercy's Work—The Creeping Things and Beasts—Reason Why this was Mercy's Work—The Vastness of this Work—Seven Different Kinds of Life—Man, Mercy's Last Work—Love one of the Creative Attributes—They all Breathe their Nature into Man—God, the Father, Represents the Soul-form—God, the Spirit, the Mind—And God, the Son, the Human Form—The Human, created in God's Likeness—The Man Distinguished from the Beast—How—Man's Seven Senses—Instinct of the Beast—The Judgment Sense—The "Carnal Mind."

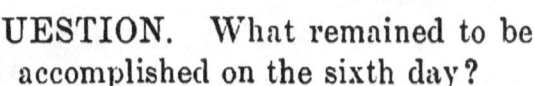

QUESTION. What remained to be accomplished on the sixth day?

*Ans.* The formation of all the beasts and creeping things that are found upon the face of the whole earth; and to close the sixth day's labor by the formation of man, the governor and ruler of them all, and over all animated life, to have absolute dominion.

*Q.* Who performed the labor of the sixth day?

*A.* In part, Mercy.

*Q.* What was Mercy's part?

*A.* First to form all the creeping things upon the earth, who in number are legions upon legions, and then the beasts of the field and forest, who fill every mountain side and valley, the tropics and the polar regions, on the earth and in the earth, an assemblage that no man can number. We thus read: "And God said, Let the earth bring forth the living creature after his kind, cattle, and creeping thing, and beast of the earth after his kind, and it was so. And God made the beasts of the earth after his kind, and cattle after their kind, and every thing that creepeth on the earth after his kind, and God saw that it was good." Gen. i: 24, 25.

*Q.* Why was this Mercy's Work?

*A.* Because man would most need the beasts to perform the work allotted to him.

*Q.* Why so?

*A.* Because, to subdue the earth and to fashion and adorn it with structures of beauty and architectural magnificence, might require greater strength than he possessed. The beasts being under his dominion must have been necessary to his work, even more so than the fowls or monsters of the deep; and this may have been a reason why Mercy was chosen to perform the labors of this day, and thereby form a link in the great chain of creation.

And further, the various forms of the brute creation arise in the scale of being, till we see in the formation of the ape and the ourang-outang the appearance or a resemblance to man quite remarkable; and should we commence in the scale of being at the smallest creeping thing that is found upon the face of all the earth, and advance step by step till we had numbered the millions of the creeping things, their various forms, habits, and pursuits in life, their colors, shapes, and motions, and extend our observation to the remotest parts of the earth, from the insect, whose peregrinations are circumscribed by a few feet or a few rods at most, to the great Mastodon of Geological history, whose gigantic proportions are almost fabulous, we would get but a limited view of the morning work of the sixth day. Man, whose dominion was to extend over all the vast monsters of the deep, as well as those of the earth, must have needed them to carry out the plan of his organization, or the design that his Creator intended.

*Q.* Must not this have been a great work?

*A.* It was wonderfully so. The human mind can form no adequate idea of the vast assemblage of animal life; go where we may, life seems almost spontaneous, filling the earth in all its length and breadth from pole to pole, and from sea to sea, so that scarce a foot of soil has not *in* it, or *on* it, the creeping thing, the insect or the beast, the carnivora or the herbivora, the strong and terrible, or the weak and defenseless, the sloth who scarcely moves, or the rein-deer or the moose, whose fleetness is wonderful.

*Q.* In what particular do we see the mystical seven in the animal creation?

*A.* There are seven different kinds of life, and in creation these are all revealed.

*Q.* What are they?

*A.* First, the *earth* brings forth the living grass and gives life to it—hence, in itself, it must be a species of life. The water also gives life, and from it life is derived, and hence must possess a species of life.

The air, also, is the support of life, gives life to the millions that breathe it, and hence, in itself, must possess a life-bestowing property, as without it is certain death, and with it is life. Here are three kinds of elemental life, and these are all the elements that inhere in life, or have life in themselves.

There is a kind of life of the tree—a life of the animal—a life of the soul, and the creative life of God.

These seven embrace all that can possibly be said to have a life-giving power.

Thus the earth, the air, the water, and all the vast surroundings had been prepared for the only object of Divine approval, the only associative creature whose parentage and lineage could be traced to the eternal attributes of God—the man—*Ecce Homo*, and to the great work of his relationship to God, the Trinity gave attention, "Let us make man."

*Q.* How was he formed?

*A.* In part from the earth, as were all the host of animated life, with this grand distinction: he was made, or created, in the likeness of God. We thus read: "So God created man in His own image, in the image of God created He him; male and female created He them."— Gen. i: 27.

*Q.* What is an image?

*A.* The likeness, show, or resemblance of another.

*Q.* How was man created in the likeness of God?

*A.* First in his triplicity—the body, the mind, and the spirit—like God, the Father, the Son, and the Holy Spirit; that is, God, the Father, represented the immortal soul, God, the Spirit, the mind, and God, the Son, the body.

*Q.* Was the human form created in the likeness of God?

*A.* Most assuredly. It would be false to every meaning of language to understand it otherwise. God the Word, or Son, was, or is, as eternal and almighty as the Father of spirits, or the Holy Spirit. He was the eternal Archetype of man—the Lamb of God, the Messiah— before the world begun. He was one of the Three that made man, and in the image of this eternal Christ man was made, and that *form* or image he covenanted to assume as a type, while He was the eternal Archetype. This human body was made or created on the sixth day.

*Q.* By whom was this President of all the works of God, this noble and exalted being, created?

*A.* In part by the Seven Spirits of God. Mercy had finished his work, and the five preceding attributes had witnessed the harmony that every-where developed itself, and with the attribute, Love, form the ever-blessed seven, and man is created, and the Seven Spirits of God breathe a measure of the image and likeness of themselves into him, and the man becomes a living soul.

*Q.* How as a creature, is man distinguished from the beast creation?

*A.* By having two more senses than they, and seven attributes.

*Q.* What are those two senses?

*A. Judging* and *talking.*

*Q.* Do not beasts judge?

*A.* Only intuitively. You place a pail of water before your horse, and when he has taken all he wants at that time, he does not judge that he will ever need more, so he not only upsets the pail, but destroys it with his feet, unless you remove it. If he were in possession of a judgment sense, he must have been guilty, in the act, but he is not, consequently he did not possess this sense.

Again, the judgment sense in man enables him to appreciate values and appropriate them to adorn his person or his home; the beast never. No matter how much cunning, sagacity, or instinct the brute may have, he can not be so educated that he will know the relative values of coin or paper. To him gold is no more precious than dirt, and even the grain that has been garnered up for his special use he destroys with impunity, and why? Because he is devoid of a judgment sense.

*Q.* Is not this also the *moral* sense?

*A.* Not at all. The moral sense inheres in wisdom, and is the operation of all the attributes; the judgment sense is the controlling power over all the senses, and is most clearly, and from the other senses most visibly, apparent in planning, contriving, inventing, and constructing.

*Q.* Do not animals construct? See the beaver, the honey-bee, the ant, do they not construct their cells and their homes?

*A.* Certainly they have an instinctive power of construction, but no judgment to alter, change, or construct, only in the same instinctive manner that the race have ever done before them. They build nothing different from their ancestors, just as the kid extracts nourishment from the mother, so instinctively they build; but *man* learns to construct, and judges as to the structure which he is about to erect, whether he may not exceed all former builders in architect or beauty, hence he possesses a judgment sense.

*Q.* Does the judgment sense combine the senses and form of them a kind of mind or acting principle?

*A.* It certainly does. The Apostle calls it in its present totally depraved condition the "carnal heart."

*Q.* Can this carnal mind, then, become subject or obedient to the law of God?

*A.* It can not. All its powers, all the senses over which it presides, are totally depraved; therefore "it is not subject to the law of God, neither indeed can be." Hence, to become holy, so far as the human senses are concerned, is as much an impossibility as it would be to escape the results of sin—the condemnation of death.

*Q.* What other sense does the man possess in contradistinction to the brute creation?

*A.* The sense of Language, or the Talking sense.

*Q.* Do not some birds or animals talk?

*A.* They do not in a language sense. They learn the meaning of certain sounds, and can imitate them, but to construct language, to write letters, to telegraph messages, is as far removed from them as they are from the tree. The harmonies of music would have been placed in the atmosphere in vain if man had not been in possession of the language sense.

*Q.* These two senses, then, must have placed

man in a very superior condition over the vast host of the animal creation?

*A.* Preëminently so; this the beast readily learns, and submits to, or flees from man in terror; even the lion, when maddened by hunger, fears the man, and dares not attack him face to face.

In man's primitive or primeval state the senses were holy, and then he had dominion over all animated creation; when he commanded they obeyed, when he called they came to his aid.

*Q.* What is the human will?

*A.* All the senses rallying around the judgment sense creates or originates the human will.

*Q.* Why so?

*A.* Because the judgment sense has to do with things earthly, and only earthly, and may err in heavenly things or in a willingness to make a sacrifice of self, though it be without sinful intent; hence the pure and holy Jesus remarked in His prayer to the Father: "Not as J *will*, but as Thou wilt." Matt. xxvi: 39.

*Q.* What relation does the language sense sustain to the human will?

*A.* It permanently establishes or diminishes the power of the will. If we use the power of language to help on the will when it is already inflamed, nothing short of superior physical force can subdue us; but if used to soften the supposed indignity, the effect is to materially change the will. "Kind words turn away wrath." The entire power of the preached word is seen in its effect upon the will, and even this, with the additional power of the Seven Spirits of God, fail in many cases to subdue it.

These are the elements of correllation in man's present fallen state: when the human will was holy, unfallen, then the language sense was also holy, and each in delightful harmony exalted the man above all the manifold works of God.

*Q.* What are the Seven senses?

*A.* Seeing, Tasting, Feeling, Hearing, Smelling, Judging, Talking.

The animal kingdom, possessing but five of the senses, became greatly inferior to man, being governed only by the irritability of the senses acting one upon another. For example: the beast hears your call, that call through the sense of hearing conveys to the sense of taste a certain prompting or a kind of irritation that instinctively hurries the beast to the place where, from such a sound, food has been dispensed. There is no judgment about it, nor does the beast think whether the giver will dispense to them corn, or swill, or water, but are ravenously propelled by the irritation, and hurry with the utmost speed toward the sound, or call, which produced the sensation.

## CHAPTER VII.

Man's Attributes are his Moral Nature—He Possesses Seven Attributes—The same as the Holy Spirit—Their Connection with the Senses—Why a Man is Crazy—A Monomania—Where the Connection of the Two—The Senses and Attributes.

QUESTION. Were the seven senses all that the primitive man possessed, and only two of these superior to the beast?

*Ans.* They were not. After man had been fashioned out of the earth and endowed as the highest order of the animal kingdom, by being greatly their superior, God gave to him of His own Spirit.

*Q.* How do we learn this fact?

*A.* By the Apostle's expression, "*That* was not first that was spiritual, but that which is natural, afterward that which is spiritual." 1 Cor. xv: 46. "And God breathed into him the breath of life, and he became a living soul."

*Q.* Why was it termed, "breathed into him the breath of life," instead of *created him a living soul*?

*A.* Because the seven attributes thereby became inosculated with the seven senses, and by this process of inosculation, or uniting, the attributes exert supreme control over the senses.

Hence moral law, which has to do with the attributes, only, is transferred to the action of the senses, and makes them also responsible.

*Q.* Does each attribute, then, connect with a sense and govern it?

*A.* It would so appear, and in man's primeval state this power was absolute, but now, if there be a derangement in their inosculation, this exempts the senses from responsibility to civil law.

*Q.* How so?

*A.* If a single attribute be diseased, or deranged in its connection with a sense, then the man becomes a monomania; if more than one, he is crazy; if all, then he is totally insane.

No moral law can recognize a man amenable to civil law when by the disease of an attribute, or when inosculation is suspended by disease, he is unable to control the judgment sense.

*Q.* In what portion or part of the human organism does this union of the attributes and special senses, probably occur?

*A.* In the cerebrum or brain.

*Q.* Why?

*A.* Because from the smaller portions of the brain, at its base, proceed certain pairs of nerves distributed to the organs of sensation, part to the special, and part to the common sensation and motion. If, then, the invisible organs of sense are thus located, may not, and indeed do not, the attributes which, to human observation, are also unseen unite at this point, and, by the "breath of God," become united?

*Q.* Is there any occurrence by which the attributes in their combination as a spirituality may be detected, in contradistinction to the senses?

*A.* There is. It is a very natural occurrence that men become *lost*, or as is commonly denominated, "turned around."

This occurrence takes place with the cultivated and refined much more frequently than with the uncivilized and the savage. The philosophy of this phenomena may be thus easily explained. The attributes form a mind—a moral or intellectual mind, of their own; the senses also form a mind, or rally around the judgment sense, but the latter is subordinate to the former; the attributes, then, becoming engrossed in the meditation of spiritual, intellectual, or scientific pursuits, may not recognize the changes of compass that have occurred during our hasty marches through the streets or forests, and are thereby disconnected from the senses, and form an opinion of their own as to north or south, and to this opinion the senses must submit. Hence, should the individual be accosted as to which way was south; when he could not see the sun or stars, would answer with much certainty of mind to directly the reverse of the facts, and in this opinion would think himself right beyond a doubt. And should he be put on oath, or affirmation, would probably testify to the points of the compass, east, west, north, or south, with as much confidence in a truthful result as if it were really so.

You might ask him, "Which way is south?" he might point to the north. You ask him, "Are you sure that that direction is south?" and he will say it certainly seems so to me; you then take him to the door and show him the sun at high twelve, and ask him again which way is south, and he points to the sun, and says that way, but it does not seem so to me. Now he judges by the judgment sense; before, he judged by the attributes, and sometimes it may be months and years before he can harmonize the two, so that the attributes will agree with the facts as revealed to the judgment sense.

The beast, not being in possession of the attributes, can not be in this sense lost or "turned around."

*Q.* What are those attributes?

*A.* The spiritual mind.

*Q.* Is that the Soul, then?

*A.* No. It is no more the soul than the senses is the body. The human body might be represented by the senses which pervade every part of the body, and the *soul* might be represented by the attributes that pervade every part of its body, but the two are two, notwithstanding.

God, the Father, made the soul; God, the Spirit, made the attributes; and God, the Son, made the humanity of man. "Let us make man."

The attributes, then, are associated with the senses, as also the senses are associated with the nerves and muscles, and control them and preside over them; hence, to suppose that the *mind*, located and, connected with the senses in the cerebrum, becomes the soul immortal, would be as contrary to reason as to suppose that the senses becomes the body by being with it immediately connected.

*Q.* The attributes, then, are unseen?

*A.* No more so than the senses. Who has ever seen another person's *taste* or *hearing, seeing, smelling*, or *feeling*, and yet they exist in the nervous tissue and find their grand center in the ganglionic nerves of the common sensation.

*Q.* What are the seven attributes of man?

*A.* The same as compose the mind of God or the Holy Spirit, dealt out to man by measure, but identical in kind.

*Q.* Do these attributes in man beget the power of infallibility?

*A.* They did in his primeval state, but not now. While the soul, the attributes, and the senses remained primeval, his acts were all infallible and right.

## CHAPTER VIII.

The Attributes of Man—What is his Light—Life—
Holiness—Justice—Mercy—Truth—Love—The
Crime of Murder—The Attributes not Depraved
—The Senses totally so—Can not be Restored—
Man a Sinner.

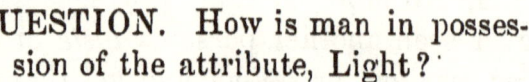

QUESTION. How is man in possession of the attribute, Light?

*Ans.* By creative ideology.

*Q.* What does he discover in the world that ranks him as the possessor of the light of God?

*A.* His conceptions of the motions of the heavenly bodies, his analysis of the causes of their motions, his idea of an all-controlling Power, and the relation he sustains to that power.

*Q.* Has he no other light than this?

*A.* In his present fallen state he is aware of an abode of life beyond the vale of death, and this state of existence is made inviting and joyous by the grace of God. In his first relation to the world, by this light, he beheld the God of all grace, and held converse with Him, and saw Him, that is, he saw the Archetypal God, and heard His voice, and drew all his designs of architect and skill from this infinite Teacher.

By this light he saw the wonderful works of God in the heavens above him, and in the earth around him; all was full of glory. By this light how marvelously had Deity mirrored himself in every thing! The mystical seven gave to light its charm in the beautiful colors of the rose-bud and the lily, and in all that he beheld he saw the allusion to that Spirit which related him to Jehovah. How delightful were the golden tints of the rising sun as it scattered the shades of night and poured its vivifying rays upon the vast fields of vegetation and animal life. He who knew no decay or decrepitude, he who comprehended in a measure the honor, dignity, and glory that he so bountifully enjoyed, could, with the light of God shining around him, and the light of the Seven Spirits of God within him, exult in his Creator's great name and great glory.

*Q.* Is this light in man self-progressive and reproducing?

*A.* Emphatically so. Step by step in the vast fields of science he progresses, and how much more so in the science of the soul; even the great Redeemer, who is the embodiment of Deity, when identified with our infantile progression, became subject to the same laws of the senses, and though He was God manifest in the flesh, yet "grew in wisdom and stature."—Luke ii: 52.

The judgment sense, even in the primeval state of man, if from infancy up, must have been progressive, and so the great Archetype of man must increase in this relation, though in his Deity, his wisdom was infinite. Nor is this light in man only expanding continuously while he lives, but it is reproducing in others, as well as hereditary, in its pro-creative nature. If a man writes all he knows on a given subject, and you learn it all, you are his superior, for you know all he knows, and also all *you* know that he does not know. Hence you know more than he does.

So the light in man expands, and develops, and lives in the schools of others after he has passed away, and in the primitive man it was also progressive; and had he not violated the law of God, this light would have still been expansive and progressive.

*Q*. In what particular does the attribute, *Life*, in man appear superior to the life of all other animals?

*A*. In its moral associations.

There is in the life-attribute a sense of right and wrong which we denominate the moral sensibility or the conscience. This power or faculty looks beyond the death-bed, beyond the grave, even beyond the judgment of the great day, and threads out an existence parallel to the existence of its great Author. This life-power combines with its present life an existence of harmonial enjoyment, where all that has made this life dreary and sad will be exchanged to the eternal delight of the soul.

*Q.* How do we know that the beasts do not think of a future state, a future life?

*A.* By the fact that they have no manner of communication among themselves to that end, no idea of moral worth or means to encourage it, no moral law either in their natures or in any code of laws that the great Creator has given them. They have none of the attributes of God in a spiritual sense, and have probably ever been subject to death, as have been the trees and the flowers.

It appears from the science of Geology that animal fossil has been found in the strata of the earth, bearing date farther by several thousand years than since the fall of man. It is, then, probable that the myriads of the insect creation became food for other animals of larger growth, and on, in this relation through the world's cycles since first created by a single attribute of God.

*Q.* Is it not equally wrong to destroy the life of a beast or a fowl as it is that of a man?

*A.* No, it is not; because he that kills a man aims the blow directly at the attributes which God has honored in the relation of a child;

hence in the sight of God this is murder, and so He has revealed the terrible crime and the certainty of retribution. He that kills the beast, the fowl, the fish, only carries out the great design of their creation for man, unless by wantonness or cruelty he sacrifices their life to no purpose.

*Q.* The act of taking human life, then, is an act against God as well as His creature?

*A.* Directly so. "Thou shalt not kill," and the great God is himself insulted and assailed when man destroys (in revenge, lust, or anger) the life of a fellow-being. By this we can clearly see that the life in man is a measure of the attribute, Life, in Jehovah, and is protected by His eternal law.

*Q.* Is man's present life and his primeval life a synonym, one a counterpart of the other?

*A.* It is; only, as seen in the condemnation of the senses, and the disorganization of the attributes. In his creation, the life of the senses were impassively united to the life-attribute, which made him a holy being, but transgression by the senses originated the disorganization of the attributes, and terminating the one left the other forever disorganized and destroyed.

*Q.* Then the attributes in the original man were infallible?

*A.* They were, and now, in the heart of a conscious believer, there is a longing for a like blessed state.

*Q.* How did the infallible attributes of man become fallible and sin?

*A.* They did not. The attributes did not originate the transgression, nor did they at all comprehend the results that the transgression affected. Man's humanity was all of earth, all his senses, all his organic functions were received from the earth, and the single attribute, Mercy, fashioned him for the earth as an animal of superior power. His senses were not infallible, hence the judgment sense could be influenced by the sense of taste or the sense of sight, and the higher position, of being a God, or controlling more than he now controlled in the innocent state of his organization, led him to the tree of the knowledge of good and evil.

*Q.* Then, if his senses sinned, his sin must have been of a finite character?

*A.* Most assuredly, and if God had not breathed into him the breath of life, and joined the moral nature to the human, he would have died like the beast, and nothing more, but having united them (the senses and attributes) the condemnation of death upon the senses disorganized the attributes, and rendered their action powerless for God. The attributes had no other outward channel but through the senses, and these were totally depraved; hence they became unavailable in the sphere of moral action, and would have forever so remained had not grace interposed.

*Q.* Can this *Life* ever regain its infallibility in this world?

*A.* Never, so long as we possess the fallen senses.

*Q.* Can not our fallen senses be restored?

*A.* They can not, "for it is appointed unto man once to die." Nothing short of a translation could effect this, and then the senses must be lost, for they are under condemnation, "for all have sinned."

*Q.* Can not, then, man's disorganized attributes be restored to infallibility?

*A.* Not in this life; they may be harmonized by the power of the Holy Spirit, but so long as they are connected to the senses can not be infallible. "If we say we have no sin, we deceive ourselves, and the truth is not in us."—1 John i: 8.

*Q.* What do we understand by the term *disorganized?*

*A.* A pint of blood taken from the arm and left in a bowl in a short time becomes disorganized, though every part that once composed its organized properties is still in the bowl; and, there being no chemical power or antidote sufficient to its restoration, it continues to be disorganized. So with the disorganized attributes. Man has no power to restore that which he has lost in transgression and sin.

*Q.* The attributes in man, then, can not morally act in concert or in harmony?

*A.* By no means, if unaided by the Spirit.

The sinner will acknowledge the importance of Holiness, Mercy, Justice, and all the principles growing out of them, and his judgment sense will corroborate in their importance, and he may even vow in his heart to live a better life, but can not rally the attributes in concert at all; and hence he "resolves and re-resolves, and dies the same," unless aided by the Seven Spirits of God.

*Q.* Is holiness an attribute of man?

*A.* It must be, or he could not understand the meaning of the term.

God commands all sentient beings to be holy; if man possessed no principle or knowledge of holiness, the commandment would be null and void—an inconsistency. When, in his unfallen state he could obey this command, and in so doing wrought and obtained favor with God; now, this attribute, being disorganized in its relation to his other attributes, affords him no power to obey the just demands of the moral law, although fully aware of God's right to demand and his duty to perform. Hence he must be in possession of the attribute, Holiness. To be in possession of gold, does not make one rich unless he can control it and use it.

## CHAPTER IX.

The Plan of Salvation—The New Birth—The Effect of the Holy Spirit—The Soul—How Contradistinguished from the Body—The Attributes are the Soul's Senses—Man's Business before the Fall—Duty to Love God—What Powers he Possessed before the Transgression—His Dominion.

QUESTION. Is not man in his present state declared to be corrupt and unholy?

*Ans.* Yes, and he perfectly understands this to be true, and, farther, that unaided by the Holy Spirit, the Seven Spirits of God, he can never regain his original power to fully perform the requirements of the moral law.

*Q.* Does not the attribute, Holiness, in man, destroy the necessity of regeneration?

*A.* Not at all; it establishes it beyond a probability. The life power in man's salvation is in the Holy Spirit. "Except a man be born (of the Spirit) again he can not see the kingdom of God."

The operation of the Spirit is not a creation, as was man's first being, but a birth into the Life of God, the harmonizing of the attributes into their original life—" born *again*."

*Q.* How so?

*A.* As the Spirit of Holiness had to do in the creation, or formation of earth for man, so now the Spirit of Holiness must aid in his preparation for heaven, and as no one attribute of God could fashion man to make him a child of God, so now no one attribute of the Spirit can fashion him for heaven.

Foreseeing this necessity, the Seven Spirits of God are sent out into all the world, that through *them*, in their separate personified relations to man, or through the Holy Spirit in *its* work, every attribute of man might be regenerated; but before the fall of man these Seven Spirits rested after the work of creation was finished. "And God rested on the seventh day."

*Q.* What effect would the seven attributes of God produce if introduced amidst the seven disorganized attributes of man?

*A.* They would be his Life, his Light, his Holiness, his Justice, his Mercy, his Truth, and his Love. This would be "the love of God shed abroad in his heart," and, by organizing them, which is giving active life and vitality to them, would constitute him "a new creature." These are the seven golden candlesticks to the individual child of God as they are to the churches.

*Q.* The individuality of the man, then, is not changed by the new birth, either in his attributes or in his senses?

*A.* Not at all. This was what surprised Nicodemus when the Saviour declared to him, "Ye must be born again." If the new birth had been a change of *ideocracy*, or individuality, we could not say, "I know that in me, that is, in my flesh (my senses) dwelleth no good thing, for to will is present with me, but how to perform that which is good I find not. For the good that I would I do not, but the evil which I would not that I do."—Rom. vii: 18, 19. So we see that the *I* is not ignored in the work of regeneration, but an attributive harmony effected by the Comforter—the Holy Spirit.

*Q.* Can not the same be said of Justice, Mercy, Love, and Truth?

*A.* It can; for in the labor of the sixth day all these attributes were united in man's formation, and imparted a measure of themselves to him in the manner the Holy Scriptures declare, "God breathed into him the breath of life."

*Q.* What was farther done on the evening of the sixth day?

*A.* The formation of the immortal soul. After God, the Spirit, had breathed into man the "breath" of the attributes he became a living soul.

*Q.* What is the soul of man, or how is it contradistinguished from the senses and attributes?

*A.* The soul is as separate of either of these as is the body, and possesses a positive, spiritual entity permeating every fiber, muscle, or property of the human formation, imponderable, and infinitely more rarified than even electricity—a spiritual substance, a body. It embraces the entire human organism, and is its whole in a spiritual sense, and is as much a spirit as is an angel, and not unlike an angel merged into the human, and giving it an immortal form. God, the Father, in this had a work to accomplish, or an object to secure, infinitely grand and incomprehensible.

*Q.* What purpose?

*A.* That of securing to Himself a *Royalty* by which he might be glorified throughout the countless cycles of Eternity. Though this is only revealed in the fullness of time, yet the mind of God was eternally fixed on this one object, that is, that a race of intelligences might lift up their hands to Him and say: "Our Father who art in heaven."

*Q.* Could he not have created a child as well as a man?

*A.* He did create a child in one sense when he created the man, but His attributes would have remained eternally pent up in his undiscovered self, if the plan of redemption had not been consummated.

*Q.* Did God, the Word, co-eternally exist with the Father?

*A.* Most assuredly. God needed not to add any thing to himself in order to be a merciful God, the Three were the eternal Three millions of ages before the creation of man, and when the eternal Word became flesh it added nothing to the essence of Deity more than a mirror placed before us adds any thing to us. It reveals us to ourselves, and the flesh revealed God to us. We read: "No man hath seen God at any time; the only-begotten Son, which is in the bosom of the Father, he hath declared." John i: 18.

*Q.* Is the soul, then, in possession of the Seven *Senses?*

*A.* No, not the senses, but the seven attributes, which to the spiritual organism is as much so, as are the senses to the body.

*Q.* Then the soul, in its spiritual existence, hears, sees, feels, tastes, smells, judges, and talks the same as the human organs?

*A.* It must be so, for "God is a Spirit, and seeketh such to worship Him as worship in Spirit and Truth," and if we are the "Temple of the living God," in which, by the Spirit, He dwells, our spiritual organism must answer to all the faculties.

In the creative work of the sixth day the senses and attributes were alike holy, but not now.

*Q.* Why?

*A.* "Because sin entered into the world, and death by sin."

*Q.* What effect, then, had sin upon the human soul?

*A.* It rendered it inoperative and impure, nor can it become co-operative with God, unless washed and purified by the application of the archetypal blood of Christ, the Son of God, the eternal Word. The soul must be cleansed by the blood of Christ.

*Q.* It needed no such fountain in its primeval formation?

*A.* No more so than do the angels of God; the *soul-form* was as completely good as was the human, for we read: "And God blessed them, and God said unto them, be fruitful and multiply, and replenish the earth, and subdue it." The whole organism was complete, and God-like, and good.

*Q.* What is implied in the commandment to "subdue" the earth?

*A.* The earth evidently had no monuments of human architect or genius; man receiving the creative attributes of God must necessarily seek the development of those faculties, and as the earth had just emerged from a chaotic state, and the creative power of God had fashioned the living millions and the vast surroundings of earth, no other work remained for him than to people the entire earth with an unfallen race, and then call out the inventive genius of that race in ornamental columns and architectural display.

The food he was to live upon embraced the kernel of every tree that God had made, without a single exception. We read: "And God said, Behold, I have given you every herb bearing seed which is upon the face of all the earth, and every tree in the which is the fruit of the tree yielding seed, to you it shall be for meat." Gen. i: 24. The cattle, also, and all creeping things and fowls, lived upon the herb itself, *man* upon the kernel or seed. He had then no food or clothing to provide for, no sickness or decay to provide against, hence had time to subdue the earth, and in so doing had the control (dominion) over all the hosts of animal life.

*Q.* How is the soul now dead in trespasses and sins if it is immortal?

*A.* The derangement or disorganization of the attributes paralyzes all its faculties; so far as spiritual worship is concerned, it can have no life to serve God without the harmony of the attributes more than can the body without the senses.

*Q.* Can the human body live without the senses?

*A.* No, it is the senses that die; the body does not die, it returns to its mother earth—decomposes—the senses die, but the senses might be paralyzed so that they could not control the body, and the body still live by the senses. So with the attributes and the soul.

The attributes become paralyzed by their disorganization, and can not control the immortal self, and hence the sinner is dead in sin.

Or, some extraneous force may produce insensibility and still the organism be alive, though no action of the senses is apparent, and under those circumstances must become unconscious, and in such a condition there could be no responsibility; if, then, the attributes should be *mechanized* by extraneous spiritual force, the soul would not be responsible to God; but God has not so dealt with His creatures, nor does he address them at all in such a condition. He has given the senses to control the body, and through the senses of language and judgment, to embrace the attributes: "Ask and ye shall receive," for "God is more willing to give the Holy Spirit to those who ask Him than earthly parents are to give good gifts to their children."

*Q.* What attribute holds a synarchy over the six, uniting them as the judgment sense unites the senses?

*A.* Love. Love is the all-controlling attribute of God, and he fashioned his moral law to reach this end, and demanded of His creatures their undivided love.

Hence, to love God supremely, and our neighbor as ourself, is the whole duty of man.

Love is the first attribute revealed—the last to be relinquished. The little babe in its first *smile* upon the mother, shows the possession of this attribute; the mother's last embrace of the little babe before leaving the world, shows that this attribute is the last relinquished.

When our first parents sinned, God, the Archetype, clothed them up against the storm and cold outwardly, and as a garment to shield them against the fiery darts of the enemy, he clothed the attributes with his garment of grace. The attributes of the soul are now under grace, and hence the proclamation of Mercy. Had not grace interposed, the attributes, too, might have sinned against God, and have been totally depraved—a devil incarnate. The tree of life, then, was guarded outwardly by a flaming sword to keep humanity from becoming thus totally and eternally depraved, and also around the attributes inwardly, that the tempter could not totally dethrone them. "The grace of God," then, "that bringeth salvation, hath appeared unto all men." "By grace are ye saved, through faith, and that not of yourselves, it is the gift of God."

*Q.* Is the man now in possession of this attribute?

*A.* Most assuredly; how could he be commanded to love God with all his soul, mind, and might (this being a moral requirement) if he did not possess the attribute addressed, if he did not understand what the term meant. If such an idea were true that man did not possess the attribute, Love, he would be no higher in the scale of being than the brute, to whom such a commandment would be the height of folly. Love was one of the seven attributes breathed into the creature man, and became the controlling principle, and upon this is predicated his eternal felicity.

It is probable in man's imparadise state, in addition to, or connected with, this attribute, he possessed a degree of *prescience* or foreknowledge and unlimited dominion over every other living creature God had made; and so far as this earth was concerned, might have possessed omnipresence, at least he had a sufficient amount of ocular power to *see* and *name* the whole host of animated life.

Thus were the labors of the sixth day completed, and here we can see the perfect union of mind and matter, of Deity and humanity, of soul and body, of sovereignty and agency, of dominion and submission, of time and eternity, of life and of death.

Here we see the noblest work of God, a being who could form and construct, could beautify and adorn, having dominion over all the animals that filled the vast ocean beds, over all the fowls that fly in the midst of heaven, and over all the beasts that fill the unpeopled forests, valleys, mountains, and continents, from the rising to the setting sun, from the rivers to the ends of the earth. He needed no steam power to propel the great ships He might build, for His dominion over the sea monsters, furnished a more reliable power.

He needed no railroad train to carry him more swiftly over mountains and valleys than he could otherwise travel, for he had dominion over all fowl and over the mightiest birds of passage, and, at his bidding, would carry him wherever he wished to go, even over mountains and oceans. He needed none of the inventions of the present age to assist him in placing in position the mightiest rocks that are found in the ancient cities of primeval days, because he controlled all the power of the strongest beasts of the forest, who were ever ready to obey his will.

And what must have been the force at his command, when he summoned the strength of a single continent to his aid. He who was of God commanded to replenish (to fill up) the earth with a race, mighty in intellect as himself; and, to subdue the earth and fashion it to his nobler taste of grandeur and elegance, had at his disposal abundant power to rear the loftiest pyramids or place in position the vast rocks in the ruined temple of Balbec.

Time wasted not the powers of his organism, for decay and decrepitude were unknown in the universal family of him who, as supreme monarch, presided over, and managed the concerns of the entire world.

Angels hailed with ecstasy the new created image of God, and heard with delightful emotions the song of the stars (Job. xxviii: 8), as from the harmonies and cadences of the spheres God's praises were heralded by the attributes of the eternal Jehovah.

Gently and softly the waves of the ocean proclaimed the tidings of the finished work of God; and the gentle zephyrs rocked the roses and lilies till their enchanting aroma filled the evening air with fragrance and delight. The morning sun, that had risen for the first day to shine upon God's image, cast its mellowed light upon the being who was "fearfully and wonderfully made," and glad anthems of praise seemed vocal from the forests and hills, that earth had now a Governor, whose glory was a little below the angels in regard to time, but vastly their superior in his relation to God.

God looked upon it, surveyed all its bearings, and declared that it was "very good." And the evening and the morning were the sixth day. "Thus the heavens and the earth were finished, and all the hosts of them."

*Q.* What was the work of the seventh day?

*A.* On that day God ended his work. The attributes of God—the Holy Spirit—had finished all that was sublime and stupendous, all that was necessary for man, and had endowed him with all the elements of greatness, the powers of reproduction; had given to him an infinite variety of vegetable and animal life, had filled the earth with precious ores, treasures, jewels, and diamonds, had given to light the adapted eye, to the ear the harmonies of sound, to the olfactory sense, the fragrance of the flowers; to the sense of touch, the knowledge of substances; to the sense of sight, the infinite varieties of formations, plants and colors; to the taste, the delightful relish for food; to judgment, the value of earth's treasures, a mathematical knowledge of distances, the comprehension, in a measure, of substances; and to the tongue the power of speech; and above all, had imparted to him and through him to his posterity for all coming time, a measure of themselves—a measure of the Divine nature—the Seven Spirits of God.

*Q.* Why did the attributes of God rest on the seventh day?

*A.* Because they had finished all their labor, and now retired in the fullness of Love (for God is Love), therefore they rested in Love.

*Q.* Has the seventh day an allusion?

A. It has many, but most of all it alludes to a time at the close of the present dispensation, when the Seven Spirits of God will *again* rest, and in that rest the trophies of redemption will join in the jubilee of heaven forever.

But more especially the attribute, Love, inspired the seventh day.

Like the judgment sense in our human operations, pervading, uniting, and giving force to all the senses, so Love, among the divine attributes, cements, unites, and pervades all. This is the crowning excellence of Deity as it is of humanity, embracing in its mystical relation to man the sum of all moral law, and the basis on which all the law and the prophets rest—love to God and love to man.

How beautiful that the seventh day is thus represented by the Love of God! How sublime and grand as the halo of this attribute surrounds the devotions of this delightful day of rest!

# PART II—TYPES AND TIME.

## CHAPTER X.

Creation's Work Finished—Why the Attributes of God Rested—The Seventh Day—The Review.

QUESTION. How many are the dispensations of time?

*Ans.* We have the record of only three.

*Q.* What are they?

*A.* First, the *dispensation of purity*—that duration or cycle of time when God rested from his works.

The second, that cycle of time or period from which the Messiah or Shiloh was promised, and during which epoch, the great Messiah's blood was typified by the types of the ceremonial law, beginning with the sacrifice of Abel's lamb and consummated by the sacrifice of our Lord and Saviour Jesus Christ—*the typical dispensation.* The third dispensation is that of

*Grace*, and commenced at the sacrifice of Jesus, and continues till the close of time.

*Q.* What is understood by the term *dispensation*?

*A.* A period during which certain laws and regulations control moral intelligences.

*Q.* What laws controlled man during the first dispensation?

*A.* He received but two commandments, the one to multiply and replenish the earth, the other to control and subdue it.

*Q.* Was he not forbidden to taste or eat of the tree of the knowledge of good and evil?

*A.* Not till near the close of this dispensation. He was permitted to eat of every tree throughout the vast globe without restraint: "And God said, behold, I have given you *every tree*, in the which is the fruit of the tree yielding seed, to you it shall be for meat." Gen. i: 29.

*Q.* How long did this dispensation probably last?

*A.* This dispensation must have lasted during the seventh day, or till the attributes had enjoyed their Sabbath of rest, which was probably four thousand years.

*Q.* Why so?

*A.* We may safely conclude that God's procedure toward man is simply consecutive steps in the accomplishment of his purposes. Each day in creation occupied the same duration of time. It would be irrelevant to his character to suppose that the duration of the evening and the morning of the first day was only twelve hours, that the second day was thirty six, and the third twenty. He does not so reveal himself. His disclosures show him unchangeable, hence all his actions are in accordance with his eternal purposes. The mystic number three may very justly refer to Him in his association, and in that reference supposes that each of the Three that bear record in heaven are of equal might and glory; and as it relates to man, body, soul, and mind, each are alike equal in their parts. So in the duration of time each of the dispensations are presumptively of the same duration. If, then, the duration of one dispensation was four thousand years, and of the last nearly two thousand have already passed, and still many prophesies are unfulfilled, and may require the whole of the four thousand years, or two thousand yet to come, before the gospel has been preached in all the world for a witness to all nations; then we may justly conclude that the duration of each dispensation is alike—four thousand years.

*Q.* How do we arrive at the certain chronology of the second or middle dispensation?

*A.* The Mosaic account of creation closes at the sixth day, and adverts to the seventh merely as a day of rest, wherein the active labors of the attributes of God rested; of the time of their rest we have only the seventh day to guide us, but as this is only typical of the eternal rest of the saints, the duration of the type can have no value when placed in juxtaposition with the antitype. Then of the *duration* of this *rest*, while our first parents and their posterity needed not the special care of the attributes, we can only discover, by the rocks, the numbers, and the book of Revelation.

Here many persons misjudge in reading the Holy Scriptures, and form an opinion that there were *two* creations alluded to, instead of one, because of the apparent hiatus, or unexplained period, that the first pair remained in purity; and the strange repetition, and the new place of their abode, and responsibilities in Eden, which garden was not mentioned in the first history, nor a remark in reference to the fatal tree. The Bible history in many respects is like any other truthful history. In taking up a history after the lapse of ages, it is expected that the historian will give a short recapitulation of the important points of interest in their connection with the following historical record. So with the great historian to whom the world is indebted for the truthful history of the world's creation. The panorama, so to speak, was first drawn to the dispensation of creation and purity, then to the dispensation of types, prophecies, biographies, and canons, and, lastly, to grace. Of course, then, the history of transgression must commence with the transgression, and, as holy men of old wrote as they were moved upon by the Holy Ghost, the labors of the Holy Ghost, or seven attributes of God, must have again commenced at the commencement of transgression.

The first history and dispensation ends with the third verse of the second chapter of Genesis; after this Moses traces only the generations of Adam, and his fallen posterity, merely adverting to another race of intelligences, but not making this the topic of history By giving the ages of the lineage down from Adam to Noah, and then on, we get the data of chronology; and upon the strength of this testimony conclude that it must have been near four thousand years from the fall, or first transgression of Adam in Eden, to the birth of our Lord and Saviour, Jesus Christ. This interim embraces the *Typical Dispensation*.

*Q.* Does this aid us in solving the problem of the duration of the first Dispensation?

*A.* In a manner it does, because if, like the days of Creation, their length is presumptively alike, then the duration of the first and third dispensations must be alike—four thousand years each.

*Q.* What race did the sacred historian allude to as contradistinguished from the fallen race of Adam?

*A.* The unfallen sons of God. These were probably the primitive children of Adam and Eve, and their children's children.

The history of this race, their transgression and fall, is undoubtedly the great burden of the book of revelation.

## CHAPTER XI.

First Dispensation Four Thousand Years—Man's Work—The Mystical Number Twelve—Cain's Wife—Adam's First Posterity—The Relicts of their Work—The Giant's Causeway—Pyramids of Egypt.

QUESTION. What would probably have been the business of man if he had carried out the command of God in his primeval state?

*Ans.* His first command was in regard to the multiplying of his species, "And God said, be fruitful and multiply and replenish the earth."

The second, to "subdue the earth.'

As the race had no sickness or death, we may readily suppose that, in four thousand years, a vast host would have been the result. If from the flood to the coming of Christ, being less than three thousand years, and under the diminishing effect of sickness and death, with human life not to exceed a hundred and twenty years, so vast a population had spread all over the globe, what must the population of four thousand years have been without these disadvantages?

We readily conclude, then, from this hypothesis, that the earth must have been peopled in all its islands and continents, in all its length and breadth, at the time that "God planted a garden eastward in Eden," wherein he placed the man he had created.

The Rev. Joseph P. Thompson, D.D., LL. D., in his recent work, entitled "Man in Genesis and Geology," thus writes: "But on the other hand there are facts that seem to call for an extension of time considerably beyond the computed chronology of the Bible, in order to admit of all that has been effected by man, and in man since his first appearance upon the earth."

The business of this vast company would have been to "subdue" the earth by subjecting it to mechanical processes, by sculpture, by magnificent temples dedicated to the living God, and by works of art as noble as the dignity of their commanding position would justify.

They were worshipers of the living God, and could see the hosts of heaven, and in the attributes were children of God, as was Adam before he fell: "Which was the son of Enos, which was the son of Seth, which was the son of Adam, which was the son of God." Luke iii: 38. If, then, Adam, in his lineage after his transgression was the son of God, how much more so before his fall, and his posterity prior to his sin would naturally be styled the sons of God?

*Q.* But how do we learn that this dispensation continued four thousand years?

*A.* By the mystical number twelve.

*Q.* How so?

*A.* If the three dispensations were of equal length, and the typical dispensation from the fall to the coming of Christ was four thousand years, then the three must have been twelve thousand years:

This will account for the choice of the twelve Patriarchs, who were the representatives of the twelve tribes of Israel. Here, then, is a representative of time, as is also the twelve apostles, the twelve foundations, the twelve angels, each and all relate to the three dispensations of time —the twelve thousand years.

*Q.* How do we know that Adam had a posterity before the fall?

*A.* By certain facts that can not be otherwise explained.

*Q.* What facts?

*A.* The sons of God took to themselves wives of the daughters of the children of men; if there had been no peculiar distinction between the two races, why this announcement?

Cain, shortly after the murder of Abel, took a wife in the land of Nod; if there had been no other race save the fallen posterity of Adam, who could she have been?

Cain was afraid of being killed by somebody, some one who was under moral law; and God, to protect him from those who might think him a beast and slay him, put a mark upon him.

And again, the remarks of Jehovah to Eve plainly showed her to have been a *mother* before the transgression, and to establish the fact beyond a doubt, Adam "called his wife Eve, because she *was the mother of all living.*"

Here are a sufficient number of landmarks to enable us to survey the whole field, and this is all that we may expect revelation to give.

*Q.* Would it not, then, be a violation of the laws of nature as well as of God for the sons of God to have taken to themselves wives of the daughters of the children of men? Gen. vi: 1, 2.

*A.* Most assuredly so, and the posterity must be a posterity of illegitimates: "There were giants in the earth in those days"—a monster race, whose sins were so great that it "repented the Lord that he had made man."

*Q.* Did not the Lord always know that just such a race would follow the transgression, then why did he repent that he had made man?

*A.* God was sorry only, as to the necessities that arose in carrying out his purposes.

*Q.* But the remark is that "it repented the Lord that he had made man on the earth, and it grieved him at his heart." Gen. vi: 6. Why was this?

*A.* It is no pleasure to God for man to sin—

is not now—never was. In all his dealings with man he has declared this truth, "that he has no pleasure in the death of him that dieth;" but now the sin was so terrible and great that man's entire nature had no redeeming quality—an offshoot of illegitimacy—who gloried in his shame, and became presumptuous, self-willed, and of monster size, and his destruction must ensue, so Mercy, Life, and Love wept over his ruin. But as this transpired in the second dispensation, we must leave it to the investigation under that age of the world's history.

*Q.* What evidence have we of the long abode, say four thousand years and less, of an unfallen race?

*A.* The remains of gigantic structures that no power now or since the flood could have erected.

*Q.* What are those relics of antiquity that surpass the achievements of later ages?

*A.* There are some five remarkable ruins found on the earth that have no record worthy of themselves, and many wonders, also, in the mammoth caves of the earth which are equally mysterious, that have long since passed for natural curiosities, which are as much the works of art as was the temple erected by King Solomon.

*Q.* What are they?

*A.* Historians have so long claimed some of these to have been the work of the elements, that to get an idea of their constructions and proportions, we will be obliged to copy a few paragraphs of what has been written. The majesty of some of the remains of destroyed palaces and structures is enough to challenge our credulity, or overwhelm us in amazement, and never has any writer attempted to reconcile it to the labor, of human hands. Let us, then, examine the *Giant's Causeway.*

This wonderful work of art (or natural curiosity, as some call it) is situated on the coast of Ireland, a hundred miles or more north of Dublin, in the County of Antrim, west of Bengore Head; the rock, as herein described, profusely covering over twelve hundred miles of coast, so great and so vast. Our historian thus remarks: "It (the columns around and near the Giant's Causeway) consists of many hundred thousands of columns, composed of hard, black rock, rising perpendicularly from two to four hundred feet above the water's edge.

"The columns, or basaltes, are generally pentagonal, or have five sides, and are so closely attached to each other that, though perfectly distinct from top to bottom, scarcely any thing can be introduced between them.

"This extraordinary disposition of the rocks continues below the water's edge; it also obtains in a small degree on the opposite shore in Scotland.

"The columns are not each of one solid stone in an upright position, but composed of several short lengths exactly joined, not with flat surfaces, but articulated into each other as a ball in a socket, one end of the joint having a cavity of three or four inches deep, into which the convex end of the opposite joint is exactly fitted. This is not visible till the stone are disjointed." Enc. Americana, vol. 5.

*Q.* Is it supposed that these peculiarly wrought stone are formed by the processes of Creation?

*A.* Some even write so, whether they have a reason for it or not. Would it not seem a little out of the method of the Creator to have erected hundreds of thousands of these columns two or three times the height of the forest trees, and to have joined them together by sections and joints five square, three square, and eight square, and left them as monuments of His skill?

One writer declares that God built these basaltic columns "just to silence the atheist." Could not the canopy of heaven, with the myriad of twinkling luminaries, have been a greater, a more overwhelming proof of the existence of God, than these columns? But, driven to account for their singular appearance, and having no key to unlock the mystery, they resolve it into the probability that the great God had a desire to surprise his creatures, and so fashioned these rocks with corresponding cavities and sockets; that is, after making worlds, He became a stone mason!

*Q.* Is the Giant's Causeway and these basaltic columns the same?

*A.* They are alike fashioned, but many of the columns are seen on the high bluff, while the same kind of stone, with the same kind of joints and sockets, are those of which the great causeway is formed.

*Q.* How is this causeway arranged or constructed?

*A.* The north channel, at its narrowest point, is some twelve miles in width, and all along north to the Giant's Causeway, and far beyond, these fragments of dressed rock are found in great abundance; that portion designated as the *Causeway* rises but a few feet above the sand, and consists of three streets, three or four hundred feet in width, each appearing about a rod apart, and the portion between the causeway streets filled with immense undressed rock, over which the tide as it arises or recedes roars with great fury. These streets are the tops of perpendicular columns, like those back from the water's edge, with cavities on the one end of every section and corresponding sockets on the other.

They descend with the slope into the sea, and some suppose they cross it, it being more than sixty miles across, and the depth of which is over thirty fathoms, or one hundred and eighty feet. As no one has ever given a hint as to who placed this pavement of closely fitted columns in such artistic arrangement, or who could have filled up the spaces between them with such enormous rocks, we venture to try, to solve the problem, by remarking that these are relics of the work of Adam's unfallen race, and the history of the object of their erection will be positively found out, only, when we have deciphered correctly the language used in this first cycle of time, as perchance may yet be found engraved upon these eternal witnesses—the rocks.

But this we may justly suppose: that a plan had been laid to entirely dam up the north channel so that the tide could not pass through. This magnificent enterprise might have been deemed expedient to the safety of vessels moored along the channel. Or it might have embraced two objects, not only to rear a barrier against which the tide might rush with its fury for ages in vain, but to so bridge the channel that persons and processions could pass over in safety.

We may guess at the magnitude of an enterprise by the preparations made in that direction. Now, along this coast are an abundance of these dressed rock to have bridged by one continuous street of columns from Port Ganniay to the Scotland shore, notwithstanding the great depth of the channel, and to a height of even three or four hundred feet above, if it needed such a height to make it impervious to the rushing tide.

Here are the dressed rock, yonder is the commencement on a grand scale, and we have only to conjecture the object by the great preparations made for its accomplishment.

That such a vast wall as this has survived the

dashing billows and swelling tides from unknown ages, and that the artistic skill indicates that intelligent laborers were employed in its construction, and that by almost superhuman precision each stone fits to its place with perfect exactness, is irrefragable evidence of the existence of a race who needed this skill, and accomplished, so far as they had proceeded, the great design of their being.

*Q.* Is this all the curiosities of the North-Irish Coast?

*A.* It is not, nor from our brief sketch can the mind grasp the wonders of these curiosities. Before we proceed farther, let us learn from another writer and eye-witness the wonders of this coast. He says: "Only imagine yourself in a little row-boat, passing around the northern coast of Ireland. In the distance you seem to look upon an immense castle, flanked by double rows of cylindrical columns.

"It seems so fortress-like, these massive structures, rising from the depth of the sea, that you expect to find guards and wardens, soldiers and arms, but as you approach nearer it loses that castellated appearance, and gradually lessens in magnitude, until there remains only a huge stone wall extending around the coast for miles.

"It is composed of gigantic pillars, cut into prisms, three-sided, five-sided, and eight-sided, side fitting to side, variously jointed, joint corresponding to joint, innumerable irregularities, conformed into such beautiful regularities that you are struck with awe at so perfect a monument of skill, and ask involuntarily, to what great artist your praise is due, what year marked the foundation-stone, what force formed each cylinder and joined in uniform contact such irregular masses; the toil of many a life-time has been spent on far meaner designs, and proud wealth has gloried in much less wonderful relics of man's invention.

"Passing onward, and still onward—for this columnar structure bounds a great extent of coast—you come upon a vast gateway of stonework like the rest, but formed into a wide arch, not Norman or Gothic, but unique, and perfect as peculiar.

"Its entrance is kept by huge waves that for centuries have been rolling higher and higher to bar the gateway that opens still; so your tiny boat rises with their swelling, and you pass through, not, as you had expected, to find the sky above you still, but into the recess of a mighty cavern, whose vaulted roof is formed of stones, many cornered and many colored. You should be there at sunset, as we were, to see dashing waters sparkling with gold, and the stones radiant with crimson light.

"One is awed into silence, for there is something fearful in the thought of a chamber built *without hands;* but should your feelings find vent in words, your ears would be stunned by the deafening sound of your voice, so heavy is the echo there.

"I had always been anxious to see the inside of this famous cave, with its ocean door and stony wall, hung with sea-weed tapestry, but I assure you I was not less eager to see the outside of it again.

"I had no ambition to interfere with solitude too desolate for aught save the cawing of rooks and the twittering of swallows.

"The average height of these basaltic columns, constituting the Giant's Causeway, are from two to four hundred feet, while the whole neighborhood is strewn with detached fragments of this species of rock, that in their picturesque confusion seem the broken pillars of some ruined temple.

"These columns in combination, these heptagons, hexagons, octagons, and triangles, all join in perfect symmetry, as if hewn from corresponding measurement, and form, when you have climbed the rocky ascent to the level summit, a tasselled pavement where one may promenade in scorn of the fierce waves that incessantly dash against their base.

"But we are forced to turn away from the Mosaic pile that owns no mason, from the old arm-chair that no cabinet-maker ever planned, from the huge bowl where none but a giant could drink, and the organ-pipes, to whose identity the roaring waves lend so real an enchantment."— *Jour. of Com.*

*Q.* Did that writer think that these columns and that cavern were made "without hands"?

*A.* So it would seem by the sketch already given.

This wonderful subterranean cavern is now called the Giant's Amphitheater, and is found near Port Noffer Bay.

Not even Rome itself can equal in beauty this grandest of all that is grand in this direction. It is in form just a half circle, and no living architect could form it more exact, and the cliff slopes precisely the same angle to the center.

All around inside of this cavern, from the upper part, extends a row of columns eighty feet high, with a broad, rounded projection, not unlike an immense bench, for the more perfect accommodation of giant guests of **Fin-Mac-Cul**.

The next row of pillars is sixty feet high, with the appearance of another gigantic bench; and so on continuously down to the bottom, and here the water is inclosed by a circle of basaltic rock, forming the limits of a grand arena. Close to this amphitheater is the giant's organ, composed of beautiful colonade pillars, one hundred and twenty feet high, much resembling the pipes of an organ, and opposite of this is his loom, where tradition asserts that the giant busied himself in weaving the fabrics of other days.

*Q.* Why do all writers judge these to be natural curiosities?

*A.* Not knowing who could have built them,

or for what intent they were erected, they, as others always have done, call them natural curiosities.

*Q.* This must be a very easy way of disposing of a work of art so significant of human accomplishment?

*A.* It certainly is, and the reason for so doing is self-evident; for, having no idea of a pre-fallen race, united in mind and interest, that needed not to sow and reap in order to obtain their bread; that had no sickness or death, that could conceive great projects and carry them into effect, that had minds that had greater forecast than our own, that could employ the leviathan of the deep, and all the amphibious races to labor in perfect accordance with their will; in short, a race that had dominion over all the fowls, the fishes, the beasts; although this *race* is plainly spoken of in the Holy Word, the solution, with them, became impossible. Hence they write of it as a stupendous work of chance or of God, and they hardly know which.

This surely could not come under the stalactites or stelagmites; volcanoes could hardly have dressed the stone so exact, or reared them so symmetrical, nor does it seem rational that the angels turned stone-masons, and much less Jehovah, who stretched out the heavens by his word alone.

*Q.* If, then, there is no record as to when or for what purpose these walls were erected since the second dispensation commenced, we may justly conclude them to be relics of the first dispensation?

*A.* That would seem very reasonable.

*Q.* What other remains of antiquity have no historical origin?

*A.* The *Pyramids of Egypt.*

*Q.* What of them?

*A.* There are three wonderful towers, or Pyramids, some two miles from the river Nile, and but a short distance from the city of Cairo, which at present has a population of over three hundred thousand. The Nile is a large river bordering the great Sahara Desert of Africa, and running nearly parallel with the Red Sea, its entire length (one thousand five hundred miles), and emptying itself into the Mediterranean sea at or near its eastern extremity.

Along this river are found the loftiest pyramids of any in the known world; the dressed stone also, that compose three of them, are of such magnitude as to almost challenge credulity as to their being the works of art. The names of these three pyramids are, Gize, Cephrenes, and Cheops. We will now give a historical sketch or two, and then proceed with our catechism. The historian says:

"When we left Gize, at one o'clock in the morning, the tops of the two largest pyramids were illuminated with the light of the moon, and appeared like craggy peaks piercing the clouds.

At half-past four in the morning we prepared to enter the great pyramid, Cheops. We laid aside our clothes, and each one took a torch in his hand, and we began to descend the long passage, which at last became so narrow that we were obliged to creep on our hands and knees. When we had passed through this passage we were obliged to ascend in the same manner, when we came to a much more spacious apartment, coated with granite, and at one end of which Mr. Savory saw an empty sarcophagus, made of one piece of stone, but without a lid. We next proceeded to a second room, which lay under the one above mentioned, and was of smaller extent. It contained an entrance to a passage that was filled up with rubbish. We now ascended through this, avoiding, not without difficulty, a deep well on the left. When we had reached the open air we were all exhausted by the heat, which we had endured in the interior of the pyramid.

"After we had rested ourselves we ascended the pyramid on the outside, and in doing so counted about two hundred stone steps, varying from two to four feet in thickness, and here from the summit we enjoyed a most delightful view."

*Q.* How much land does this pyramid cover?
*A.* About thirteen acres.
*Q.* How high is the highest of these pyramids?

Herodotus gives eight hundred feet as the

height of the tallest of the three; Diodorus six hundred; Strabo makes it six hundred and twenty-five feet, and later discoverers declare it four hundred and fifty feet perpendicular at the center, and about eight hundred up each of the four sides to the top. One writer claims the top stone to be sixty feet square and five feet thick, weighing not less than nine hundred tons. Another historian gives the following graphic sketch:

"After walking the columned avenue of this great mausoleum, we began the ascent of the larger pyramid, known as the Cheops.

"We found the ascent extremely difficult, indeed, in ancient times it must have been impossible, when its polished and beautiful casing, remained entire; but this having been removed by time and accident in many places, and purposely in others, a path, if it may so be termed, is made to the summit.

We were aided by attendants from the temple, who, from long practice ascend with ease, assisting also those strangers who wished to climb the perilous height.

"As we reached half way a block, which had been removed from its place, either by the irresistible force of a sirocco from the desert, or by lightning, gave the high priest and myself a resting-place.

"As we stood here a few moments I looked down upon the prospect below; the sight at first made me dizzy, for we were elevated four hundred feet above the base.

"Again we mounted upward, and after incredible fatigue gained the summit, not without peril, for a slip of the foot, or hand, each block being as high as a man's neck, would have been fatal.

"How shall I describe the scene that burst upon my vision as I gazed about me from this mountain-like elevation? As I ascended the prospect of the country enlarged at every step, but now I seemed to behold the earth itself spread out beneath me.

"The place where I stood, which looks from below like a sharp apex, is a platform several cubits across, on which twenty men could stand or move about with ease. I can give no adequate conception of the scene I beheld.

"First the valley of the Nile was visible, extending many leagues to the right and left, and resembling a green belt a few miles wide, through which the river flows like a silver band, while upon its borders cities appeared like precious stones. It was a gorgeous and magnificent assemblage of cities, temples, palaces, obelisks, gardens, monuments, sphinxes, barges, causeways, and a multitude of people."—*Pillar of Fire.*

*Q.* Is there no idea when, or by whom, these pyramids were erected?

*A.* Certainly. There are an abundance of opinions, but by what *power* these mighty rocks were conveyed there and placed in such perfect harmony, each step being of equal thickness on all sides, as well as being a perfect slope, has very much confused speculation. Some think, from an engraving of modern language, that it took a hundred thousand men twenty years to build it; but with all the strength of Egypt, five hundred thousand men could not have placed those rocks so mountain high; no class of being but those who had dominion over all the beasts of earth and fowls of heaven could have done it.

## CHAPTER XII.

THEBES ON THE NILE—EL KANARK—EL UKSUR—BALBEC—GARDEN OF EDEN PLANTED—MARRIAGE—THE WORLD PEOPLED BEFORE THE FALL—PALENQUE—COPAN—CAVES OF KENTUCKY—FINGAL'S CAVE.

QUESTION. What other ruins of preterlapsed ages do we find along the Nile?

*Ans.* At Memphis we find a colossal statue of unknown antiquity which is eighteen feet across the breast, lying in the dust, the statue being that of a man, and supposed to represent some giant of olden time, like busts of modern years, the legs of which have long since been removed.*

---

*GIANTS OF THE OLDEN TIME.—A giant exhibited in Rouen, in 1830, measured nearly eighteen feet. The Chevalier Scrog, in his voyage to the Peak Teneriffe, found in one of the caverns of that mountain the head of the Gunich, who had sixty teeth, and was not less than fifteen feet high. Gorapius saw a giant that was ten feet high. The giant Galabra, brought from Arabia to Rome, under Claudius Cæsar, was ten feet high. Fannum, who lived in the time of Eugene II., measured eleven and a half feet. Near the castle

What a gigantic monster of a man this must have been when standing upright, as probably it once did, formed out of solid limestone rock, if proportioned in height to the breadth across the shoulders as it now appears.

*Q.* Are these, all the wonders of the valley of the Nile?

*A.* By no means. Let us ascend the river a few hundred miles and look at the ruins of the ancient THEBES.

The author of *"Remarkable Places and Characters in the Holy Land,"* Rev. C. W. Elliott, thus remarks of the ruins in the vicinity of Thebes:

"Let us ascend the Nile to THEBES.

"When it was first founded is lost in the centuries of the past; but fifty centuries ago Menes found it a city.

"On the eastern bank of the Nile stood, and

---

in Dauphine, in 1623, a tomb was found thirty feet long, sixteen wide, and eight high, on which was cut in gray stone these words, "Ketolochus Rex." The skeleton was found entire, twenty-five and a fourth feet long, ten feet across the shoulders, and five feet from the breast bone to the back. Near Palermo, in Sicily, in 1516, was found the skeleton of a giant thirty feet high, and in 1559 another forty-four feet high. Near Mazrino, in Sicily, in 1816, was found the skeleton of a giant thirty feet high, the head was as large as a hogshead, and each of his teeth weighed five ounces. The giant Farragus, slain by Orlando, nephew of Charlemagne, was twenty-eight feet high. In 1814, near St. German, was found the tomb of the giant Isorent, who was not less than thirty feet high. In 1599, near Rouen, was found a skeleton whose skull held a bushel of corn, and who was nineteen feet high. The giant Bacart was twenty-two feet high; his thigh bones were found in 1703, near the river Moderi.

still stands, the Temples El Kanark. At the entrance of the Temple El Uksur, half a mile from Kanark, stood two superb obelisks of red granite, with hieroglyphic writings engraved upon their apex. Within is a magnificent avenue of fourteen columns, sixty feet high, with capitols sculptured with the bell-shaped flowers of the papyrus.

"The great Hypostyle Hall, in the Temple of El Kanark, is the most elaborate work in Egypt, or even in the world. In length it is a hundred and seventy feet, in width three hundred and twenty-nine feet, and it is supported by one hundred and thirty-four columns, the loftiest of which rise seventy feet, and are thirty-six feet in circumference.

"These grandest columns form an avenue in the midst of the court, and the others form transverse avenues.

"In the Ramesium, at the edge of the desert, is a Colossal Statue, hewn out of a solid rock of red granite, which, in weight, is over nine hundred tons. The foot of this statue measures eleven feet, and across the shoulders over twenty-two feet.

"This ponderous mass was in some way transported from its bed in the quarries of Syene, and placed in the courts of the Temple—How?"

*Q.* Do we suppose that these columns were erected by man?

*A.* Most assuredly they were, and as we have

not at our command power or unity of effort sufficient to transport or erect them, if transported, we naturally place them among the undeveloped ages, or as the last named writer calls it, the "rude Egyptians" who "dared to do" what we, with all our science and inventions, can not or will not do. But we do not presume to say that the Egyptians ever knew any more about the time of their erection than we do, only in their traditionary record, which may be very unreliable.

*Q.* What has been the wonderful history of this portion of the earth?

*A.* That this portion of earth has been the center of the revelations of God, ever since the flood, and in it is still found the great river Euphrates, of Eden notoriety, as well as Jerusalem and Judea, of which are written all the miraculous revelations concerning not only the Jews, but of the redemption of the world itself, none can even question.

That immense deserts border both the Nile and the Euphrates is also a geographical fact; that in this portion of the earth are the most positive evidences of the ruins of mighty temples and of giant men and monster beasts, no educated mind can doubt.

If, then, we ever learn its earlier history, its history before the fall of man, when the garden of the Lord was not Eden, but the world, we shall then develop the fact that the great deserts of this land were made so only after the "sons of God took to themselves wives of the daughters of the children of men," and the earth became doubly cursed for their sake.

*Q.* Are there any other ruins of mighty temples that have outlasted the records of time?

*A.* BALBEC, the ancient *Heliopolis*, or City of the Sun, in Syria, forty miles from Damascus, is surrounded with ponderous walls that are of astonishing dimensions, and must have been erected by men who had access to power and unity of effort, not now known upon the earth.

The *Encyclopedia Americana* thus describes the wonderful ruins. The writer remarks: "Whether the magnificent temple of the sun, a great part of which is still uninjured, and which is one of the most splendid remains of antiquity, was built by the Emperor Antonius Pius, or by Septimius Severus, upon whose medals it appears to have been first represented, is uncertain. Of fifty-four lofty columns there are only six standing; their shafts are fifty-four feet high and nearly twenty-two feet in circumference, and the whole height, including the pedestal and capitol, is seventy-two feet. The size of the stone of which the walls of the temple are constructed, is astonishing. No mechanical expedients now known would be able to place them in their present position."

Other writers have given their dimensions as over thirteen feet square and sixty feet in length, of one solid dressed rock. This would place their weight at between six and seven hundred tons each, the shafts equally great and ponderous.

In the quarry, some two miles distant, is one of those dressed stones, protruding out from the solid mass of rock more than seventy feet, and is supported in this horizontal position by the strength of itself, as it still remains in connection to solid rock in the quarry. This dressed rock is thirteen feet three inches square; the whole mighty projection supports itself aloof from any abutment on which to rest, having been dressed, on all sides, back some seventy feet. Should that rock or dressed stone become disengaged from the parent rock, what force could again raise it or convey it to the wall, where many like it remain a wonder to those who visit the ruins of Balbec?

*Q.* What testimony do these rocks give?

*A.* The testimony these mighty rocks bequeath to us is that skill, labor, strength, and wisdom placed these stones in everlasting perspicuity, so that the nations of the earth might learn that in their transgression they inherited a weakness and incompetency, that with all their knowledge of arts, inventions, and mechanical power, they are left as pigmies and children when compared with the men of primeval ages—men of the first dispensation.

We have now examined the wonders of what we call the old world, and found many testimonies of the rocks to corroborate the testimonies of the Mystic Numbers, and as much so, they testify of the skill and labor that reared them as do any works of art now known, and the sudden and complete overthrow of the nations that reared them, in the apparent midst of their erection, or while they were rejoicing over the great achievements of sculpture and strength, leave us but little doubt that the judgments of God were poured out without a mixture of mercy upon their land and upon their cities, upon their temples and their palaces alike, when by revolt and sin they became the children of wrath.

*Q.* What would probably have been the employment of the sons and daughters of Adam (the sons of God) for the first four thousand years of their sinless purity?

*A.* It is not positively known, nor has revelation indicated the exact spot of earth where Adam and Eve were first created, but it is supposed to have been near to Eden, or in that portion of the world. Indeed, it is our opinion that the country of the Nile might have been the favored spot; and if the garden of Eden, which we believe was subsequently planted "eastward in Eden," was located near the great river Euphrates, this locality would have been eastward of the Nile. We gather this idea also from the fact that temples of the most astonishing grandeur and workmanship are found erected along the course of this ancient and mighty river.

The progress, then, of the human family during the first four thousand years, would have exhibited itself in their temples erected to the living Jehovah, and in the songs and anthems of praise they might have offered up to Him—their Father and their God.

Having no sickness, no death, and but little sorrow, needing no food, save that, that grew spontaneously, no need of clothing, for the humanity they possessed was their clothing, as even ours will be, when raised up to meet the Lord in the air; their undivided attention might easily have been directed to the first and only universal language of the world—the language of poetry and of music.

*Q.* Did they marry, and were they given in marriage from their first creation?

*A.* We can get a better understanding of the regular steps in the history of man by reading to the seventh verse of the second chapter of Genesis, and for the eighth verse read the eighteenth, and so on to the close of the chapter, and then finish that portion omitted, *i. e.*, from the seventh to the eighteenth verses.

We do not say that the present arrangement of the verses in the chapter are intentionally wrong, but we think they have been misplaced, and by reading as above we plainly see the relation of marriage in its appropriate place, and the time that the first pair were united in marriage, God himself solemnizing the holy relation. Our Saviour remarked to the Pharisees: "Have ye not read that He which made them at the beginning made them male and female, and said, for this cause shall a man leave his father and mother and shall cleave to his wife, and they twain shall be one flesh. Wherefore they are no more twain, but one flesh. What God hath joined together let not man put asunder."—Matt. xvix: 3–6. We then learn that what Adam said to his wife, Gen. ii: 24, was the command of God, and that they both married, and were given in marriage from the time mentioned in Gen. i: 28 to the present time—no change in the holy relation of the man to his wife. In their first married relation the union was formed between the attributes, which were infallible, and this constituted the union an infallible and inseparable connection, so much so that even Adam could not avoid the dilemma into which the fallible senses had led the "bone of his bones and flesh of his flesh," though he tried to excuse the association before God by saying, "The woman whom thou gavest to be with me, she gave me of the tree, and I did eat."

*Q.* The marriages, then, of the first dispensation were very peculiar?

*A.* No more so than now, only in this relation; the attributes now being disorganized, we are not in possession of infallibility, and the senses being depraved, we can not judge of another, and hence, unless assisted by the Seven Spirits of God, we may make a very unwise choice, either of husband or wife. But this was impossible in primeval ages, "for the man was not without the woman, neither the woman without the man, in the Lord."

*Q.* Do we not suppose that the population of the earth extended to the western continent before the great transgression?

*A.* There are many evidences of an intelligent race of human beings, of whom there is no record left, either traditional or historical, on the western continent, and the remains of ruined cities and temples clearly show the artists to have been familiar with Egyptian and Grecian architecture, some specimens bearing great similarity.

We call a certain style of architecture Grecian or Egyptian, but both the Brahmans and Buddhists claim an ancestry more remote than modern Greece, Egypt, or Rome, for they go back to a time when gods were victorious over gods, and in these contests whole constellations were involved.

How wild the traditional record of events must be that occurred before the deluge, and of which only the daughters-in-law of Noah could communicate to their children, and thus hand it down from generation to generation, continually being augmented, as all traditions must be, in passing from mouth to ear for ages. Still we may learn something from the traditions of the unchristianized nations of the earth.

If, then, any style of architecture extant is called Grecian it may have existed thousands of years before Greece had a nationality; so we may say that the oldest relics of antiquity cast are very similar to those found in ruined cities in Central America.

*Q.* Where are those ruins that are unknown to history, or tradition, as to their first erection?

*A.* We find some of them in Central America. PALENQUE is the most noted, it having more statues and singular engravings, a richer display of mason-work and architecture than any other, and also resembling the obelisks and engravings of Thebes, and El Kanark, and other ruins along the Nile.

*Q.* What would we infer from this similarity?

*A.* That the probability is that the arts and sciences had in a measure their origin in the eastern hemisphere, and prevailed westward at first in their progress as they have of later ages.

*Q.* Do the columns of stone and ruined walls of these unknown cities indicate the force of strength that must have been accessible when Hypostyle Hall, in the Temple of El Kanark, on the Nile, was erected?

*A.* There have none as yet been discovered so vast and ponderous, but as there has been but little search in this direction in the interior of Central America, we need not be surprised if colossal structures may not yet be found of equally marvelous proportions.

The ruins of the Temple of Copan, as shown by the sketches of Mr. John L. Stephens, in his work, entitled *"Incidents of Travel in Central America, Chiapas, and Yucatan,"* published by Harper & Brother, 1842, illustrate in a very forcible manner the skill to which engraving had advanced in this remote age of the world; and in a clearer manner than on any other ruins found, indicate an alphabet either of hieroglyphics or of characters, to represent certain sounds, as does our own alphabet, and the same to have existed so far back in the earlier ages of our world as to have no record now left in ancient history or even tradition, so sudden and complete have been their overthrow.

Mr. Stephens' remarks in reference to the ruins of Palenque, and especially the tablets of hieroglyphics, that "the impression made upon our minds by these speaking but unintelligible tablets, I shall not attempt to describe. From some unaccountable cause they have never before been presented to the public. Captains Del Rio and Dupaix both refer to them, but in very few words, and neither of them has given a single drawing. Acting under a royal commission, and selected, doubtless, as fit men for the duties intrusted to them, they can not have been ignorant or insensible of their value.

"The Indians call this building an escuela, or

school, but our friends, the padres, call it a tribunal of justice, and these stones, they say, contained the tables of law. There is one important fact to be noticed: The hieroglyphics are the same as were found at Copan and Quirigua. The intermediate country is now occupied by races of Indians, speaking many different languages, and entirely unintelligble to each other, but there is room for the belief that the whole of that country was once occupied by the same race, speaking the same language, or, at least, having the same written characters."

*Q.* Is there any thing in the formation of these deserted ruins that are similar to those on the shores of the Nile?

*A.* The pyramids are somewhat alike, though of much less proportions; the carved work on the walls and statues, obelisks, and dressed columns, indicate that the workmen of each had been educated in the art of cutting stone in the same school, resembling them much more than did any work of the American Indians, the Europeans, when this continent was first discovered.

*Q.* What do we gather from this of the history of the first dispensation?

*A.* Only one fact, that the entire earth was once occupied by a race of human beings, whose education in the arts were similar, who erected edifices or temples to Deity, and that the same became habitations of beasts and fowl, and that the race perished, and with them the arts they understood so well, and that the American Indians are not their descendants; hence this race must have existed before the flood, if not before the fall, and as such were of one language, one school of arts, and were devoted to similar pursuits.

*Q.* Have we any relics of antiquity or of superior artistic skill, in any part of the United States that history gives no record as for what purpose they were arranged, or for what object they were fashioned?

*A.* We surely have, in the caves of Kentucky, and in other subterranean wonders, a brief sketch of which we will give: The three principal caves in Kentuckey are located in Barren and Edmonson Counties, about ninety miles from Louisville. They are truly the wonder of the world, and he who can place them as natural curiosities can easily consider a steamboat or railroad engine a natural curiosity also; and let us here remark that no writer would do so if there were any other way to account for the wonderful works of sculpture and skill, revealing design and grandeur alike marvelous.

The names of the caves are the Mammoth, the Diamond, and the Hundred Dome.

The Mammoth Cave is about eighty rods from Green River, with quite an ascent from the river to the entrance of the cave. Here is an opening in the hill-side of some twenty feet, and the descent is at one-eighth of a circle, or forty-five degrees, which continues for more than a hundred feet, and passes near to a great chasm of seventy or eighty feet in depth, close beside the passage way. The avenue through which the visitor must pass in order to reach the wonderful cavern is about thirty feet wide, the sides of which are as white as if newly plastered, being of white limestone rock.

The *avenues* have all been named by the owners of the caves, thereby giving a very spicy exhibit of nomenclature. The first avenue we pass is called Audubon, and is some half a mile in extent. The floor along the main avenue is rough and irregular, and great piles of loose rock are found all along the passage, while farther on the floor seems to glitter with crystals which can not be described, so grand is their appearance.

We now come to a spacious room called the Church, which has a large recess in the rock for a pulpit, with projections very much like a gallery, and a little farther on is a rock much resembling a coffin, which is named the Giant's Coffin; then we come to Martha's Palace, the ceiling of which is limestone, and the room some twenty-five feet in diameter, the lofty exhibit of which is very picturesque and beautiful, and the more so as near it flows a delightful fountain of cool spring water. Our passage now is beautifully arched in the most workman-like manner, but near it is another pit or chasm fifty feet deep, which, if not being in possession of a lamp or flambeau, we should most assuredly make it our last resting-place on earth.

Here is Minerva's Dome, which is about thirty feet high, and so lofty is the vast arch or ceiling, that its appearance is sublimely grand.

Our journey now for half a mile is through crooked passage ways, and over rough rocks, and near vastly deep chasms, one of which is called the Bottomless Pit, which is not less than a hundred and fifty feet deep, and were it not for a protection of modern days, along its brink no one could pass in safety; but, having passed the pit, we are almost startled at beholding the magnificent dome over our heads.

We now come to what is called Reveler's Hall, where the floor is quite smooth and the room spacious and grand. A very peculiar stone, eight feet across and one foot thick, standing on one edge; the point of the other edge holds the stone from falling by touching a projecting rock, under which dead-fall we must pass if we wish to farther proceed; but on we hurry through this trap, and through that narrow passage till we find ourselves in the Odd Fellows' Hall, which is so named from the fact that three links of a chain of purely stalactite formation are here to be seen, the whole chain being about six feet in length.

Bacon Chamber is an oddity, for the entire ceiling is hung with apparent hams of bacon, tied up in white sacks, and so suspended from the lofty roof. These are said to be solid stone, and near them is a round cavity as if a chaldron kettle had been pressed into the rocky ceiling, bottom up. Here is a body of water twenty feet deep, called the Dead Sea, along the slippery shore of which we must creep if we would pursue our journey till we come to the Mammoth River, which is filled with eyeless fish, and is forty feet wide and twenty feet deep, and doubtless somewhere empties into Green River, but no one has yet ascertained the place of intersection.

One singular phenomena of this cavern is that the air is pure and refreshing, notwithstanding we are several miles from the mouth of the cave, and a thousand feet below the surface.

The Star Chamber is a most magnificent sight, as the roof is more than sixty feet above our heads, and by a dim light the projecting white rocks look like stars, being entirely surrounded by black gypsum, which covers the entire ceiling. The stalactite formations are numerous and very picturesque, being formed by carbonate of lime, and suspended from the roof-like icicles of one to two feet in thickness, reaching from the ceiling to the floor, named, of course, after the ancient worthies of bygone ages, such as Hercules, Cæsar, Pompey, etc.

This cavern is among the wonders of the world, being in all its avenues more than a hundred miles in extent; but as we have only passed through some ten miles of the cave, we can form but a limited idea of the vast recesses of Mammoth Cave; but this we shall learn, that human beings could make their homes in this cave, and enjoy fresh and wholesome air, as well as refreshing springs and rivers of water.

*Q.* Do we suppose that all these avenues, domes, water-courses, arches, and stairways were fashioned by volcanic forces?

*A.* Nature has some very singular phenomena, but we believe that the unfallen race of Adam, in the first dispensation of time, while in possession of unlimited dominion over all living animals, could have as easily set them at work in excavating these channels in the then soft, clayey rock as to have used them in the erection of more noble but not less wonderful achievements.

But before we judge, let us examine the Diamond Cave. This cave is a very recent discovery, only having been known since 1859.

It is situated in or near the center of a large basin or tract of land descending from every point of compass, and at its deepest point the water from heavy rains will remain on the surface only a short time.

The country around the cave is adapted to grain raising, and even to the very entrance could thus be used, though from the center of this depression to the mouth of the cave is near one-fourth of a mile.

We descend by a substantial stairway through the rock some forty feet or more and reach the rocky floor of the magnificent rotunda, thirty feet high and seventy feet in diameter. The form of this rotunda is not regular, but from the roof and sides hang stalactites in great variety, of from a few inches to many feet in diameter. It might be an easy matter for us to reconcile the stalactite formations from the roof, as the dripping of water, when impregnated with calcareous spar, might possibly produce this hollow icicle; but to reverse the position and see thousands of them out in a direct line on the sides and stalagmites, that is, icicles springing from the bottom upward, as Cleopatra's needle, being only six or eight inches in diameter and some five feet high, our ideas of the icicle formation are quite out of place, and we begin to think they are vegetable formations, and receive their nourishment and grow out of the rock. Some of these stalagmites are incrusted with a kind of coral formation, some are covered with clayey oxide of iron, which renders them a light brown color, and some again are as clear as crystal.

In some places the entire floor is covered with these stalagmites, from an inch to ten inches in height; and again the rocks exhibit, by the aid of our light, far up above our heads, consecutive steps covered with this strange icicle formation, points being upward, and look the perfect image of a cascade.

Here is the appearance of the upper jaw of a huge serpent, and these stalactites hanging from the jaw, in appearance, as poisonous fangs.

There is a mammoth stalagmite as large as a farmer's hay-stack, twenty-five feet in diameter and fifteen feet in height, the largest in the known world. The ceiling in many places is nearly as white as snow, and full of little holes half an inch deep, and as large across, which are called the Vermiculated Ceiling, and looks somewhat like the honey-comb.

The grand avenue through which we pass is filled with marvelous formations, some like a flag partly unfurled, and others like sheets, through which our lamps cast a mellowed light, exhibiting beautiful colors. Here is hanging from the ceiling a monster magnolia flower, four feet in diameter and six or eight feet long; there we behold beautifully ornamented columns, with cornices, moldings, and carved work of the most exquisite taste. A little farther onward we find a stalagmite about four feet high, perfectly resembling a female shrouded in white, which figure is called Lot's Wife. We now come to a Gothic archway, and thence into the Palace of Crystals, around us, above us, and beneath us, the most exquisite and delicate formations present themselves to our astonished vision.

But the most marvelous is the Hundred Dome Cave in the same vicinity.

We will give only a few of the thousand wonders here unfolded:

The entrance to these caves are all on a slope of forty-five degrees, and from fifty to a hundred feet to the first grand entrance or magnificent hall. This reception room is a grand rotunda, fifty feet in diameter and fifty feet high. Here is Solomon's Throne, draped in a magnificent manner by stalactite formations down to the floor, twenty feet; here we see the edges of shelving rock, scolloped at the outer edge, some four feet in diameter, which gives to the hall a romantic and pleasing appearance.

Let us now visit the Ladies' Avenue, and here the walls are decorated in a new and unprecedented manner. Clusters of apparent grapes are hanging from the walls in singular profusion. Forty rods farther, and we see Brock's Monument—a huge column of smooth limestone; then look at Dripping Dome, more than a hundred feet high, and fifteen feet in diameter at the bottom; the sides are elegantly fluted.

The walls of Court's Avenue, still farther on, are marvelously ornamented by little globules of marble attached to the rocks by a very slender stem of stone, from one to two inches in length.

We will now enter Vineyard Avenue, and

look at the curiously wrought grape-vines, extending over our heads, and loaded with clusters of calcareous grapes; the circumference of some of the clusters are nearly five feet, being twenty inches in diameter. This vine has a perfect resemblance to the grape, and appears loaded with its autumn luxury. Passing on, we come to the Twin Domes; the first is about sixty feet high, having a uniform diameter of fifteen feet; the other is eliptical, eight by fourteen feet, and rises to the enormous height of two hundred feet, the sides of this rock being fluted in the grandest style.

What a vastly high ceiling is over our heads when a spire, towering nearly as high as the tower of Bunker Hill, in Boston, fails to reach it. Here again is Everett's Dome, fourteen feet in diameter and three hundred feet high, and Clay's Dome, sixteen feet square,.and as high as Everett's.

The last and most remarkable dome is that called the Mammoth, it being twenty feet in diameter at the base, and stands perpendicular, and rises more than five hundred feet.

Who can tell how it was reared, or how this vast arch and all these innumerable wonders were wrought!

We will now glance at another Mammoth Cave, recently discovered in Nevada, in which very similar formations exist as in those already noticed. Of its wonders a recent writer remarks that it bids fair to outrival Kentucky's great wonder. He says:

"It is situated in the Buckskin or White Mountain range; and the entrance, which is situated near the base of an isolated butte or hiacacho, and so low that a man must stoop to enter it; but twenty feet in this vault of limestone, it widens rapidly, turning toward the east, and you pass through chamber after chamber of immense proportions, some of them of such vast height that the light of the torches show no signs of a roof. It has been penetrated to the extent of a mile, and no end has yet been discovered. The exploring party saw many chambers in which tongues of limestone hung from the roof, in places almost touching the floor; and in others stalactites and stalagmites abounded, as in the Mammoth Cave of Kentucky. They found burnt sage-brush, showing that the Indians had been there as far as they went. Since that time, the Indians, on being interrogated, say that they have been five days' journey into the cavern, where they found a lake full of fish, and yet saw no end to the succession of lofty chambers stretching out before them."

No doubt that when this cave has been carefully explored the wonders of this hidden recess of the earth, will tax the ingenuity of man for a solution of its sculptured mysteries.

Nor are these caverns all the remarkable phenomena of the history of caves. We will mention one other, and that is *Fingal's Cave.*

This singular musical instrument, for we can call it nothing else, is found in the Island of Staffa, one of the group of the Hebrides. This vast hall, from the ocean into the earth, and the basaltic columns on either side that support the arch, are so peculiarly constructed that the dropping of water from the roof upon the waters underneath produce all the perfect harmonies of a loud-sounding organ. The hall or cave is two hundred and twenty-seven feet long, one hundred and sixty-six feet high, and forty feet wide. Of all the wonders of art this is surpassed by none in this direction. The cave near the Giant's Causeway has its wonders; the caves of Kentucky have their wonders, but to build a vast hall, supported by columns that have resisted the dashing waves of the ocean for unknown ages, and to so arrange it that the ocean never recedes by its tides so far as to leave it too shallow to echo the sound of the falling waters from the dripping roof, and to so construct it that always its harmonies should exist, and in the midst of these basaltic columns one can listen to the remarkable *echoes*, so far transcending any other pre-fallen work of art, as to challenge the world to produce such beautiful harmonies of music, so perpetual and perfect.

On each side the entire length of this cave these basaltic columns rise from the bottom in the sea, to one hundred and sixty-six feet to the roof above, and only a few of them are even now in a broken condition, the position of the echos still remaining a wonder to the world, and an unceasing organ of musical tones.

## CHAPTER XIII.

God's Purpose in Redemption—The Plan Laid—The Covenant of Grace—The Parties in the Covenant—Christ, the Archetype, Suffers—The Human Saviour a Type of the Eternal Archetype—Why the Garden of Eden was Planted.

QUESTION. When in the eternal purpose was the plan of human redemption laid?

*Ans.* We should always remember that *time* is only a revolving wheel of continued rotation, and that, as it counts off its revolutions, so periods are marked; and from one period to another we measure time, and this, too, by the velocity with which this whirling sphere makes its annual and daily motions. But back of this, before this orb emerged from Chaos, there were cycles, epochs, periods, from which the eternal Jehovah drew his designs and measured out his purposes.

Of his thoughts and his purposes, we can only learn of him and of his word.

God speaking by the prophet Isaiah, (xliii: 13, 14), thus remarks, "Therefore ye are my witnesses, saith the Lord, that I am God. Yea, before the day was, I am He." Here he refers to a cycle of time before the King of day had shone upon the earth. Our Saviour also adverts to a period far back of the records of time: "Father," said He, John xvii: 5, "glorify thou me with thy own self, with the glory which I had with thee before the world was." The Apostle Paul also reverts to a similar time or period in his letter to the Ephesians i: 4, "According as he hath chosen us in Him, before the foundation of the world."

We then conclude that there was a cycle or a point on the dial of eternity, when the great Jehovah determined to surround himself with a royalty, who should bear his image, should be spirit of his Spirit, form of his form, and children of the Most High.

*Q. How* was this plan laid?

*A.* By a wonderful sacrifice in the harmonial courts of glory.

The Apostle, in his letter to the Hebrews, ix: 14, thus declares the manner of this sacrifice. He says, after showing the inferiority of the types in their relation to the flesh, "How much more shall the blood of Christ, who, *through the eternal Spirit* offered himself without spot to God, purge your conscience from dead works to serve the living God."

The Revelator, speaking of the sacrifice of Jesus, saw "a lamb as it *had been slain,* having seven horns and seven eyes, which are the Seven Spirits of God, sent forth into all the earth." Rev. v: 6. He also speaks of him as a "Lamb slain from the foundation of the world." Rev. xiii: 8.

*Q.* Did the plan of Redemption embrace a Covenant?

*A.* It would so seem by reading the 89th Psalm, 26–7–8: "He shall cry unto me, Thou, my Father, my God, and the Rock of my salvation. Also, I will make him, my first-born, higher than the kings of the earth. My mercy will I keep for him for evermore, and my covenant shall stand fast with him."

*Q.* Who were the parties to this covenant?

*A.* They were God the Father, and Spirit, and Son.

*Q.* Could God, who was only ONE, make a covenant with Himself?

*A.* Most assuredly; we often make a covenant with our *memory* to remember certain events, with our lips to never profane His name, and with our attributes to forever love Him.

How much more reasonably, then, could He make a covenant with Himself, when He had in his great mind so wonderful an object to accomplish.

*Q.* How was this plan accomplished?

*A.* It was first announced in the Temple of

the great God by the sacrifice of the Archetypal Messiah?

*Q.* How?

*A.* God, the Infinite, Eternal, unseen Form—the Deity—so divided Himself as to separately personify each person of the Trinity. In that relation the attributes of God became the council, God the Father the judge, and God the Archetypal Son the sufferer.

*Q.* Can Deity suffer?

*A.* Why not? Could remission of sin be applied to the immortal part of man, which is a spirit, without a spiritual sacrifice?

*Q.* But is not the human body of Jesus the great, the *only* sacrifice?

*A.* For our human nature it is, but our spiritual nature needs a higher, a nobler sacrifice than a "vail," a type. Heb. x: 20.

*Q.* Was the humanity of Jesus a type?

*A.* Most assuredly. He himself declares that "before Abraham was I am." "The beginning and the ending, the first and the last."

If he was the eternal Word, and He took upon himself flesh, the flesh could not be the Archetype—the model; but he whose geneology is not reckoned is the Wonderful, the Counselor, the Mighty God, the great Redeemer.

*Q.* Was this Archetypal Sacrifice, made in heaven?

*A.* The apostle declares that "it was necessary that the patterns of things in the heavens should be purified by these, but the heavenly things themselves with better sacrifices than these."—Hebrew ix: 23. Just in proportion to the value of the soul's salvation, above the salvation of the body from human peril, so is the Archetypal blood above the human blood of Jesus. The one is applied to the soul by the Spirit, the other to the body at the resurrection.

*Q.* Was this sacrifice made in the Council Chamber of the eternal God before the earth was fashioned for man?

*A.* It surely must have been; and in that covenant the Holy Spirit was to not only fashion the world of matter, but reprove the world of mind, and also apply the Archetypal blood of Christ to the soul of the penitent believer.

In this covenant, God the Father pledged a successful issue—the Church of the first born—"a royal priesthood, a peculiar people," and that the Eternal Word should see the travail of His soul (His Archetypal travail) and should be satisfied.

*Q.* How could Deity suffer by his own choice, or one part of Deity suffer from the action of another?

*A.* In the same manner that we can choose to suffer for another. Your house is in flames, you see your darling boy in the peril of death, and by suffering some pain yourself you can save his life. You choose to suffer, and you make your own voluntary powers carry you into suffering and peril for another. So great was the love of God for us, that He spared not his own Son; and so great was the love of Jesus, that for the glory that appeared in the plan of redemption, He could suffer for us, and in the realms of glory make the atonement.

*Q.* Did not the Deity in Christ, then, suffer on the cross?

*A.* Not at all. The Attributes of God withdrew from the sinless senses of Jesus, and He cried, "Why hast thou forsaken me?" that is, his human senses cried to his attributes as *they* laid the sacrifice upon an earthly altar. "He had power to lay down his life and power to take it again."

In this covenant the Archetype submitted to suffering from the spear and sword of Justice, and Light. Thus, all the attributes of God accepted the condition which the great Redeemer covenanted to fulfill, and to complete on earth the work of grace begun in heaven. He also pledged to vail himself in humanity, to fight with and conquer death, and bring life and immortality to light.

Upon this covenant the attributes of God fashioned the earth for man, and these, after forming man, breathed into his nature an invisible and perpetual likeness of themselves, while, in his physical formation, he was the image of the archetypal Christ.

*Q.* Then man, in his primeval state, was an exalted and semi-deified being?

*A.* He "was fearfully and wonderfully made," embracing the earthly and heavenly, the human and divine nature.

To him the glory of God was visible, and the songs of the cherubim his inheritance. He was lord of the entire world, and the governor of all on earth that he beheld.

*Q.* But was he not placed in a garden and commanded to dress it?

*A.* Not at first; not until he had filled the design of the great God in matters that pertained to a world, and his superintendence over the host of earth no longer necessary; then, and not till then, did the Creator see fit to plant a garden in which to put the man he had created, and give him a new law, a new condition to happiness, a new occupation, a responsibility involving his earthly existence.

*Q.* When, then, was the garden of Eden planted?

*A.* We have no positive data on which to predicate an opinion, but it is safe to say that it was planted during the period of the first dispensation, and probably near its close.

*Q.* What is a garden?

*A.* An inclosure where fruits, and flowers, and herbs are cultivated.

*Q.* What were the remarkable trees of this garden?

*A.* The tree of the knowledge of Good and Evil, and the tree of Life.

*Q.* Were these trees anywhere to be found on the earth till now?

*A.* It does not seem from the history given us that they were planted during the days of Creation. Nor do we find any restriction as to any tree till now, but this first dispensation must close, or the earth would become infinitely too small for the vast population that must, in the very nature of things, be produced; so, as a vesture or garment soiled and worn, He folded it up and laid it aside.

*Q.* Why was this garden planted for man and he placed there, amidst the temptations, to dress it?

*A.* To test the responsibility of the seven senses of man.

*Q.* How so?

*A. First*, the sense of *sight;* it was indeed a fascinating tree to look upon; and, *second*, the sense of *taste*, for it was delicious; and, *third*, the sense of *language*, for report said it was good to make one wise; and, *fourth*, the *judgment* sense, because thereby they would be as gods, knowing good and evil; and, *fifth*, it was talked in the *ear* by the serpent that God did surely know that they would not die, and they heard it; and, *sixth*, the *aroma* of this fruit led them to pause beneath its shadow; and, *touching* it by the seventh sense, all the senses rallied to the judgment sense, and the mortal organism could not, or did not, resist it. The attributes being ever-living, anticipated not the nature of fear, shame, and despair that the fruit of this fatal tree would produce.

# CHAPTER XIV.

The Second Dispensation—Genealogy of Cain—Tubal-Cain, Master of Arts—Jabal, Organist—Sons of God and Sons of Men—The Book of Revelation—Who is the Devil—How he became a Devil—The Unpardonable Sin—The Mystery of the Woman Clothed with the Sun—The Beast—The Number of his Name—Mark—Image—Babylon the Great.

QUESTION. When did the second dispensation commence?

*Ans.* With the transgression of our first parents.

*Q.* What are the peculiarities of this dispensation when contrasted with the dispensation of purity?

*A.* They are many and wonderful. In the first place, Adam and Eve were ejected from the garden, their senses totally depraved, and their dominion over the beasts, birds, and fishes lost; the earth cursed by being adapted to their fallen natures, and the attributes disorganized, and the soul, immortal, polluted.

In the second place, their happiness gone with their purity, and death their inheritance.

*Q.* Did they suppose that their fallen and depraved senses would be inherited by their children?

*A.* They did not; for Eve, at the birth of Cain, remarked, "I have gotten a man from the Lord," or this is a son of God; but of the sorrows of the mother, when she afterward saw him a fratricide, a murderer, who can tell?

*Q.* What is the history of Cain?

*A.* His history is brief and peculiar.

After Jehovah had given out a law to protect him amidst the unnumbered sons of God that had populated the entire globe, lest they, seeing him with senses so debased, might think him a beast, and kill him; and placed a visible mark upon him, to secure to him the right to life, and had bid him depart from his presence to the fugitive land, or land of Nod; it would appear that very shortly he secured to himself a wife of some of the daughters of the sons of God, or of Adam's unfallen posterity.

*Q.* Have we any chronology of the generations of Cain?

*A.* Only till the birth of Seth, which was one hundred and thirty years, and in that period we have six generations. This places the age of Cain, at the time he slew his brother, at twenty-one years; his brother Abel, nineteen. We then have from Cain to Enoch one year, from Enoch to Irad twenty-two years, from Irad to Mehujael twenty-two years, from Mehujael to Mathusael twenty-two years, from Mathusael to Lamech twenty-two years; and from Lamech to Jabal and Tubal-cain twenty-two years; making in all one hundred and eleven years, which will extend the genealogy of Cain to some few years after the birth of Seth; and here the sacred historian leaves the history of Cain with six generations in about one hundred and ten or twelve years, and Lamech a polygamist.

*Q.* Did Adam and Eve have any other posterity during this century?

*A.* We have no record of any; they might have had daughters, but no sons; the Holy Record asserts that for eight hundred years after Seth was born, they lived and begat sons and daughters.

*Q.* Do we suppose that Seth begat Enos as his first-born?

*A.* Not as a certainly; for Cain is not mentioned in the genealogy of Adam, and but one son is mentioned by name, and that may not be the first son or the last.

On the other hand, we have no genealogy of the mothers, only as their names occur in connection with those whose record is given.

*Q.* What was the probable condition of the world at the commencement of the second century after the fall?

*A.* We may reasonably suppose that the earth was more extensively peopled than at the present moment. We find that Jabul, Lamech's son by his wife Adah, became the father or instructor of those who used the harp and organ. So we may conclude that these instruments were in use even before the transgression, for that time had not then passed to exceed a hundred and fifty years.

Tubal-cain, Lamech's son by his other wife, Zilla, became an instructor of every artificer in iron and brass. So, at this early period, iron and brass were in use, and we have no doubt from the sketch, in reference to the garden of Eden and the rivers that flowed through it, that gold and other precious metals were in use as ornamental and valuable necessaries in the erection of temples, and for musical instruments, two or three thousand years before Eden was planted.

*Q.* Were the first posterity of Adam (the sons of God) located in the same vicinity, and immediately familiar with the sons of men?

*A.* It would seem so, by the allusion made to them and their subsequent action.

*Q.* From them, then, the sons of men may have learned many of the useful arts of earlier years, such as embalming the dead, the mixing of fadeless colors, etc., which now are lost to the world?

*A.* So it would naturally appear; and as their

form was the same as the fallen race, and as through the sense of language they conversed with each other, as did Adam and Eve before their transgression, we have the greatest reason to suppose that they were familiar with the condition of the fallen race, and may have assisted in the burial ceremonies of Abel and others, who died at an early period of the world's history of transgression.

*Q.* Why do we not have the history of this race if they were the descendants of Adam?

*A.* We have as much, yea more, of their history than we have of the angels in heaven. The history of redemption from transgression could not commence before the transgression; the condition of sinners could not precede their sin; and as the revelation of God, in Creation, is as much a revelation as is the Apocalypse or the Prophecies, we can not expect the history of fallen man to commence earlier than the revolt. Hence the earth was peopled by the sons of God when our first parents were placed in the garden of temptation. We also learn of the notoriety of some of the sons of God by reading Gen. vi: 4, that these "were of old men of renown," and this remark would appear the more singular when we reflect that this almost universal revolt of the sons of God took place not later than six hundred and sixty-six years after the transgression. So, if the sons of God were of old men of renown, they must have been artists, designers, or musicians; for the earlier languages were spoken in tones and song, and this may be the reason why their idiom of language is lost, for we find abundance of evidence of their skill and achievements, their sculpture and architectural knowledge, but have not yet deciphered their language.

*Q.* How long a period of time did the earth remain after the fall and before the flood?

*A.* Chronology indicates that it was sixteen hundred and fifty-five years, but there is much uncertainty in reference to the exact time; we think the period to have been sixteen hundred and sixty-six years.

*Q.* Have we any history of this long period of the world's achievements?

*A.* Nothing but a bare genealogy, unless given by the Book of Revelation.

*Q.* How could the Apocalypse relate to this age?

*A.* As easily as could the writings of Moses relate to the Creation.

*Q.* What part of Revelation refers to this age of the world's history?

*A.* The Lord, in giving instructions to John what to write, remarked, "Write the things that thou hast seen, and the things that are, and the things that shall be." We must, then, understand one thing, *i. e.*, that the Book of Revelation is not all prophecy, but it is a statement of facts and visions, and, as the "beast that arose out of the sea was, and is not, and yet is," when it became the object of his greatest wonder, we must, to understand it, believe it to have existed antecedent to this period, and necessarily could not have been the Catholic Church, however great her sins may have appeared before God.

*Q.* At what period of time do we suppose he saw this beast—the great Red Dragon?

*A.* It is our opinion that this seven-headed beast made its appearance in full power about six hundred and sixty-six years after the fall of man, and one thousand years before the flood.

*Q.* Where do we find this number?

*A.* The revelator gives it as the number of the beast: "Here is wisdom. Let him that hath understanding count the number of the beast; for it is the number of a man; and his number is six hundred three-score and six."— Rev. xiii: 18.

*Q.* How do we understand the mystical number seven, so often alluded to in the seven vials of wrath, seven last plagues, and the seven trumpets?

*A.* There is one thing we should remember, that under the covenant of grace, whether in the typical dispensation or in the triumphs of redemption, the seven attributes of God are at labor for man; and a withdrawal of any of these nationally is a national calamity, and the only *wrath* the world has ever experienced from God is the withdrawal of these intercessors. A sin, then, against the Holy Ghost is a sin against the attributes of God; and, as they are our intercessors, and we are in possession of these attributes, the sin is perfectly suicidal; because, if they withdraw from us, we are irrecoverably lost. Hence the Saviour remarks: "All manner of sin and blasphemy shall be forgiven unto men, but the blasphemy against the Holy Ghost shall not be forgiven unto men."—Matt. xii: 31. And it is repeated in still stronger terms in the thirty-second verse.

*Q.* The withdrawal of the attributes of God from the mind, then, reduces it to hopelessness and despair?

*A.* So God hath revealed the heinous nature of this sin.

*Q.* But the mystical seven is also revealed in the seven-headed beast—how is this?

*A.* The seven heads of the beast are the seven depraved attributes of the devil, when the seven attributes of God have been withdrawn.

The devil is totally beyond the reach of the love of God or the influence of His attributes, hence his septenary head is the vile attributes of his demoniac nature.

*His* attributes (having a spiritual body or an organic form in his angelic state) became the mind to his spirit, and his sin resulted in the total depravity of his attributes; so mercy could not reach his case; man's attributes being only disorganized or disconnected through their moral relation to the fallen senses, God's mercy could reach his case; and the Seven Spirits of God, when sought after and obtained, through the archetypal sacrifice, could restore him to Divine favor.

*Q.* How is one "possessed of the devil," or of "seven devils," or of "legions?"

*A.* By the withdrawal of the controlling spirit or attributes of God, the attributes of man are helpless and have no power to resist the devil; but if we are under the influence of the Holy Spirit or the attributes of God, we can resist the tempter, and in and through the name of the Archetypal Christ, whom he fears, and who has become our advocate and intercessor, we can drive him from us, or, "resist the devil and he will flee from you." But this must be accomplished through the name of Jesus.

*Q.* The devil, then, is the embodiment of a spiritual form and spiritual attributes, totally depraved?

*A.* This view is correct; and no doubt the revolt in heaven, by which he forever placed himself beyond the reach of redemption, occurred very nearly at the time of the revolt of the sons of God on earth.

*Q.* Why so?

*A.* Because we read in connection with that revolt that he was cast out into the earth.

*Q.* Why do we go to the Book of Revelation to learn the wickedness of the first ages?

*A.* Because revelation is all that is left to indicate the character of the wickedness of that age.

A thousand years of the most horrible revolting sins and crimes ever committed on the earth are summed up in a single chapter; and had not revelation told us of the heinous nature of the sin, we might wonder at the necessity of the flood; and again, we should forever have been uninformed as to the *sin* that caused the great Creator to "repent that He had made man."

*Q.* What was that sin?

*A.* First, in the act of repudiating and ignoring the law of God in reference to marriage, and, secondly, in erecting idolatrous temples and dedicating them to devils.

*Q.* Will the Book of Revelation bring the sin out in its untold heinousness if rightly understood?

*A.* We think it will; and the Book of Revelation can be clearly explained only, by looking at it from that stand-point.

*Q.* Where does the Revelator draw the panorama of this age of the world?

*A.* To get a clear view of the facts, let us read, commencing with the sixth chapter of Genesis: "And it came to pass, when men began to multiply on the face of the earth, and daughters were born to them, that the sons of God saw the daughters of men that they were fair; and they took them wives of all they chose. And the

Lord said, My spirit shall not always strive with man, for that he also is flesh; yet his days shall be an hundred and twenty years."

*Q.* "He also;" who does this refer to?

*A.* To the sons of God; they were flesh, and for sin must die as much as others, for the Apostle says, "Death reigned from Adam to Moses, even over them who had not sinned after the similitude of Adam's transgression."

God then says of them, "He also is flesh;" that is, he was from the earth, as was Adam, being of his posterity, and though the sin of this amalgamation was not just like Adam's sin, it was nevertheless sin, and death must follow.

In order to obtain a clear view of the Apocalypse, it is necessary to remember that all nations, all kingdoms, all people of whatever tribe or tongue, in heaven or on earth, *must* have rulers; a king, a potentate, a president, or a chief; all the nations that have ever existed have seen this necessity, and have either chosen such rulers, or have subscribed to their birthright to power.

Again, it is an established law, that all rulers are held responsible to the laws of God for the manner in which they govern the people, and that their national character is shown by the actions and transactions of their kings.

And again, whatever calamity befalls the king or ruler, or whatever heinous offense he commits, is visited also upon the governed. If he is conquered, they are conquered; if he is victorious, they are also victorious.

We may then rest securely on this fact, that the sons of God must have had a king—a sovereign, and he being infallible, the government must have been peaceful and glorious. And as there was no sin in the world at that time, there could have been no sickness or death, hence the government must have been singularly prosperous. This may have excited emulation, or even rivalry in other dominions; and the regard paid to this race of sentient intelligences, might have provoked complaint from other intelligences. We of course do not directly infer that the "accuser of our brethren," as spoken of by the Revelator, had reference to this particular, yet there were complaints made, and accusations brought against the children of God; and when the devil and Satan were repulsed and driven out of heaven, there were great rejoicings over him, on the account as above remarked.—Rev. xii: 10.

*Q.* Who was the king—the sovereign of the race of the pure and holy, who peopled this earth in all its vastness, when it also was free from all curse and pollution?

*A.* We may possibly solve this question by examining the twelfth chapter of Revelation, in all its bearings. In doing so, it will be necessary for us to read only a verse or two, and then make the application:

"And there appeared a great wonder in heaven; a woman clothed with the sun, and the moon under her feet, and upon her head a crown of twelve stars."—Rev. xii.

We will now suppose that we are reading the Book of Revelation, instead of the Book of Mystery, and take the woman to be, as she is represented, a woman; and in this relation, the mother of all living.

*She is clothed with the sun.* There can be no glory so bright as the glory of pure and virtuous womanhood. Around her are the tenderest ties of life, the highest honors of heaven. To her every element of greatness among the hosts of the saints on earth, or in heaven, is subsidiary; even the plan of redemption found its completeness through woman, and His glory was veiled in her glory, and hence she was clothed with the sun—the light of heaven.

*The moon was under her feet.* The moon derives its glory from the sun, the child from the mother. The moon, then, became a beautiful representative of her posterity, who were honored by the glory of the woman.

*And upon her head a crown of twelve stars.* The *crown* refers to dominion, and the twelve stars to the period of that dominion. Then if the mystical twelve refers to the duration of time, which is probably twelve thousand years, we can readily understand the comparison. Each star a period of one thousand years, and the woman indissolubly united to the destiny of the race through every period of time.

Her glory centered in two objects, one the sovereign, who should lead and govern the pure and sinless through the first dispensation of time—four thousand years; and the second the King immortal, who should lead and govern his people, not only through the typical and gracious dispensations of time, but through all eternity.

Thus clothed with the sun, the woman became the center of wonder and surprise; and as the purposes of God were constantly unfolding, showing that he designed through the "seed of the woman" to vail himself in humanity, "Lucifer, son of the morning," (Isa. xiv: 12) began his meditation of revolt.

*Q.* Can an angel sin?

*A.* Most assuredly; the Scriptures give us the facts concerning their transgression: "And the angels which kept not their first estate, but left their own habitation, he hath reserved in everlasting chains under darkness unto judgment of the great day."—Jude 6.

*Q.* What could tempt an angel?

*A.* A rival, whose exaltation in the scale of being might excel his own.

*Q.* What rival had Lucifer?

*A.* The seed of the woman; to see a being just above the brute, a day-laborer, a substance animated, a man of the earth, earthy, soon to be the child of God, to be exalted to royalty and honor, and this, too, through no worthy act of his own, but solely through the election of grace, induced him to rebel.

*Q.* How can the attributes sin?

*A.* By rebellion. When the attribute, Light, rebelled against the light of the Spirit of God, God's Spirit of light withdrew its brilliancy from the attribute, which left the attribute in the agony of darkness forever. So when the attribute, Mercy, was withdrawn from the association, then Satan became a murderer. And when Truth was withdrawn he became a liar, and the father of lies. So with all the seven attributes.

*Q.* Can the attributes of man sin?

*A.* They can, and this is the unpardonable sin; it can never be forgiven, either here or hereafter. Satan committed this sin, as the first great transgressor, and can never be forgiven; for the attribute that thus sins (and as there is but one attribute that unites and combines them all, and no one, can act without this combination), then they are all embraced in the one transgression.

*Q.* If Love is the uniting nucleus, around which all the attributes rally, how could this attribute sin?

*A.* Just as we have remarked. Love, loves to be supreme in its own exaltation as well as to see others exalted. So this attribute, already having a comprehension of the glory of the woman's seed, fancied that this would eclipse his distinguished greatness, and determined for a mastery, as soon as the man-child reached the throne in glory.

"And there appeared another wonder in heaven, and behold, a great red dragon, having seven heads and ten horns, and seven crowns upon his heads."—Rev. xii: 3.

It was truly marvelous to see the change—the wonderful transformation that the rebellion of the seven attributes occasioned.

These now appeared as seven heads: for *Light* appeared Darkness; for *Life* appeared Death; for *Holiness*, Blasphemy; for *Justice*, Lust, Murder, Theft; for *Mercy*, Revenge, Cruelty; for *Truth*, Lies, Falsehoods; and for *Love*, all the elements of Hate, Anger, Wrath.

This transformed him into a hideous monster, whose character in all its depth of infamy no language can express—the Great Red Dragon. He "stood before the woman to destroy the child as soon as it was born."

*Q.* Did he accomplish his design?

*A.* It appears that he did not, for the man-child became a sovereign and reigned with absolute power and in perfect harmony with his duty to God and his governed, and the old serpent kept his pent-up purposes in check till the man-child was caught up to God and His throne.

*Q.* Who was the mother of this sovereign?

*A.* Probably Eve, for she was so named because she was the mother of all living, and the eldest son has ever been heir to the throne, and probably this was her first-born.

*Q.* Have we any clew to his name?

*A.* Only the name of Michael, and this at the time of the great victory in heaven, for the revolt embraced nearly one-third of the stars or angels of heaven, who were, with the great red dragon, cast out of the glorious habitations of light.—Luke 10–18.

*Q.* What reason have we to suppose the mother of Michael was Eve?

*A.* She had a remnant of seed against which the great red dragon directed his war of extermination. "He went to make war with the remnant of her seed, which keep the commandments of God and have the testimony of Jesus Christ."—Rev. xii: 17. This remnant may have been the believers in Christ, as were Abel, Seth, Enoch, and Noah.

But the term does not imply a single woman, but holy womanhood in its earlier generic sense. Hence, holy womanhood did not fall at the transgression of Eve, more than did the sons of God at the transgression of Adam; and woman, which the great red dragon hoped to destroy when the first pair transgressed, remained still clothed with the sun in her native purity, for "a time, times, and the dividing of a time," or nearly to the Noachian deluge. Before this time, the number of the dragon's name, or the mark Cain had received, or the idolatrous image tattooed upon the face or hand, became universal, as we have shown, and this was four hundred and six years after the transgression of our first parents, and the time that holy womanhood remained on earth after this period was twelve hundred and sixty years. Now, if the chronology we have adopted is correct, it was sixteen hundred and sixty-six years from the fall to the flood; then, adding the six hundred and sixty-six to the twelve hundred and sixty, we have nineteen hundred and twenty-six; and by subtracting sixteen hundred and sixty-six from the latter number, we have two hundred and sixty years before the fall of man as the period when Michael was translated through the efficacy of the archetypal atonement. At the same time was the war in heaven, and during this period the garden of Eden was planted. By this supposition we learn that human nature may have become worn with years, and the garden of Eden fitly became our first parents as a homestead provided for them, that they might retire from the wider field of labor, to only dress and cultivate a small but beautiful inclosure, where fruits of the most exquisite flavor, and flowers of the richest tints and sweetest aroma, might cheer their age and crown their ripened years.

*Q.* Do we suppose that our first parents inherited decrepitude with their years?

*A.* Not what might be called decrepitude, but it is a law of nature that time wears upon all terrestrial substances; and as Adam was from the earth, earthy, terrestrial, he also must be subject to the same general law.

*Q.* What was the wilderness into which holy womanhood was driven?

*A.* Probably the mountain fastnesses, or the caves and dens of the earth.

*Q.* How did she make her journey thither?

*A.* By flight. Having dominion over all the fowls of heaven, the whole host of the feathered tribe were summoned to bear her to the quiet resting-place where she was fed during the prophecy of the two witnesses, twelve hundred and sixty years.—Rev. xii: 14.

*Q.* Who were those witnesses?

*A.* They were the successors of the man-child, and of their labors and conflicts we shall better understand as we farther investigate the great Babylon.

*Q.* How was the victory over the Great Red Dragon celebrated in heaven?

*A.* We read, "And I heard a loud voice, saying in heaven, Now is come salvation, and strength, and the kingdom of our God, and the power of his Christ; for the accuser of our brethren is cast down, which accused them before our God day and night."—Rev. xii: 10.

*Q.* How could there be "day and night" in heaven?

*A.* It does not so positively assert, for "our brethren," to whom this alludes, were those who lived in a world of day and night, and the accuser had circulated slanders against them, which crimes he asserted that they had committed both day and night.

*Q.* How did they overcome the accuser?

*A.* By the archetypal blood of the Lamb, which blood had been shed before the world was inhabited by mortals, and this blood, when applied by the Spirit, rendered them the sons of God, that is, children of the eternal Father; and as this covenant embraced Adam and his posterity, and not angels, this blood could be thus applied.

*Q.* Could the sinless of Adam's race be translated?

*A.* Why not? Does sin make humanity any better than holiness? Were not Enoch and Elijah translated?

Now, if the archetypal blood of Christ could be applied to the sanctification of the Spirit, and He, by covenant, had sealed it with his human blood, why could not the work of translation precede his human sacrifice as easily in the case of the sons of God as in the case of Enoch?

We read of those who were presumptively the translated ones, as follows: "And they sung as it were a new song before the throne and before the four beasts, and the elders; and no man could learn that song but the hundred and forty and four thousand which were redeemed from the earth. These are they which were not defiled with women, for they are virgins. These are they which follow the Lamb whithersoever he goeth. These were redeemed from among men, being the first-fruits unto God and to the Lamb. And in their mouth was found no guile, for they are without fault before the throne of God."—Rev. xiv: 3–5.

*Q.* Then there were a class of intelligences redeemed from among men who were faultless?

*A.* It would so appear, and, as we all believe that little children, of all ages of the world, who have died in infancy, were made partakers of the benefits of the sacrifice of Jesus and admitted to realms of glory, so we see no good reason to reject the idea of the translation of this one hundred and forty-four thousand.

*Q.* When did this translation take place?

*A.* Immediately before the flood. God withdrew all His elect and His attributes from the earth at the time of the deluge, saving only Noah and those with him in the ark, where the divine attributes tarried during that period of storm and rain, and at its close restored the earth again to its original relations to seed-time and harvest.

*Q.* What do we understand by the "flood of water" that the dragon cast out of his mouth after the woman?—Rev. xii: 15, 16.

*A.* The moral stench of the curse he had

power to produce was too great for uncontaminated humanity to endure, and he thought he could reach the whole earth with his "flood," but the curse could travel no faster than the success of his armies or sources of temptation, which were legionary; hence he did not reach the "woman in the wilderness" during her stay, or the period of twelve hundred and sixty years.

*Q.* Why was the dragon "wroth with the woman?"

*A.* Because he could not corrupt holy womanhood in the first daughters of Eve as he had by temptation destroyed her and her posterity; and as he had been driven out of heaven by her first son, he feared her second; and as he supposed that the promised King of kings and Lord of lords might spring from this holy womanhood he was wroth, and now turned his attention to the making of humanity as bad as bad could be; having only "two witnesses" to contend with for twelve hundred and sixty years. These witnesses baffled every effort on his part, and had power to shut heaven that it rained not, and to send plagues on the earth during the period of their prophecy, at the end of which the holy seed—the one hundred and fourty-four thousand—were permitted to stand with the Lamb on Mount Zion and sing their song of victory over the beast.

We have now examined the peculiar condition of the world from before the fall to the flood, in one aspect, viz.: Holy womanhood; and have seen the marvelous goodness of God in preserving His elect of the first-born, and their glory when the conflict was over. We shall review the same scene again, under another aspect, and see the vileness of the same beast in another direction:

"And I stood upon the sand of the sea, and saw a beast rise up out of the sea, having seven heads and ten horns, and upon his ten horns ten crowns, and upon his heads the name of blasphemy: and the dragon gave him his power and his seat, and great authority."—Rev. xiii: 1.

*Q.* Are the *heads* of this beast the same as those who were represented to have come down to earth after the conflict in heaven?

*A.* The same in another aspect. Here the dragon gives the beast power, or in another sense the dragon personifies the civil and religious character of fallen humanity, and introduces to men a system of idolatry which he desires all men to respect, but which is opposed by the *two witnesses:*

"And I saw one of his heads, as it were, wounded to death, and his deadly wound was healed; and all the world wondered after the beast."—Rev. xiii: 3.

This *head* of the beast was probably directed against the law of marriage, but was repulsed by both the sons of God and the sons of men; but the wound was finally healed by the introduction of polygamy, which new phase of moral evil gained ascendency both among the sons of God, and also the descendants of Cain.

*Q.* At what time in the history of the world do we suppose this deadly wound was healed?

*A.* Probably six hundred three-score and six years after the fall; for we read that none were allowed to buy or sell that did not have the *Mark, the Image,* or the number 666. This event of the universal apostasy of man was so vast in its surroundings that they said, "Who is like unto the beast? Who is able to make war with him"?—Rev. xiii: 4. When the sons of God, in their associated relations to each other, decreed to take wives of the daughters of the children of men, the consummation of the dragon's power was effected, the rest was only a matter of time.

"And he opened his mouth in blasphemy against God, to blaspheme his name, and his tabernacle, and them that dwell in heaven."— Rev. xiii: 6.

*Q.* What is meant by the tabernacle?

*A.* It was probably ancient temples, or a city erected and dedicated to the great God; and declared by the Revelator to be the Holy City, which was trodden under foot forty and two months, or twelve hundred and sixty prophetic years.

The great power of the beast was exerted against the saints, and for two reasons: First, the *two witnesses*, who were the governors of the saints, had taken their position in defiance of the power of the beast, and for twelve hundred and sixty years withstood every assault brought against them. It is very probable that one of these witnesses occupied a position on the western borders of the Nile, or where the great Sahara Desert now is, the other on the eastern side of the Red Sea, where the great Arabian Desert now is located.

These great men had power over the simoons of those deserts, and thereby slew all that attempted their overthrow.

We read in reference to these two witnesses, of their costume and their power:

"And I will give power unto my two witnesses, and they shall prophesy a thousand two hundred and three-score days, clothed in sackcloth. These are the two olive-trees, and the two candlesticks, standing before the God of the earth. If any man will hurt them, fire proceedeth out of their mouth and devoureth their enemies: and if any man will hurt them, he must in this manner be killed."

*Q.* This must have made them very formidable enemies, and their destruction to have been a great triumph?

*A.* It is very remarkable of them that they were at length slain, and their dead bodies should be resuscitated, and they in the presence of their enemies ascend into heaven. Their death also is located in "Sodom and Egypt," where also our Lord was crucified, which conveys the idea that their locations must have been, as above stated, near the Nile and Euphrates— near to where Sodom now is, and near or adjacent to Egypt. They were overpowered, by their enemies, simultaneously.

"And they of the people, and kindreds, and tongues, and nations, shall see their dead bodies three days and a half, and shall not suffer their dead bodies to be put in graves."

*Q.* Their influence, then, as the opponents of the beast, must have been world-wide?

*A.* It can be better understood in reference to this particular by reading the next two verses: "And they that dwell on the earth shall rejoice over them, and make merry, and shall send gifts one to another, because these two prophets tormented them that dwelt on the earth."—Rev. xi: 10.

*Q.* Were their dead bodies on exhibition three years and a half?

*A.* It is generally supposed by commentators and Biblical scholars, that prophetic days are years; and indeed if it were not so, every year's transaction must have been half untold, or so abridged as to have given only a brief, instead of a history. So much of history, or so many years of history as are found in the Bible, could not have been written only in that manner, making each year a prophetic day.

We read of this beast, in Rev. xiii: 7, that "It was given unto him to make war with the saints, and to overcome them; and power was given him over all kindreds, and tongues, and nations."

*Q.* Who were the saints he overcame?

*A.* Probably the remnant of the sons of God and these two "olive-trees, or candlesticks;" for they were not permitted to fight with carnal weapons, hence their translation became a necessity.

*Q.* What was the second beast that came up out of the earth, who had two horns like a lamb, but spake as a dragon?

*A.* It might have been the corrupt example of "Cain, who was of that wicked one, and slew his brother." The descendants of Cain were bloody men and polygamists. These two horns were sufficient to establish his power in unison with the beast before him, who had received the deadly wound and did live. He also erected an image to the beast, and by necromancy, or legerdemain, caused the image to speak, or it may have been done by ventriloquism; at all events it was a deception.

We have now again passed over the same period, in another aspect, and still we have not discovered all the deep-laid and treacherous designs of the founder of Babylon the great; nor have we spoken of the plagues, nor have we seen the effects of the vials of wrath, or the sound-ings of the seven last trumpets. All these woes are immediately connected with the antediluvian abominations, and had their fulfillment in the days of other years—in the days when men's lives exceeded five hundred years—and when their sin reached to heaven in regard to its heinousness and abandonment.

The fourteenth chapter of the Book of Revelations gives us another aspect of the same conflict and victory, with also the warnings and threatenings of God toward all such as received the mark, or number, or image of the beast; showing the active work of the Holy Spirit or the Seven Spirits of God during all this corruption and sin. To this let us now direct our attention.

# CHAPTER XV.

THE ANGEL PREACHER—THE COVENANT WITH NOAH—NOAH'S FAITH—THE BOOK OF JOB—WHAT IT TEACHES—THE TWO WITNESSES—THE HOLY CITY TRODDEN UNDER FOOT—ROME NOT BABYLON—THE ONE HUNDRED AND FORTY-FOUR THOUSAND—THE FOUR BEASTS—THE VIALS OF WRATH—THE GREAT BATTLE OF BABYLON.

THIS chapter (Revelations xiv) calls our attention to the fact that every national calamity is, and must be, prefaced with great anxiety, both from God and his people; the latter being a channel of the former. We read, "And I saw another angel fly in the midst of heaven, having the everlasting gospel to preach to them that dwell on the earth, and to every nation, and kindred, and tongue, and people, saying, Fear God, and give glory to him; for the hour of his judgment is come: and worship him that made heaven, and earth, and the sea, and the fountains of waters."

*Q.* Who do we suppose this angel to have been?

*A.* It was probably Noah, for he was "a preacher of righteousness;" and in this immediate connection of building the ark we are informed that "he condemned the world."

If the knowledge of his works, and why he builded the ark, was world-wide, then his gospel preaching was alike world-wide.

We read, Gen. vi: 13: "And God said to Noah, The end of all flesh is come before me; for the earth is filled with violence through them: and behold, I will destroy them with the earth." V. 17: "And behold, I, even I, do bring a flood of waters upon the earth, to destroy all flesh, wherein is the breath of life, from under heaven; and every thing that is in the earth shall die. But with thee will I establish my covenant; and thou shalt come into the ark; thou, and thy sons, and thy wife, and thy sons' wives with thee."

It must be remembered that the population of the earth at this period was vastly great, and that the sins of the nations, and languages, and kindreds of the earth were exceedingly great, so much so that no future age of the world could ever approximate it, or equal it, so daring, so corrupt, so loathsome.

In the midst of this corruption Noah walked with God, as did Enoch, who preceded him; and being perfect in his generations, God was pleased to warn the world of their approaching fate, as we see in the fourteenth chapter of Revelation.

*Q.* Does the picture here given in Revelation accord to the moral condition of the earth, when God commanded Noah to build the Ark?

*A.* Perfectly so; the earth was corrupt before God, and his awful judgments were no less merited than severe. Every effort to save had been sought out and improved; the elect one hundred and forty-four thousand, hid from the face of the serpent twelve hundred and sixty years, must now be released; the two witnesses must now suffer, the world's jubilee of triumph must now be full, and the patience of the saints must now be rewarded. "Here is the patience of the saints, here are they that keep the commandments of God and the faith of Jesus."— Rev. xiv : 12.

*Q.* How could Noah keep the faith of Jesus, for Jesus was not then revealed to the world?

*A.* Not then revealed? How strange. If the Messiah's flesh, or vail, was all that the Shiloh possessed, how could he say, "Before Abraham was I am?" How could he say, "Give me the glory that I had with thee before the world began?" No, verily,

"Jesus shall reign where'er the sun
Does his successive journey run,"

whether before the flood or since. We also understand that his *name* was called Immanuel, the better to associate it with the humanity of man; but he was God manifest in the flesh, and God manifest in the bush, and the God with whom Noah walked, and who also talked with Noah; the same Saviour Jesus, upon whose shoulder rested the covenant of grace. Immediately with this condition of things a promise is given to those who die in the Lord from that period on, their works should be awarded to them even after death: "Blessed are the dead who die in the Lord from henceforth: yea, saith the Spirit, that they may rest from their labors; and their works do follow them."

It is probable, however, that the only *written word*, that had the title to inspiration at this period, was the book of Job. It is, also, more than a probability that this book was saved in the ark with Noah, for it refers to an age that must have been antediluvian.

*Q.* How so?

*A.* Before God revealed his name to be Jehovah, the book of Job must have been written; for this appellation is not found anywhere in the book, though in more than thirty places he is called Shaddai—God Almighty. Then, again, the book of Job is of apparently Hebrew origin, yet there are so many strange words of some other language that leaves the impression upon the mind of the reader that no immediate analogy exists between it and post-diluvian times. It is also seen that he knew nothing of Israel, or of Sinai, or of God's chosen people, hence he certainly must have been a Gentile, and not a Jew. He delineates a character of life, manners, and habits that are universal and common to all places. He portrays Egypt with its Pyramids, he describes the mining art of Phœnicia, he mentions the caravans of the wandering nations, the excessive heat of the tropics, and the icy regions of the north.

His friends might have made a strong point by adverting to the flood, but not a word of it do we see. But in the absence of this we have strange un-Hebrew traditions and mythologies, announcing the giant's war, Orion imprisoned, and the dragon wounded. This, and its reference to the sons of God, convey very clearly the impression that it was written in antediluvian ages, because it speaks of a time when "the sons of God came to present themselves before the Lord, and Satan came also among them."— Job i: 6.

If Satan went up with the sons of God, it must have been at a time when the sons of God were uninfluenced by his presence, and also at a time when sinful man was trying to ascend to heaven by works of righteousness. Job was, no doubt, as good a man as could at that time be found among the fallen of Adam's posterity outside of the lineage; and by God's suffering the *tempter* to try him by terrible calamity, he established three things, viz.:

1. That God could save his people from falling even when all others cast them off.

2. That the possessions of worldly goods and honors are not the reasons why his people love him; and,

3. That worldly calamities are no evidence of a depraved heart.

The Lord justified Job in his integrity, though not in the estimate he placed upon God's own character and purposes.

*Q.* What other reasons have we to believe that the book of Job was written before the flood?

*A.* The singular fact that neither he nor his friends refer to the ten commandments or to any code of laws, save love to God. Job disclaims worshiping any idol, or being in any manner recreant to his marital vow.—Job xxxi: 1–10.

Job must have been informed as to the covenant of promise made to Adam, for he declared his faith to be in God, that even after "worms had destroyed his flesh" he should behold God in the possession of purified humanity: "For I know that my Redeemer liveth, and that he shall stand at the latter day upon the earth." Job xix: 25.

*Q.* The antediluvians, then, possessed the knowledge of the promised Messiah?

*A.* Undoubtedly; this was the theme of Enoch's and Noah's preaching, as well as the two witnesses who prophesied twelve hundred and sixty years, clothed in sackcloth.

The multitude and magnitude of events, so fearfully apparent, a short time prior to the flood, is indeed overwhelming, and the picture drawn by the Revelator gives us no exaggerated idea of the crimes and blasphemies, the untold apostasy and pollution of this God-forsaken race.

*Q.* Where was the Holy City, spoken of by the Revelator, that was trodden under foot forty and two months (twelve hundred and sixty years) located?

*A.* This city was perhaps a continuous assemblage of temples dedicated to God by the sinless children of Adam, or the sons of God, and may have extended along the Nile from El Kanark, or Thebes, to the Mediterranean Sea, several hundred miles, and was undoubtedly the grandest association or collection of architectural display that has ever appeared upon the earth.

The magnitude of this ancient city should merit more than a passing notice. The learned Doctor Pocock, after examining these ruins of the "city of a hundred gates," remarks in reference to its overthrow, "the date of whose destruction is older than the foundation of other cities, and the extent of whose ruins, and the immensity of whose colossal fragments still offer so many astonishing objects, that one is riveted to the spot, unable whither to direct the step, or fix the attention."

Another writer remarks: "The glory of

Thebes belongs to a period prior to the commencement of authentic history. It is recorded only in the dim lights of poetry and tradition, which might be suspected of fable did not so many mighty witnesses remain to their truth."

Champollion, in his work on *Hieroglyphics*, remarks, "That the magnificent ruins of El Kanark, El Uksur (by some writers called Canarc and Luxor), and Medinet Abu, are the remains of the hundred-gated Thebes, the earliest capitol of the world, can not be doubted."

The distance of these ruins, according to the French measurement, from the Mediterranean Sea on the north, extends eight hundred and fifty (850) miles, and from Elephantine on the south two hundred and twenty-five miles. This also agrees with the measurement of Herodotus.

*Q.* But is not this also the place where the great Babylon was located?

*A.* The same place precisely; for the Holy City was trodden under foot forty and two months.

When the great Red Dragon had obtained partial supremacy, four hundred and six years after the fall of man, or the transgression of our first parents, these altars, these temples, this city, was re-dedicated to Diobolus, and thereby the "Holy City" was trodden under foot twelve hundred and sixty years, or to the time of the flood.

*Q.* This must have been a great city, indeed,

if it extended from El Kanark to the Mediterranean Sea?

*A.* Immensely so; for the Revelator justly calls it *Babylon the Great;* and it may truly be said that there never was before it a city so vastly great, nor will there ever be another city that can compare with it in magnitude and population.

*Q.* Do not some writers call Rome the great city of Babylon?

*A.* Most assuredly they do; but the analogy between Babylon (as the Holy Bible has given it) and Rome is scarcely as reasonable as it would be to suppose that Dunkirk, N. Y., was London or Pekin. The Revelator heard and declared the number of the horsemen, or cavalry, in the grand army that marched across the great Desert of Arabia to the battle of the great God, and the number was two thousand millions.—Rev. ix: 13-21.

We get some idea of the greatness of this sanguinary conflict, by reading Rev. xvi: 17-21.

*Q.* What facts do we farther learn, by reading the fourteenth chapter of Revelation?

*A.* We learn that God was then gathering his redeemed—the first-born—the elect who had been hidden from the face of the serpent twelve hundred and sixty years. They were only a handful—a little flock, a remnant who had kept the word of "His testimony," and of whom the world was not worthy, for they were without fault before the throne of God. This one hundred and forty-four thousand were a part of the first-fruits of the plan of redemption.

*Q.* What are we to understand by the term first-fruits?—Rev. xiv: 4.

*A.* The plan of redemption could not be complete unless the humanity of man could be immortalized. This corruptible or earthly form could not be deified unless honored of Deity, and this necessitated the covenant seal, the archetype and type, sealed by the blood of the eternal covenant, and the promise of God to man in giving to him the Immanuel. When this covenant had been established in the courts of glory, its application became not only an expectancy, but a Divine purpose.

And, as the sons of God had valiantly withstood the trial of their faith in God's promises, they were considered worthy of immortality and endless glory. The application, then, of the blood of the promised Messiah to the unfallen humanity of Adam's posterity resolved itself into the first-fruits of that atonement, which was the translation of the remnant of the "woman's seed." (See Heb. 12, 22, 23.)

This translation of the "Church of the firstborn" may have embraced a vast number, abundantly sufficient to fill the places of all the revolting angels, a holy assemblage, and this may have occurred simultaneous with the war in heaven, also the cessation of the multiplication of the sons and daughters of God on earth, and this may have tempted those not chosen to fill the places made vacant in heaven by the revolting angels, to marry the daughters of the children of men. Still God reserved the one hundred and forty-four thousand (as he did the seven thousand in the days of Elijah) as the representatives of the twelve tribes of Israel, or the twelve thousand years of time, till near the time of the world's overthrow—the flood.

Every possible manifestation of God's abhorrence to the beast, the mark, or the image is now most visibly manifest. The angel flies through the midst of heaven, declaring that "If any man worship the beast and his image, and receive his mark in his forehead or in his hand, the same shall drink of the wine of the wrath of God, which is poured out without mixture into the cup of his indignation; and he shall be tormented with fire and brimstone in the presence of the holy angels and in the presence of the Lamb."—Rev. xiv: 9, 10.

And another lesson we may learn from this chapter, and that is, that it required the sacrifice of human life to resist this Satanic power.

*Q.* The earth at this time must have been full of violence?

*A.* It could not have been more so, for the voice from heaven declares that the harvest-field is fully ripe, and that the angel should thrust in his sickle and cause the earth to be reaped.

And another angel gathered the clusters of grapes of the whole earth, and had the wine vat filled to overflow by the great source of the drunkenness of "the mother of abominations."

*Q.* What do we learn from the fifteenth chapter of Revelation?

*A.* We learn from this chapter that the Seven Spirits of God are about to be withdrawn from that portion of the earth that they had fashioned for man, and the results that must follow, viz: "The seven last plagues."

Here is an emblem of the last and final gathering of the entire Church of God: for this "remnant" is now gathered to the transparent shores of the sea of glass mingled with fire, to await the awful doom of the great city of Babylon—to the "Armageddon"—the "mountain of the Gospel."

*Q.* Who are the "four beasts" and the "four and twenty elders" that we read of in Revelation, one of which gave to the "seven angels the seven golden vials full of the wrath of God?" Rev. xv: 7.

*A.* The four beasts, or as some render it, the *four living creatures*, may refer to man in his pure and sinless state, and may have had for each separate part a representative character.

1. Man as a spiritual organism.
2. Man in relation to the attributes.
3. Man in relation to the senses; and,
4. Man with a human body.

This division in man's mysterious form is self-evident and easy to understand.

Christ, having assumed man's nature, may have personified these representatives, and hence the four parts, called beasts, or living creatures connecting with and constituting a human body, may have been thus represented before the throne. The twenty-four elders may have been the twelve representatives of the Typical Dispensation, as were the twelve tribes of Israel, and the twelve representatives of the Gracious Dispensation, as were the twelve apostles who were chosen by our blessed Saviour. The representatives of the two dispensations united constituted the twenty-four elders.

*Q.* But these four beasts fell down before the throne and worshiped God ?

*A.* That is the reason why we think them to be representative characters of man. The Holy Word, in all its bearings, has to do with man. Man is its central sun and its majestic surroundings, God in man and man in God. "I in you and you in me."

The prostration of the four faculties or properties in man before the throne illustrates the effect of sin in his fallen nature, it brings down the noblest of God's creatures to dust and ashes. And then man is identified with all God's doings, and each individual property in his mysterious organism holds its relation to God, and must accord to the cup of suffering, of which we all must drink; and man must give the vial of God's grieved Spirit to each and to all who drive that Spirit away, "Warning every man, and teaching every man in all wisdom, that we may present every man perfect in Christ Jesus."

"The saints shall judge the world." "And one of the four beasts gave unto the seven angels seven golden vials full of the wrath of God, who liveth forever and ever."—Rev. xv : 7. Hence a harmony existed, even in heaven, when Babylon the Great drank the bitter cup of God's wrath.

*Q.* What do we learn from reading the sixteenth chapter of the Book of Revelation?

*A.* We learn from this chapter the effect the withdrawal of the attributes of God would produce in the moral, as well as in the natural world. The first vial was poured out upon the earth, for the moral character of the world was indeed loathsome. Marriage was almost universally ignored; Noah, only, and his sons found favor with God; less, indeed, than ten righteous persons of Adam's fallen posterity remained upon the earth. Drunkenness universal. Idolatry the only religion. Blasphemy honored, and earth a brothel. We should remember that the safeguards of the attributes of God, are like to gates that hinder the floods from rushing upon our dwellings with irresistible destruction, and that, when withdrawn, the maddened waters rush on with terrific force, carrying destruction and dismay in every new-made channel. So with the vials of wrath. When the attribute, Holiness, had withdrawn his health-giving power from the atmosphere, those who breathed the tainted air were diseased, a grievous sore fell upon all who had received the mark of the beast or the number of his name.

*Q.* What effect did the contents of the second vial produce?

*A.* The second withdrawal was to take from the waters of the sea its life-giving property, which resulted in the death of every living creature in the sea: "And the second angel poured out his vial upon the sea, and it became as the blood of a dead man; and every living soul died in the sea."—Rev. xvi: 3.

*Q.* Do we understand that the seven last seals broken, the seven last trumpets, the seven vials, all refer to the withdrawal of the attributes of God from the world?

*A.* The world, and things therein, are kept and preserved by the power that formed them. If the attributes of God formed the various combinations that have changed this world from chaos to its present animated state, then the withdrawal of this power would be equivalent to the judgments of God; and if these attributes are at labor for man in view of his restoration to God, and to glory, when they withdraw from their moral work, evils of the most direful character must follow. In the first vial, let us suppose that Holiness, being that power to the mind of man that exhorts to rectitude of conduct, is to be withdrawn. It no longer warns, reproves, intercedes. Man is thereby left to the powers that control totally depraved attributes. The result and effect must be upon those who by flagrant sin had driven this attribute away; consequently a grievous sore must fall "upon all who had received the *mark* of the beast, and upon them who worshiped his image." If a man burns up his house, the result that follows is that he has no shelter from the storm; if a man takes poison, the result is pain and distress; so if men drive from them the attribute, Holiness, judgments must follow as a natural result.

Let us now suppose that the second vial is the partial withdrawal of the attribute, Life. Then, if applied to the water, its life-giving relation to creatures must cease; hence a curse must permeate all the vast depths of the sea, and all animated life hitherto vitalized by the life-power of water must die; therefore "every living soul died in the sea."

We will suppose that the pouring out of the third vial is equivalent to the withdrawal of the attribute, Justice, from the rivers and fountains of waters. This withdrawal, then, together with the attribute that preceded it, must bring about the calamity spoken of; and thus the waters are being arranged in their chemical relations, shortly to flood the entire world.

*Q.* What is meant by the angel of the waters? "And I heard the angel of the waters say, Thou art righteous, O Lord, which art, and was, and shall be, because thou hast judged thus."

*A.* As to each of the Spirits of God, there had been a work assigned to do in creation; so each of the attributes defended the wisdom of God in the judgments that fell upon the ungodly.

Here the attribute, or angel of the waters, declares that the blood of God's chosen people had been profusely shed by this murderous city of Babylon, now about to be destroyed; and the declaration from this angel induced the echo of another angel, or attribute, perhaps, as we have remarked, *Holiness*, to join with *Life* in declaring the equity of God in thus withdrawing his Spirit from the waters.

*Q.* What attribute of God is identical with the pouring out of the *fourth vial?*

*A.* The attribute, Truth.

As he had enveloped the sun with the element of light in the fourth day of Creation, so now he pours out his vial upon the sun, and the flames of that luminary penetrate our atmosphere with fearful heat: "And men were scorched with great heat, and blasphemed the name of God, which hath power over these plagues: and they repented not to give Him glory."—Rev. xvi: 9.

The attribute, Truth, had fixed the bounds of the volume of heat that fell upon our earth from the grand luminary of day, and had said to the solar rays, Thus far canst thou go, but no farther; but now he increases the boundary by withdrawing his control, and the scorching heat is unindurable. Morally, the restraining attributes being withdrawn, men blaspheme God though suffering excruciating pain.

*Q.* Judgments, then, do not always restrain men from sin?

*A.* They never do, unless they come as intercessors, and this character they only assume when they become reproofs, not really in their nature judgments.

Thus good men, like Job, may be terribly afflicted, and in all the calamity no visible act of displeasure is attached to the suffering; they are chastisements necessary to our spiritual growth and prosperity, and in no manner represent God's wrath.

*Q.* What attribute of the Spirit poured out the *fifth* vial?

*A.* This was probably the attribute, Light. Up to this time there had remained, even in polluted Babylon, the intercession of moral light, for all the attributes of God are intercessors, but now this intercessor is withdrawn from the seat of the beast—from the great Babylon—and as a result the darkness of despair falls upon it: "And the fifth angel poured his vial out upon the seat of the beast; and his kingdom was full of darkness; and they gnawed their tongues for pain, and blasphemed the God of heaven because of their pains and their sores, and repented not of their deeds."—Rev. xvi: 10–11.

Immediately following this plague the *sixth* attribute of God, viz.: *Mercy*, is withdrawn, and the great river Euphrates is dried up that another woe might come upon doomed and polluted Babylon:

"And the sixth angel poured out his vial upon the great river Euphrates; and the water thereof was dried up, that the way of the kings of the east might be prepared."—Rev. xvi: 12.

*Q.* What is meant by preparing the way of the kings of the east?

*A.* We can better understand it by reading of the same design under the figure of the seven trumpets.—Rev. iv: 13–16. "And the sixth angel sounded, and I heard a voice from the four horns of the golden altar which is before God, saying to the sixth angel which had the trumpet, Loose the four angels which are bound in the great river Euphrates. And the four angels were loosed which were prepared for an hour, and a day, and a month, and a year, for to slay the third part of men. And the number of the army of the horsemen were two hundred thousand thousand: and I heard the number of them." God had designed that great Babylon should receive her just deserts, so that all succeeding ages might fear to fight against him who made the heavens and the earth, the sea, and the fount-tains of waters; so he withdrew the attribute, Mercy, and at once the rival spirit of rapine and of war revealed itself, and, as if propelled by some irresistible power, marshaled to fight against Babylon a cavalry force of two thousand million.

Babylon is now to be the center of carnage and of death, and as a fitting rebuke upon creatures totally depraved both in their senses and attributes, God calls for the fowls of heaven to come to the world's great carnivorous festival.

Connected immediately with the pouring out of the sixth vial, we read: "And I saw three unclean spirits like frogs come out of the mouth of the dragon, and out of the mouth of the beast, and out of the mouth of the false prophet. For they are the spirits of devils, working miracles, which go forth unto the kings of the earth and of the whole world, to gather them to the battle of the great day of God Almighty."—Rev. xvi: 13, 14.

When Mercy is withdrawn, devils can do wonders; but they are now preparing for the terrific slaughter that preceded the dreadful deluge.

*Q.* To what attribute does the seventh vial allude?

*A.* To the only remaining attribute of God, and the grand center of them all, namely, Love. This Divine intercessor lingers long at the door of the human mind, and can only leave when all the others are withdrawn. Nothing that

God had revealed, no judgment he had inflicted, no terror he had threatened, had for a moment forestalled the corruption of the great Babylon, or received the least attention; and now her sins, mountain high, come up before God, and his pleading, interceding, and beseeching attribute, Love, is withdrawn from the doomed city; but not even now, till he had gathered the spotless of earth to the gospel mountain, Armageddon. We read, "Blessed is he that watcheth and keepeth his garments, lest they see his shame. And he gathered them together into a place called in the Hebrew tongue Armageddon."—Rev. xvi : 15, 16.

The attribute, Love, is now withdrawn from the atmosphere, and there are no longer the harmonies of musical sound, penetrating this element in heavenly cadences.

No longer the voice of praise, of joy, of rapture, as was heard by the shepherds on the plains of Judea, no glory to God in the highest, but a voice in heaven declares, "It is done." The cup is full, the attributes are withdrawn, the convulsions of nations and nature must now overwhelm the world with awe.

*Q.* Do the same results follow in the three different aspects, namely: The *Seals*, the *Trumpets*, the *Vials?*

*A.* As nearly so as could be reasonably expected?

To get their resemblance and the result that

would follow the withdrawal of the attributes as they appear in the arrangement of Creation, let us look at them in their order and apply them, and then we can get the answer.

First, *Holiness.* See the effect of the opening of the *first Seal.* Revelations, fifth chapter to the fifth verse of the eighth chapter.

Then look at the sounding of the *first Trumpet.* Revelations, eight to eleven, including six verses of the eleventh chapter.

Then the *first Vial.* Revelations, fifteenth and sixteenth chapters.

Then take the attribute, Life, for the second, and read the results as before in the chapters mentioned.

Then take *Justice,* then *Truth,* then *Light,* then *Mercy,* then *Love.* Now apply the results of this withdrawal, and you have the *wrath* of *God.* "If we forsake him, he will forsake us."

*Q.* How do the seven seals harmonize with this idea?

*A.* Let us see. The first seal presents to our vision, Rev. vi: 2, a white horse with a rider, who had a bow, and a crown, "and he went forth conquering and to conquer."

*Holiness* is a crown of glory, and in it is the bow of promise: "He that is holy, let him be holy still." "Without holiness shall no man see the Lord." The withdrawal of this attribute from the earth would be the cessation of the offered crown and the promised glory.

The *second seal*, when opened, took peace from the earth. "They should kill one another."

The attribute, *Life*, withdrawn, death must follow.

The *third seal* presented the balances, hence may fitly allude to Justice, which, if withdrawn, must result in the absence of all that is just and right on the earth.

The *fourth seal* brings out the figure of death, and hell follows in his train. The Truth of God hath declared that in the "day thou eatest thereof, thou shalt surely die." "Death and hell followed with him." Hence the attribute, Truth, may be the allusion, its withdrawal the consequences.

The *fifth seal* being opened, we behold the souls of those beheaded for Jesus' sake, the robes given to them, and the promise made.

Here is *light* on the spiritual condition of the souls of men, and this light still is lingering and shining for others. If taken from the earth, all would become darkness. Hence the attribute, Light, may have been represented by the opening of the fifth seal.

At the opening of the *sixth seal*, great consternation follows. The stars of heaven fall, the heavens depart as a scroll, men hide themselves, are afraid of the wrath of the Lamb. This may very properly allude to the withdrawal of *Mercy*.

This attribute of the Spirit, or this spiritual

attribute, fortifies our attributes against the wiles of the devil; and if withdrawn, terror and dismay must come upon us.

We now come to the number of the woman's holy seed, who had fled into the wilderness, and had been preserved from the power of the beast and dragon for twelve hundred and sixty years, viz.: the sealing of the one hundred and forty-four thousand, their exaltation to glory, their place before the throne of God, and their eternal freedom from hunger, want, or dismay; and then the *seventh seal* is opened.

This is the attribute, *Love*. The Revelator gives no other result than "*silence.*" There may not be in the opening of these seven seals any direct allusion to the withdrawal of their sustaining power, but simply the bringing out of the attributes themselves, that we may see their relation to the moral as well as the natural world; their relation to mind as well as matter.

We have now arrived at the last dreadful tragedy before the flood, the seventeenth chapter of Revelation.

In this chapter we have a clear and painful view of the character of the doomed city of Babylon. Can there be a darker picture drawn of living intelligences this side of hell? Can it be honestly written upon the cathedrals of Rome, "MYSTERY, BABYLON THE GREAT, THE MOTHER OF HARLOTS AND ABOMINATIONS OF THE EARTH"?

Was she the mother, the origin of harlotry?

Was there no abomination in the earth when God determined to destroy every creature in whom is life? When he repented that he had made man?

Did Catholic Rome ever repudiate the bands of matrimony?

Then let us apply this dreadful character to those whom God abhorred and destroyed with a terrible overthrow, and, wherein any church or nation follows this wicked Babylon, in that particular, they are like it, but not Babylon itself.

*Q.* Was Babylon destroyed by the flood?

*A.* It does not so appear; and we see a reason why it should not so occur; for had it, the penalty attached to her crimes could not have appeared to others; nor would the results of her crimes been revealed as their heinous nature demanded.

## CHAPTER XVI.

THE DURATION OF THE GREAT BATTLE—OTHER CITIES BESIDE BABYLON FELL—THE CARNIVOROUS FESTIVAL—THE BEAST TAKEN—SATAN BOUND—THE FIRST RESURRECTION—THE SPIRITS IN PRISON—BAPTISM OF THE HOLY GHOST—PROPHECY OF THE BOOK OF REVELATION—THE ARK—GOD'S ATTRIBUTES RESUME THEIR ORIGINAL RELATION TO MATTER—NOAH'S FOLLY—EFFECT OF STRONG DRINK—BABEL—CONFOUNDING OF LANGUAGE — ABRAHAM — MELCHISEDEC — THE TWO COVENANTS—CIRCUMCISION.

HERE we look upon the *great* city, the city of the nations, the city against which an army of horsemen are approaching from the east, from beyond Euphrates, of two thousand million. "The woman thou sawest is the GREAT CITY." What pomp, what delicacies, what odors, what gayeties, what mirth, what boasting. "Who is able to make war with the beast?" Great ships are sailing into her ports, richly laden cargoes are being moored at her wharves, all nations are enriched by her lewdness, and all say, "What city is like unto this great city." A peace has been conquered, the two witnesses are slain.

*Q.* How long did the battle of Babylon last before the overthrow of the city?

*A.* The Revelator says that the whole preparation of the siege was an "hour, and a day, and a month, and a year."

We suppose this must have embraced the whole time that the two thousand million troops were marching across the great Arabian Desert to the scene of battle, for it does not appear that the battle lasted over two weeks, "one hour." "For in *one hour* so great riches is come to naught."—Rev. xviii: 17.

And, again, we read that Babylon came to naught by the powers that brought about immediate destruction: "And a mighty angel took up a stone like a great millstone, and cast it into the sea, saying, Thus with violence shall that great city, Babylon, be thrown down, and shall be found no more at all."—Rev. xviii: 21.

We have no adequate conception of the heinous nature of the sins of this city.

Every good man was murdered, all devotion to God prohibited, all virtue ignored, all vice and immorality deified.

*Q.* Was this terrible battle fought to secure any principle of truth?

*A.* Far from it. The great army that came

against Babylon was just as corrupt as Babylon itself, and the only battle cry being, "She hath said, who dares to contend against this great city"?

Lust, anger, and revenge propel the great army onward, while God was carrying out his own purposes, to make the city of corruption and blood, the battle-ground of carnage.

The Revelator in the nineteenth and twentieth chapters beholds the mighty Ruler of the world, unfolding his purpose, even the archetypal Christ, whose name is KING OF KINGS AND LORD OF LORDS.

*Q.* Was Babylon the only city that fell at the time of this great battle?

*A.* It would seem from the description, that it was not. It reads that the "*cities of the nations fell.*"

All nations had become corrupt, and had re-dedicated the sacred temples erected by the pure sons of God to the beast, who had power to make an image speak. These cities were scattered all over the world, and hence their temples were defiled. Balbec, the walls around which still remain of huge dressed rock, thirteen feet square and sixty feet in length, placed in a wall, as it now appears, twenty feet high, with all its pomp and glory, fell. The mighty structures near the Giant's Causeway fell; the mighty cities of Palanque and Copan fell, and great Babylon came up in remembrance before God.

But above the smoke of battle God rules supreme; beyond the purposes of men he leads His armies.

Now, that the city has fallen, and the almost unnumbered dead are lying unburied, for the Lord fought against both armies, and prevailed, and by great hail-stones slew them; a mighty angel calls "all the fowls that fly in the midst of heaven to gather themselves together to the supper of the great God."—Rev. xix: 17.

"The beast was taken, and with him the false prophet that wrought miracles before him, and both were cast alive into the lake of fire burning with brimstone, and all the fowls were filled with their flesh."—Rev. xix: 20, 21.

*Q.* It would seem, then, that the entire battle-field would have been covered with their bones?

*A.* It is probable that they were washed by the flood into the deep, deep sea, for we read in reference to the resurrection that "the sea gave up the dead that were in it," placing it first, as though the *vast* host of humanity were there buried.

*Q.* How many years was the earth the abode of man before the flood?

*A.* Probably five thousand six hundred and sixty-six years. By this reckoning we have from the fall of our first parents to the flood, sixteen hundred and sixty-six years. Our chronology, however, makes it eleven years less, sixteen hundred and fifty-five.

*Q.* How long was the dragon, that old serpent, the devil, bound?

*A.* A thousand years. We can not tell whether the years are reckoned by lunar months or not, but probably the years were thus computed: twelve lunar months to the year. This would bind Satan till the law was given on Mount Sinai, or nearly to that period.

*Q.* When was the first resurrection?

*A.* Probably at the time of the commencement of the flood or general deluge.

It would seem quite reasonable to suppose, from allusions in Scripture to the old world, that the sainted dead had been resuscitated or resurrected. Enoch, the seventh from Adam, prophesied of the Lord coming with ten thousand of his saints (Jude xiv), and undoubtedly this occurrence did not long tarry. The Revelator saw the King of kings and Lord of lords, with his great host of redeemed, very nearly simultaneous with the terrible battle of the great God.

If these suppositions are correct, the first resurrection has already past, and this idea confused the minds of some, even in the apostles' day, for they asserted that the "resurrection had already passed, and overthrew the faith of some." If Christ, by his death, released the prisoners that were bound, if he preached to the dead that they might be "judged according to men in the flesh," their resurrection at the time of His, may have been the "rest of the dead," and this embraced the first resurrection, completed.

This is not the resurrection spoken of by the Saviour and the apostles, for this is yet to come—the second resurrection.

*Q.* Who could, then, have been raised from the dead?

*A.* All the worthies who had called upon the name of the Lord, and who had believed in the atonement through Christ, from Adam to Noah, perhaps a mighty host. The translation of the one hundred and forty-four thousand, the remnant of the woman's holy posterity, preserved of God from pollution and sin in the wilderness, probably occurred at the same time.

*Q.* Then who were the rest of the dead that lived not again till the thousand years were finished?

*A.* These might have been the "spirits in prison," spoken of by the Apostle Peter.—1 Pet. iii: 19, 20.

*Q.* Why so?

*A.* The "sons of God," who mingled in unholy wedlock with the daughters of the children of men, became thereby sinners: "So death reigned from Adam to Moses, even over them who had not sinned after the similitude of Adam's transgression." They, after their sin, may have believed in the great Messiah, who was to come to redeem the world, and dying in faith received not the promise, and could not ascend from the grave until Christ had led captivity captive, and released them that were bound in the prison-chamber of death. "The rest of the (redeemed) dead lived not again till the thousand years had expired." Nor does the Revelator say that they lived even then, but it is presumable that these were the saints that rose after the resurrection of Christ, for our Saviour remarks: "Other sheep I have who are not of this fold, them must I also *bring*, and they shall *hear my voice*, and there shall be one fold and one shepherd." Christ alone could conquer death and open the prison doors to them that were bound.

*Q.* How long was Satan loosed?

*A.* To the time, in all probability, that the Holy Spirit descended, on the day of Pentecost. The Revelator saw this as a fire coming down from God out of heaven. This was a sublime and glorious light, as it approached our dark and sin-ruined world, for it even appeared to those who saw it in its blessed effulgence (and the Revelator himself was one that saw it), like a flame of "fire, and it sat upon" each of the apostles, and inspired them.—Acts ii: 3.

This Spirit drove the devil from his stronghold of bewitching men, to the atmosphere of discord and of darkness.

*Q.* What is the difference between the work of regeneration and the Baptism of the Holy Ghost?

*A.* In the action of the Spirit in regeneration God's holy attribute, Love, touches our love attribute, thereby harmonizing all our devotions with love. From this attribute, then, we joy and rejoice in the hope of the glory of God—this faculty only is inundated by the Spirit, and "we see as in a glass, darkly:" or to illustrate; we see a person rushing past us on horseback at high speed, and, from only the knowledge we derive and apply to our judgment sense, we may say it is cruel to the beast for that man to ride so fast; but another person informs us that this rider's house is in flames, and his family asleep; then we no longer say he is cruel to the beast in riding so fast, but we shout, go faster! go faster!!

In the latter case, all our senses were informed of the peril, in the former only our sight.

Now the baptism of the Holy Ghost was the inundation of all the attributes of the soul with the Seven Spirits of God. Hence the earnestness of the disciples led others to think that they were full of new wine.

*Q.* Did not the apostles find some who were possessed of the devil after the descent of the Holy Spirit?

*A.* There were some who had the power to attach their demoniac natures to the senses of men, and continued to hold that relation till they were cast out by the advancing light of the Gospel, and it is probable that the gifts of the Holy Spirit ceased to be a necessity at the time that Satan ceased to have power to attach his demoniac nature to mortals.

*Q.* Will Satan ever again have that power?

*A.* Never, while time lasts. Judah's Lion has conquered and taken the field. The Holy Spirit has become vocal in the songs of redemption, and the churches of the living God are marshaling their forces to conquer.

Now the Spirit needs perform no miraculous display to render his attributes intelligible. The law of the Spirit is now written in the heart, and there the love of God is shed abroad, hence we no longer need the baptism of the Holy Ghost, but the communion of the Spirit in our hearts, whereby we can cry, Abba father.

*Q.* To what does the remaining portion of the Holy Scriptures of the Book of Revelation allude?

*A.* To things to come, to the progress of the Gospel, and the triumphs of grace. To the final judgments of the great day—to the final separation of the righteous and the wicked—to the glorious millennium, when the new heavens and new earth—the new Jerusalem—makes its appearance in the cloudless realms of glory.

*Q.* But does not the Revelator say that "fire came down from God out of heaven, and consumed them"?

*A.* Truly it does, and John the Baptist remarks (Matt. iii: 11, 12): "I indeed baptize you with water unto repentance; but he that cometh after me is mightier than I, whose shoes I am not worthy to bear; he shall baptize you with the Holy Ghost, and with *fire:* whose fan is in his hand, and he will thoroughly purge his floor, and gather his wheat into the garner; but he will burn up the chaff with unquenchable fire."

"And fire came down from God out of heaven and consumed them."

Thus we see that the forerunner, John, saw the same fire come down from God out of heaven, before the descent of the Holy Spirit, as did the Revelator when he saw the "things that are."

Both agree as to the character of "that light," and the results of that wonderful gift. The prophet Isaiah speaks of the same occurrence, after this manner: "For behold, the Lord will come with fire, and with his chariots like a whirlwind, to render his anger with fury, and his rebuke with flames of fire. For by fire and by his sword will the Lord plead with all flesh: and the slain of the Lord shall be many."—Isa. lxvi: 15, 16.

We have now, under the character of Babylon the Great, reviewed the enormous crimes alluded to in the sixth chapter of Genesis, and have learned that what God has been pleased to call *revelation*, is indeed REVELATION; and in all our investigations thus far have seen no reason for believing this to have been the *Mystical* Babylon, but the real, the corrupt, the abominable, the mother of abominations of the earth, the great city of Babylon, and in so doing have spoken of the beast that "was and is not."

Of the beast that now is, or the Mystical Babylon, our readers are referred to the various authors who have written elaborate volumes upon that topic.

It does not occur to us that the *Mystical Babylon* belonged to the age of the inspired writers; hence to synchronize the power that now worketh in the hearts of the children of disobedience with the character of Babylon the Great, the before-mentioned authors have only to show the analogy between the two, and the proof is irrefragable. This we believe, has, beyond a doubt, been most ably and conclusively accomplished, for all the allusions point to Rome, as the needle to the pole, but the *pole* is not the needle.

We will now pursue our investigation of the Word.

*Q.* What was the length, and breadth, and height of the Ark?

*A.* If we now are in possession of the exact distance, or extent, of a cubit, as it was understood before the flood, the length of the ark would be five hundred and fifty feet, about thirty-three rods; the width of the ark ninety-two feet, or about five and one half rods; the height of the ark fifty-five feet.

*Q.* Could an ark of that size have held seven of many, and two of all the rest of the species of animals, birds, and insects, "and of every thing that creepeth upon the earth"?

*A.* Mr. Hugh Miller, in his *Testimony of the Rocks*, is very sure that it could not. But it must be remembered that prophetic measurement may have differed from the real, as much as do prophetic *days* or *years*, and as Jehovah (from whose word alone we learn of the flood, and all that pertained to the ark, and to the animals that were saved in the ark) has declared it to have been large enough to hold the six thousand and more species of animals, and Noah and his family, together with food sufficient for this great host of animated life; who are we that we should question the dimensions of the ark, or the sizes of the animals saved?

*Q.* But how could all the different species of animals have reached their native habitation from the ark?

*A.* This question, involving, as it does, many grave interrogatories, it might be well for us to look at a few of them, before we proceed to the answer. Mr. Hugh Miller remarks:

"But how are such facts reconcilable with the hypothesis of a universal deluge? The deluge was an event of the existing creation. Had it been universal, it would have broken up all the diverse centers, and substituted one great general center instead—that in which the ark rested; or else, at an enormous expense of miracle, all animals preserved, by *natural* means by Noah, would have had to return by *supernatural* means to the regions whence, by means *equally supernatural*, they had been brought. The sloths and armadillos—little fitted by nature for long journeys—would have required to be ferried across the Atlantic to the regions in which the remains of the megatherium and glyptodon lie entombed; the kangaroo and wombat, to the insulated continent that contains the bones of the extinct macropus and phalcolomys; and the New Zealand birds, including its heavy flying quails, and its wingless wood hen, to those remote islands of the Pacific, in which the skeletons of *palapteryx ingens* and *dinornis giganteus* lie entombed. Nor will it avail aught to urge, with certain assertors of a universal deluge, that during the cataclysm, sea and land changed their places, and what is now land formed the bottom of the antediluvian ocean, and *vice versa*, what is now sea had been the land on which the first human inhabitants of the earth increased and multiplied. No geologist, who knows how very various the ages of the several table-lands and mountain chains in reality are, could acquiesce in such an hypothesis." "How, we may well ask, had the flood been universal, could even such islands as Great Britain and Ireland, have ever been replenished with many of their original inhabitants?"

Dr. Pye Smith, in reference to this same grave objection to the universality of the deluge, remarks: "All land animals having their geographical regions, to which their constitutional natures are congenial—many of them being unable to live in any other situation—we can not represent to ourselves the idea of their being brought into one small spot from the polar regions, the torrid zone, and all the other climates of Asia, Africa, Europe, America, Australia, and the thousands of islands, their preservation and provision, and the final disposal of them, without bringing up the idea of miracles more stupendous than any recorded in Scripture." Still the Doctor must have known that even this stupendous record is in the Holy Scriptures.

Dr. William Hamilton remarks: "If I yet find it recorded in the Book of Revelation that in the deluge '*every living thing in which is the breath of life perished, and Noah only remained alive and they which were with him in the ark,*' I could still believe it implicitly, satisfied that the difficulty of explanation springs solely from the imperfection of human knowledge, and not from any limitation in the power or wisdom of God, nor yet from any lack of trustworthiness in the document given us in a revelation from God, a document given to men by the hands of Moses, the learned, accomplished, and eminently devout Jewish legislator."

We have now examined the objections to the

universality of the flood in part, and now let us examine it in the light of the Seven Spirits of God, and science. The seed of an apple will, when certain other associations assist it, produce an apple-tree; this tree produces fifteen bushels of apples of a season, of two hundred to the bushel, making three thousand apples. These apples yield, say six seeds each, equal to eighteen thousand seeds. Now all these seeds find their generant, in the single seed that first produced the tree; nor did that seed alone produce the tree, only from the life power lent it of God. Then if the life power of God retire the life power of all these eighteen thousand seeds to its original representative, no greater miracle would ensue than did in its extension, only in the time allotted to its development.

We may make something that much resembles the seed of an apple, but we can not give it the life power; then, who can? We answer, God only; and as the life power, or Seven Spirits of God, fashioned all matter in which is life, and as this life energy is of God only, he can retire that life from the eighteen thousand seeds to the one generic, and, in so doing, suspend the life till the Spirit of God again resuscitates the powers suspended.

So with the animals. They having been created of matter, and the life power being of God, when that life power retired to the ark, the representative beasts and creeping things, from which the myriad formations sprang, followed that life power to the ark, where the generic seed of every plant and tree in its root and origin had, by the command of God, been gathered for the food of all the animals saved in the ark; the life power of God retiring from matter to the ark, suspended the life of every thing in the earth, air, or water, and "every living thing in which is the breath of life perished"—died.

As soon, then, as the storm ceased, and the wind passed over the waters, and the atmosphere drank up into itself the vapor, the mountains appeared; the Seven Spirits of God reproduced the animated life, till now suspended, and seas were again filled with the teeming millions, the air was again vocal with the fowls of heaven, and the earth moved with animated life.

*Q.* Would not this be transmigration?

*A.* No; it would only be retiring the life of the tree to its original seed, the bird to its first created species, and all the creeping things in like manner; for if, as we have shown, the creative attributes of God retired to the Noachian ark, then the root of the life of all things that had life must inhere in the same ark, or in the life power of the attributes of God.

*Q.* Why was not man resuscitated in the same manner?

*A.* Man had sinned, and for his sin alone all the beasts, birds, and fishes, suffered, and to save the species to him, and for him in the future revelations of God to man, they were retired to the seven, and to the two of a kind.

*Q.* Would not this be a resurrection of the beasts and birds?

*A.* No, not a resurrection, but a resume of life, a resuscitation from unconsciousness to conscious existence. We read, "Of every clean beast thou shalt take to thee by sevens, the male and his female; and of the beasts that are not clean, by two, the male and his female. Of the fowls also of the air by sevens, the male and the female; to keep *seed* alive upon the face of all the earth."—Gen. vii: 2, 3.

These are here represented as the genitors of all the races on "*the face of all the earth.*"

*Q.* Then, Mr. H. Miller's wingless wood hens and heavy flying quails, of New Zealand, could, when the creative attributes left the ark, be as easily reproduced as they were killed?

*A.* Certainly; and the long voyages of being ferried across the Atlantic, be dispensed with.

It might be profitable for us to investigate this matter still further. The existence of the seed of certain plants in a latent condition, or whether there are seeds in the earth at all, till certain chemical changes have been effected, has been a question easier to ask than to answer. Here, to illustrate, we go miles into the forest, and fell a portion of timber, and burn over the ground where it stood, and thousands of plants, called fire-weed, will spring up from the earth spontaneously.

*Q.* What produces these plants?

*A.* The same as produces life in any thing else. The Seven Spirits of God created all the relations, natural and chemical, that exist. The combinations of these produce life; for all matter, so long as the attributes of God pervade matter, has bequeathed to it the power of life. Hence ourselves, and every living thing, and tree, plant, and flower, owe their origin to the life power of God, and the chemical affinities of matter, by which life is produced in the lower orders of animals, is as much the creative power of the Spirit as is our own life.

This combination may exist in the latent, as well as the active state, and may be developed into life by chemical processes; but the author of matter has fixed these laws as perfectly as they are marvelous.

There are thousands of chemical combinations that produce or develop life, and God is as much the author of that life as he is of the elements that are the unfolding exhibition of it. Hence the fire-weed only existed in latent chemical affinities, and was brought forth by the action of heat upon the decayed vegetable matter of the forest.

*Q.* This, then, does not necessitate even a seed, as the root of the fire-weed?

*A.* Certainly not; as the life-spirit of God

pervades all matter, and holds it subject to life under certain affinities.

We thence learn of the resuscitation of vegetables and trees; similar to those engulfed in substances derived from the atmosphere hundreds of feet below the surface, when the Seven Spirits of God partially withdrew from matter; and their appearance is *identical* with those which were submerged with coal, or rock deposit from the atmosphere, becoming crystalized or petrified beneath the water.

Hence the problem is solved, if the attributes of God pervade all matter.

*Q.* What do we learn by reading the seventh chapter of Genesis?

*A.* We learn that Noah obeyed God in all things, and, as the attributes of God were withdrawn from the temporal things they had made, that all terrestrial things were changed; the elected beasts flock to the ark, the fountains of the deep are broken up, the air and water unite to fifteen cubits above the highest mountains, and all flesh outside of the ark died. "And every living substance was destroyed which was upon the face of the ground, both man and cattle, and creeping things, and fowl of heaven; and they were destroyed from the earth: and Noah only remained alive, and they that were with him in the ark."—Gen. vii: 23.

*Q.* What do we learn from the eighth chapter?

*A.* That when God's purpose had been accomplished, the attributes resumed their former creative and restorative power, and that the "Lord smelled (or breathed) a sweet savor" upon the various connections, originally established by his Seven Spirits—the seven attributes of God.

Thus the waters returned to their original channels, the mountains reared their lofty peaks, the rivers assumed their wonted paths to the ocean, and vegetation began its luxuriant growth.

*Q.* Were there no changes in the earth's surface effected by the flood?

*A.* Perhaps not by the flood, but immediately preceding the deluge there had been great changes and convulsions in the earth. Islands and mountains had disappeared, for God withdrew his attributes from their controlling power over the boundaries they had fixed, and seas and oceans rushed madly on, impelled by fierce volcanoes, and the confused elements submerged whole provinces of rank vegetation, turning them into coal and petrified rock in a moment of time. These and a thousand other evidences remain to tell us of the confusion that every-where prevailed when God withdrew the powers that fashioned them for man.

Thus the assuaged waters left them as they are, but not as they originally were.

*Q.* What do we learn in the ninth chapter?

*A.* We learn that the dreadful deluge, which

had swept the inhabitants of the old world away, had not restored the seven senses in man to purity or perfection.

The former doings of the race were not forgotten, their practices not entirely ignored, nor the vile use of intoxicating drinks abandoned.

Even Noah became inebriate by the wine from his newly planted vineyard, and his second son, Ham, is placed under the curse of his hoary years.

*Q.* What effect does fermented liquors produce upon the attributes?

*A.* It drives them from their natural abode in the body to the several points of inosculation, or to the ganglia of the special sensation.

*Q.* Would not this destroy man's moral responsibility?

*A.* Not wholly so, for the use of alcoholic drinks he could have dispensed with, for he knows the result. You leap from the window in a five-story building, you are not really responsible for the gravity that draws you down with such rapidity, but you are responsible for placing yourself under the force of that gravity, so the inebriate may not be ashamed of his drunken debauch while intoxicated, but is not rendered irresponsible thereby, because he brought this condition upon himself.

*Q.* Why does a man stagger and fall down when intoxicated?

*A.* Four sevenths of the senses find their nerve center in the brain; three only are diffusive.

These, here connect with the attributes, which permeate the senses and make them morally responsible. If driven, then, from the system to this nerve center, the brain is surcharged with a force not its own, and this force unbalances and intoxicates the cerebrum.

*Q.* If the attributes are thus driven to the brain, why does not this produce insanity?

*A.* It temporally produces a species of insanity, and does not ever leave the brain in as good condition as it found it; but Divine compassion has so ordered, that this suicidal attack upon the attributes does not always result in insanity, but by frequent abuse in this relation a disease may be produced at the point of inosculation, and then the man is insane—dies of mania a potu.

*Q.* Why is it that so many get drunk so often, yet are apparently sane when not under the influence of strong drink?

*A.* Because three-sevenths of the senses do not inhere in the cerebrum. If in the brain was found the nerve center of the common sensation of feeling, talking, and the judgment sense, the effect must be fatal to the organism.

Every man who has watched an inebriate has readily observed that the *language* sense is rather developed than destroyed, when a man is partially intoxicated. The operation of the attributes, being diffusive when of the nature that inheres in the connection with the common sensation, can not be driven to any center. Hence the language sense, the judgment sense, and the sense of feeling are greatly debilitated, but not intoxicated.

*Q.* Are the attributes so ponderous in their nature as to press the organism to the earth when driven to the brain?

*A.* The attributes are as imponderable when in connection with the senses as is the air in which we move, though this element exerts a weight upon us of from fifteen to twenty-two pounds to the square inch. If, then, the head could feel the weight of the atmosphere on a surface of thirty square inches, the aggregate weight upon the neck would be about five hundred pounds, which very few persons could carry, but, like the attributes, this aerial substance permeates the system, and we do not sense the ponderability, but, could we drive out this atmospheric substance, and upon the head only try to balance it, it would not be unlike trying to balance the organism, when, by alcoholic drinks, the attributes, that is, four-sevenths of them, are driven to the brain.

*Q.* Why is this a sin?

*A.* Because God has formed this connection for moral and religious purposes, and when we render this relation inoperative, God is dishonored; hence the "Woe unto him that giveth his neighbors drink, that puttest thy bottle to him, and makest him drunken also."—Hab. ii: 15.

*Q.* What peculiar information do we obtain by reading the tenth chapter of Genesis?

*A.* We here learn the generations of Noah and his sons, the rapidity of their increase, and that all the tribes and nations of this multitude spoke but one language.

*Q.* What new idea is contained in the eleventh chapter.

*A.* We learn in this chapter that the idea of another Babylon (for Babel and Babylon are the same), with a tower so mountain high that no deluge could sweep it away, and one that might last against the wastes of time forever, so largely became universal, that already they were at work on the tower—that brick and slime answered the place of stone and mortar.

Hitherto Satan had power to unite the depraved senses in carrying out every demoniac object that his depraved attributes might suggest, but now he was restrained from such power, he was bound a thousand years; hence the attributes could be deranged, that is, their relation to the senses could be so turned around, or disunited, that east might appear west, north seem to be south, or an idiom convey directly the reverse of its original meaning. Hence the language sense was confounded. They heard the same word that they heard before, but now, the attributes and senses being disjoined, or turned around, it conveyed to them other meaning, till the whole seven senses had originated as many languages.

Dr. Thompson, in discoursing on the unity of the race, from the stand-point of, at first, *only one language*, makes this statement: "The lines of language converge toward Central Asia, and in the far past its many threads can be woven into a small number of strands, which the science of comparative philology may yet succeed in twisting together in a single cord, but cautious philologists doubt whether conclusive testimony for or against the unity of the human race will ever be derived from language alone."

One can easily see that it requires no miraculous power to lose a man as to the points of compass, and surely the judgment sense could as easily be disarranged from the attributes in reference to language, as in the points of compass, and this change would involve the necessity of seven primitive languages, all of them commencing simultaneously with the building of Babel.

Dr. Thompson farther remarks: "If there was one primitive language of the race, the Biblical story of the confusion of tongues at Babel would account for the diversity of human speech. But when the trustworthiness of the Biblical narative is under consideration, we have no right to assume the miraculous element as a mode of meeting difficulties that seem to embarrass the narative itself. That it is difficult to provide for a normal division of tongues from one primitive root within the period of our received chronology, must be obvious to any who will reflect upon the elements that enter into the construction and growth of a language."

By the same reasoning Adam could never have understood any language at all, and the trustworthiness, that is, the truthfulness of the whole record, goes by the skepticism. The "Biblical story" thus reads: "Let us go down, and there confound their language, that they may not understand one another's speech. So the Lord scattered them abroad from thence upon the face of the earth: and they left off to build the city."—Gen. xi: 7, 8. Now we see no good reason to doubt this truth of God, more than that the Messiah made his appearance on earth, and by the Mystic Numbers the phenomenon is as easily explained as are occurrences of every-day life.

This confounding of their language confused all their plans and dispersed them abroad upon the face of the earth, and Babel was left to ruin and decay.

This eleventh chapter of Genesis closes with the marriage of Abram, afterward called Abraham, and their journey to the land of Ur, of the Chaldees, the land of Canaan.

*Q.* What do we learn from the twefth chapter of Genesis?

*A.* We learn that Abram, by the command

of God, left Haran, when he was 75 years of age, went to the land of Egypt; and that Sarai, Abram's wife, by judgments upon Pharaoh's house, was restored to him, and then he left Egypt with all that he had.

*Q.* What do we learn by reading the thirteenth chapter?

*A.* That Abram dwelt in Canaan, and Lot in Sodom. That the Lord gave to Abram all the land lying northward, and westward, and southward as far as his eyes could see. He also received the promise of an abundant posterity, and removed to Mamre, where he builded an altar to the Lord.

*Q.* What is learned in the fourteenth chapter of Genesis?

*A.* The great battles of five kings against four kings, and their capture of Lot, Abram's brother's son. That Abram pursued them and recovered Lot. That Melchizedek met Abram and blessed him in the name of the Most High God, through whose power he had gained the victory over Chedorlaomer.

*Q.* What strange conduct do we see in the sixteenth chapter?

*A.* The principles of polygamy advocated by Abram's wife, Sarai.

*Q.* Did Sarai do right in offering Hagar to Abram for a wife under the pretense of barrenness?

*A.* Indeed, she did not, nor did Abram in

accepting her proposal; but as the law and the Gospel must be separated, God chose this method to represent the two covenants.

*Q.* What were the two covenants?

*A.* The one pertained to earthly things, the other to the heavenly—the one answereth to ritualism, the other to grace—one to Jerusalem below, Ishmael; the other to the Jerusalem from heaven, Isaac. (Gal. iv: 24–30.)

*Q.* How old was Abram when Ishmael was born?

*A.* Eighty-six years of age, being fourteen years prior to the birth of Isaac.

*Q.* What does the seventeenth chapter of Genesis teach?

*A.* The origin of the act of circumcision—a bloody, cruel, and indecent ritual, made necessary by the stubbornness of the people to whom it related, and a "yoke of bondage," by which the Jews were to be distinguished from all other nations. To describe this rite of circumcision would blush the cheek of modesty, although it is still practiced by Jews and Mohammedans.

*Q.* Has circumcision an allusion?

*A.* It has, as it alludes to the land of Canaan, and is a sign of the covenant to that inheritance: "And I will establish my covenant between me and thee, and thy seed after thee, in their generations, for an everlasting covenant; to be a God unto thee, and to thy seed after thee. And I will give unto thee, and to thy seed after thee, the land wherein thou art a stranger, all the land of Canaan, for an everlasting possession; and I will be their God."—Gen. xvii: 7, 8.

Hence, the covenant that God made with Abraham was an everlasting covenant, and the land of Canaan an inheritance equally everlasting.

*Q.* But the Apostle saith that Abraham "received the sign of circumcision, a seal of the righteousness of the faith which he had, yet being uncircumcised."—Rom. iv: 11. How could this be, if circumcision was a sign of that covenant which gave to the Jews only an earthly inheritance?

*A.* It must be remembered that all God's promises to man, where covenant blessings are offered, are conditional. Here he offers to Abraham the glory of being the father of all the faithful, both of the circumcision and of the uncircumcision, if he would carry out the stipulation, accept the sign of circumcision. Abraham accepts the condition, and is himself circumcised, and also Ishmael, and all the males that were in his house, fourteen years before Isaac was born. Upon the fulfillment of this stipulation God promised him an heir, even Isaac, with another promise that through this lineage all the earth should be blessed.

The great Redeemer must appear through

some lineage, and God chose Abraham; and he again confirmed this promise to him when his faith had been tried in the offering up of Isaac upon the altar as a sacrifice. But the seal of a title is not the sign; circumcision was the sign, faith in God the seal to the inheritance, so far as the promised Messiah related to that covenant; hence, circumcision was a sign of a covenant in the flesh to a portion of land known as the land of Canaan.

*Q.* Circumcision, then, was really a national rite—not a religious ordinance?

*A.* It was truly a national ritual, and could have no relation, either *pro* or *con*, of a moral character, as the male infant was to be just eight days old when this strange ritual or surgical operation was performed, and at such an age moral character has no visible existence.

## CHAPTER XVII.

Moral Law—The Ten Commandments—The Ceremonial Law—Polygamy—Legends of the History of Creation — Prophecy — Spiritualism — Typical Dispensation—Sacrifices—Numerals Twelve—Numerals Forty.

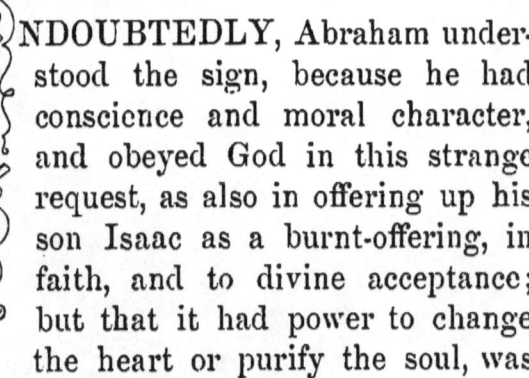

NDOUBTEDLY, Abraham understood the sign, because he had conscience and moral character, and obeyed God in this strange request, as also in offering up his son Isaac as a burnt-offering, in faith, and to divine acceptance; but that it had power to change the heart or purify the soul, was as foreign to it then as it is now; neither circumcision nor uncircumcision will avail any thing, but only a new birth, a new relation to God by faith in our Lord Jesus Christ.

The *moral law* knows no act of circumcision, nor does the *law of grace;* for it is declared that faith in God is alone the method of salvation.

*Q.* What is the moral law?

*A.* The moral law relates directly to the seven attributes of man, and as love is the controlling attribute, its relation to the moral law is apparent. It reads: "Thou shalt love the Lord thy God with all thy heart, and with all thy soul, and with all thy mind, and with all thy strength, and thy neighbor as thyself."

*Q.* If God addresses the moral law to this attribute, this attribute, then, must have the control of all the attributes?

*A.* It certainly has, and the Author of our entire moral nature knew full well of the powers we possess and of the access of his Love attribute to ours, in the acceptance of this devotion to him.

*Q.* But, if the senses are totally depraved, how can the attributes be reached through them?

*A.* By the power of the atonement of Christ in his archetypal relation to our spiritual organism. Access to the attributes are twofold: first, by the Divine Spirit direct; and, second, through the judgment sense, which embraces all the senses.

*Q.* What law, then, refers to the senses, if the moral law refers to the attributes?

*A.* The law of the decalogue, or as is generally known, the law of the ten commandments.

This law is mostly a law of negatives: "Thou shalt not kill, thou shalt not steal, thou shalt not covet, thou shalt not bear false witnesses," etc. The senses being totally depraved, the restraints of law became necessary (thou shalt not) instead of positive. The law to the attributes became positive ("thou shalt love the Lord thy God"), because they were not absolutely under the reign of depravity.

*Q.* What, then, is the ceremonial law?

*A.* The ceremonial law is the blending of the two laws together, but they could not, even thus blended, make the comers thereunto perfect. "For if there could have been a law given that could have given life, verily righteousness should have come by the law;" but no law that could be given could affect total depravity, only as a restraint through fear; not to the sanctification of the soul. The devils are restrained by fear of penalties, but this does not make them better.—Jas. ii: 19.

*Q.* Were all these laws experiments, then?

*A.* No. They were "schoolmasters;" "The law," says the apostle, "was our schoolmaster, to bring us to Christ." They were restraining necessities; but the "law made nothing perfect," the law itself was holy, just, and good, as are all laws emanating from God; even a law to exterminate a tribe, or the inhabitants of a city, if it emanates from God, must be a necessity, and the law is therefore holy, just, and good.

*Q.* Are there any other laws besides the moral law, the ten commandments, and the ceremonial law?

*A.* There is a special system of grace, the law of salvation, which was really the first revelation of God, "for it is the end of the law for righteousness," and this law is wholly and only revealed in the covenant of grace. The act of obedience to this law is, faith in the promised Messiah, the offering that eternal love accepted before the world began. This law readeth thus: "If thou shalt confess with thy mouth the Lord Jesus Christ, and shalt believe in thine heart that God raised him from the dead, thou shalt be saved."—Rom. x: 9.

*Q.* If the moral law related only to the attributes, how does the violation of any other law become sinful?

*A.* The other laws are restraints upon our totally depraved senses; and the penalties attached to the violation of these commandments are of a finite character, so far as they relate to human objects. For illustration, the command that says, thou shalt not kill or murder, has a penalty: "He that sheddeth man's blood by man shall his blood be shed." When this penalty has been endured, the law of restraint is satisfied; but by the connection of the senses and attributes, this crime had a moral type, and this moral relation is transferred to the Supreme Court in heaven; hence the violation of any law of God has a moral responsibility as well as physical.

*Q.* Then the law governing marriage, as given

to Adam, must have had a moral character as well as human?

*A.* It undoubtedly had; but as it was perfectly obeyed, it received no notice in the Mosaic account, till the sons of God violated this holy relation, as also did the sons of Cain, and here is the first scriptural allusion to polygamy.

*Q.* Why was polygamy tolerated in the first ages of the second dispensation?

*A.* For one thousand years before the flood, even from the descendants of Cain, and through the entire career of the antediluvians, this corrupt system had received the most hearty indorsement. In fact, those who were not guilty of this sin were reduced to the smallest minority before the flood, for we may infer from the teachings of sacred history that Noah was the only man that was perfect in his generation.

Restraining law in this particular had no moral effect whatever, and on, till this and other heinous sins culminated in the destruction of almost an entire world. Shem, Ham, and Japheth, Noah's sons, had lived a hundred years before the flood, and their wives also were well instructed in the habits and character of those with whom they lived. Universal evils, by being of every day's occurrence, growing up with our growth from childhood, lose their heinous nature, and thus it had become the custom of the masses, and they gloried in it. Hence polygamy became a part of the depravity of man.

*Q.* But it would appear to have been necessary for God to have positively forbidden this evil?

*A.* All unrighteousness is sin, and as this sin was no more heinous in his sight than other sins, and as God disapproves of all sin, we are inclined to the belief that some code of law did exist, and that this act was positively prohibited, as was idolatry. But it is a fact that in less than five hundred years after the flood, both these evils had so entered into the customs and practices of the vast majority, that the corruption of polygamy was almost universal, and no *moral* barrier presented itself of sufficient note to make it even a religious test; hence it passed to the patriarchs and teachers of the law, as we look at original sin, a moral calamity, not a virtue.

*Q.* But was it not a sin then as much as it is now?

*A.* Most assuredly it was, but the light of truth had much to eradicate from the totally depraved senses before a law that would effect a reformation on that point could, with any hope of success, be promulgated.

*Q.* Were not the "sons of God," in their transgression, polygamists?

*A.* So Dr. Kitto informs us, but he supposes that the sons of God were the worshipers of God, and that the daughters of the children of men were open sinners or unrepentant sinners. If this rendering be true, the worshipers of God were the basest men, which illy comports with their title.

We think, however, that the sons of God were the prefallen race of Adam, that this was their first sin, and that this sin placed them under the condemnation of death; for if Adam's sin caused death to reign, then the sin of his unfallen children must be equally offensive to God, and should receive the same penalty.'

We believe, however, that at no time since the flood has a majority of all the nations countenanced polygamy, and, as Satan was bound for the first thousand years, no united or universal decree could be given in favor of such a practice, and the evils resulting from this "doctrine of the Nicolaitans, which thing God hated," became apparent to most of the nations of the earth.

*Q.* How long did the world's history remain only in legends and traditions?

*A.* About twenty-five hundred years after the fall of man.

*Q.* Who wrote the history of Creation?

*A.* By the teaching and power of the Seven Spirits of God, Moses was enabled to give the wonderful history.

*Q.* How could the depraved senses be so controlled as to write a perfect sketch of events and biographies that occurred more than two thousand years before the writer lived?

*A.* Writing, as well as prophesying, was anciently a peculiar association with the Spirit, somewhat after the manner of somnambulism, only the one occurred during the wakeful hours, and the other during the hours of sleep. The fulfillment of the prophecy was a sure test of its inspiration, though some wicked men prophesied; even Balaam prophesied favorably for Israel, though bribed by an enemy, and an enemy to Israel he proved himself to be afterward, and is called in Scripture wicked Balaam.—2 Pet. ii: 16. Rev. ii: 14.

*Q.* Prophesying, then, was accomplished, in ancient times, much after the manner of modern spiritualism?

*A.* Not at all. False prophets were influenced by the thrill of demoniac spirit, or by the devil's attaching his totally depraved attributes to man's totally depraved senses, and thus by the consent and will of the senses became their oracle.

True prophets, on the other hand, placed their attributes in unison with the attributes of God, that is, "holy men of old" (wrote and) "spake" (prophetically) "as they were moved upon by the Holy Ghost."—2 Pet. i: 21. In this union the senses became passive to depraved action, for the Holy Ghost rendered them so, through the supreme desire of the Love attribute, with which the Spirit of God united. Their writings, then, were the writings of God, for God inspired them, and one of the harmonious attributes of

God is truth. Then all prophecy must come to pass, for the prophet, through his love to God, had rendered his senses as submissive as a pen in the hand of the writer.

Modern spiritualism is no more nor less than the harmony of the seven senses with others in some speculative object of no real value.

*Q.* Do they not foretell events by clairvoyance?

*A.* Only by the judgment sense combined with the judgment sense of another. While one sleeps, another prompts him to tell about some given thing, all they both know; and of such things separately, they may neither know; but this is all of a trivial character, for when a clairvoyant tells you where money is hidden in the earth, if you believe him, you make a fool of yourself, unless he or you know of its location. If so, what is gained by clairvoyance; for he could have communicated to you the secret without clairvoyance just as well.

*Q.* But does not the devil contribute to this delusion?

*A.* No. He does not even have this honor; for the devil is bound and tongue-tied. He can thrill our depraved senses, because he is the prince of darkness, as well as the prince of the power of the air, but he can not make the senses talk.

*Q.* Do not a great many people believe in so-called spiritualism, and do they not believe that they converse with departed loved ones?

*A.* Of course there are thousands of just such fancies, and as it can do but little good or hurt to think so, it is not worth contending about; but when darkness reigned to a greater extent than now, when people believed in witches and wizards, and ran mad over the delusion, spiritualism would have been a frightful monster. But as it is now, the senses are no worse when combined than when separate, and as education forms the judgment sense, and no one expects the other possessed of the devil, but little ill can come of it.

*Q.* But how is it that one person can have so much control over another as to place him under his will as a clairvoyant?

*A.* The human will, *i. e.*, the judgment sense, is induced into its passive state by electricity. This element can be detected as we are becoming drowsy, by its effect upon the nervous system, which shock, sometimes awakens us to consciousness; or, by watching a person when first going to sleep, we can detect an effect similar in its operations upon the nerves to slight shocks of electricity; and thus man is himself electric, forming, when hand is united to hand, an electric chain of humanity to any conceivable extent, so that if the first person receives the shock, all receive the same simultaneously.

Now if we are thus circumstanced, the condition of the human nerves not only self-induce electricity, but receive it of others; then, if the will power or judgment sense passively submits to its influence, the human nerves, and to some extent the senses, act with the operator, and, combining, unfold some peculiar things that separately neither of them knew.

*Q.* Is this psychological power, then, a science?

*A.* No, it is not. It is only a speculation. If it was a science, when one was apprehended for crime, he could, by the clairvoyance process, be made to confess his crime, and thereby the real party to the crime discovered. But clairvoyance knows no secret, either moral or religious, that is at all reliable. Who would purchase stock, grain, farms, or merchandise, simply because a clairvoyant said the prices of that article would advance? No one. Then modern spiritualism is neither prophetic, scientific, nor reliable.

*Q.* Are we not cautioned in Scripture to "try the spirits, to see whether they are of God?"

*A.* We certainly are; but there is no use of calling a phenomena as easily accounted for as telegraphing, a spirit. But the passage to which allusion is made in the question, has reference to doctrine, and not disembodied spirits. It is called the spirit of antichrist, the spirit of error, etc.—1 John iv: 1, 3, and 6.

If clairvoyance, biology, or spiritualism, was the action or transaction of disembodied spirits, by whose extraneous force men were driven to acts of desperation and crime, then it would be necessary to have them incarcerated in an insane asylum or a mad-house, but no such fears need be entertained when, by the order of the great God, such forces are chained and inaccessible.

*Q.* Does not a religious excitement proceed from the same combined action of the senses as does the "spirit rappings?"

*A.* Not a genuine revival spirit.

The whole work of a religious interest, if it is truly religious, is effected by the intercession of the attributes of God upon our attributes, and are conveyed to the connecting points of inosculation, with such soul-stirring appeals that the judgment sense involuntarily promises a better life, and our fallen senses hope even by that *promise* to gain relief; and when the power of the Holy Spirit, which some calls *excitement*, thrills every connecting sense with fear and dismay, there *must be* a terrible struggle if the senses resist so benign and so blessed a spirit. If, on the other hand, the offered grace is through the senses accepted, the joy will be unspeakable and full of glory.

But, in either case, it differs widely from the mesmeric effect of hobgoblin and imaginary spiritualism.

*Q.* Have we now no prophets?

*A.* The age of prophesying has closed, for the reason before alluded to. Satan is bound and shut up, so far as his controlling power is concerned.

There are two classes of influences at work upon us constantly: First, every thing we see, hear, taste, or feel, in fact, every thing that comes in contact with our seven senses has an influence upon us, either of a pleasurable or of a disagreeable character, either to make us better or worse. Hence bad associations result generally and naturally in bad habits: "With a furious man thou shalt not go, lest thou learn his ways;" as, also, good associations result in a correspondingly good life: "Train up a child in the way he should go, and when he is old he will not depart from it."

Second, we are, from the senses, subject to temptation from unexplained and internal causes. We think wrong by some wrong effect upon our attributes, and sometimes it would seem that they are totally unprotected against this internal influence. These the apostle calls "the motion of sins."—Rom. vii: 5.

To remedy this evil God has given us his Word, which is a lamp to our feet and a guide to our path; to this guide every man is exhorted to lend a listening ear. If we would circumscribe our passions by the boundary of God's word "we should not materially err."

As this is the last dispensation of time ("the last time") we need no other prophet. When spiritualism assumes to have found some other book better than the Bible, some other revelation that is of more value than God's Word, or some system of ethics that have a better tendency to save the soul than God's method, as in his Word revealed, then, and not till then, does it effect the character of men more than a belief that stones fall to the earth from the moon. It is pure speculation.

*Q.* How long did the power of prophesying last?

*A.* During the entire second dispensation, that is, from the fall of man to the cessation of the miraculous gift of the Holy Spirit.

*Q.* What are the peculiar distinctions between the second and third dispensations of time?

*A.* The second dispensation, that is, the typical dispensation, had all its types and rituals in connection with nationality; the third dispensation calls out of all nationalities, languages, and tongues, a people saved by grace.

*Q.* Were not all that ever were saved, saved by grace?

*A.* Certainly; but "they are not all Israel that were of Israel;" the nation to whom God gave his law on tables of stone were no more Christians, in a Gospel sense, than is Scotland or England, nor were their religious views more in unison than are the views of the people of any State in the United States. Still some were the salt of the earth—the chosen of God, and faithful; the laws of the second dispensation subjected saint and sinner alike to the obedience to the rituals. A burnt-offering, a sin-offering, and all the ceremonies, were as applicable to the infidel as Christian; to Korah, Dathan, and Abiram, and all the revolters, as to Moses and Aaron.

The third dispensation brings out, in a public profession of faith, all those of all nations who believe in our Lord Jesus Christ, and obliges no man, not a believer, to obey the ordinances of the church; nay, it forbids any to partake of the Lord's Supper but such as discern his body.

*Q.* Was not the Saviour of mankind, our Lord Jesus Christ, believed on in the world during the second dispensation?

*A.* He was as a lamb slain from the foundation of the world; slain for man. In his archetypal nature he suffered, and in his human nature he died—was slain. In his archetypal nature he revealed himself to Adam, Enoch, Noah, Abraham, Elijah, Isaiah, Daniel, Malachi, and all the prophets.

These and the tens of thousands who, through their prophesying and preaching, believed on the Messiah, received the Spirit, and were washed from their sins in the archetypal blood of the Lamb, and entered the realms of glory triumphantly before the "man of sorrows" had been offered up as an atoning sacrifice, consequently their salvation was not based upon a promise, but upon a satisfaction already made, a covenant already sealed, a release already secured, as much then as now, so far as the sanctification of the soul and the harmony of the attributes were concerned. The type of the human blood of Jesus was then represented by the blood of goats, and of lambs, and as much expressed the divine purpose as does "the bread we break, or the cup of blessings which we bless."

*Q.* Do we understand that the attributes and souls of men were cleansed by a fountain then already opened?

*A.* The Psalmist, speaking of it, says: "For with thee is the fountain of life; in thy light shall we see light."—Ps. xxxvi: 9.

The promises to man were based upon the satisfaction accomplished in the covenant of grace. Could the promise of washing a garment make that garment clean? Could the promise to cleanse the soul from all sin cleanse it? Surely not. The work of salvation is alone seen in the cleansing of the soul from pollution and sin.

This was the work of the Holy Spirit, in harmonizing the attributes, and in applying his archetypal blood, as much before the coming of the Messiah as now.

*Q.* But how could blood be applied before the blood was shed; in other words, what is the archetypal blood of Christ, and how applied?

*A.* As we have before shown, God the Father can not be seen by any of his creatures more than my spirit, or your spirit, can be seen by our offspring. The form that hides the Godhead (who is a consuming fire), is the WORD—the Lamb of God—the Wonderful. This Word, by offering a pure spiritual fountain, the archetypal blood of that *form*, called the Word of God, for the purification of the heirs of promise, placed its application within the power of the Holy Spirit.

The Holy Spirit, then, at the harmonizing of the attributes of man, applies this fountain to the soul, which cleanses it from all pollution, and in its dual nature, enters glory as a redeemed trophy of the victorious Christ.

Thus the plan of salvation was complete without the resurrection of this body—the redeemed would then be like the angels of God, only a little more exalted, as they bear the image of the King of kings and Lord of lords.

*Q.* The number seven, then, in its primary allusion, inheres in the seven attributes of God, but to what does the mystic twelve allude?

*A.* This number, or combined numerals, is first brought to our notice prominently in the twelve patriarchs; but this would not appear of great moment if it did not occur so typically obvious in the Saviour's choice of the twelve apostles, as also the prophecy of one to fill the place of Judas, who, by transgression, fell from the office of Bishop, which he had so unworthily filled; and still, to confirm the probable allusion of this number, the foundations of the New Jerusalem, the gates of the city, and the twelve angels at those gates, leave us little doubt that the mystic twelve has an allusion.

We have before shown that the second dispensation lasted four thousand years, and that the third dispensation would probably last four thousand years, and to harmonize the first dispensation with these, *it* must have existed four thousand years. Adding these together we have twelve thousand years, the probable duration of time.

*Q.* When, then, will the millennium commence?

*A.* The exact time when the "swords will be beat into plowshares, and the spears into pruning hooks," we may not know, but it is very probable, as we have no prophets of whom we can inquire as to this time, that its solution may be learned from the word of God, already given. The prophet Zechariah has given the clearest description how this change will be effected of any of the prophets. He says: "And it shall be in that day that living waters shall go out from Jerusalem; half of them toward the former sea, and half of them toward the hinder sea: in summer and winter shall it be. And the Lord shall be King over all the earth: in that day shall there be one Lord, and his name one. And the land shall be turned as a plain from Geba to Rimmon, south of Jerusalem, and it shall be lifted up, and inhabited in her place, from Benjamin's gate unto the place of the first gate, unto the corner gate, and from the tower of Hananeel to the king's wine-presses. And men shall dwell in it, and there shall be no more utter destruction; but Jerusalem shall be safely inhabited."—Zech. xiv: 8–11. The same prophet informs us how this work will become universal. We read: "And it shall come to pass that every one that is left of all the nations that came against Jerusalem, shall even go up from year to year to worship the king, the Lord of hosts, and to keep the feast of the tabernacles. And it shall come to pass that whosoever will not come up of all the families of the earth unto Jerusalem to worship the king, the Lord of hosts, even upon them shall be no rain. And if the family of Egypt go not up that have no rain, there shall be the plague wherewith the Lord shall smite the heathen that come not up to keep the feast of the tabernacles. This shall be the punishment of Egypt, and the punishment of all nations that come not up to keep the feast of tabernacles. In that day shall there be upon the bells of the horses, HOLINESS UNTO THE LORD; and the pots in the Lord's house shall be like the bowls before the altar."—Zech. xiv: 16–20.

We understand by this that the wicked are to waste away before the light of the Gospel, and that personal safety can not be found outside of the people of God; that the plague shall destroy all living creatures where the reign of Christ is not complete.

It is probable that the last thousand years of time, or eleven hundred and thirty years hence, the light of the Gospel will be sufficiently worldwide, so that "a great tumult from the Lord," as the prophet hath said, "shall be among the people," and the influences of the Church of God will be so universal that wickedness can not survive. Then the millennium will commence—no more war, no more wickedness, no more suffering in all God's holy mountain.

*Q.* We understand, then, that the last thousand years of time will be the thousand years of the reign of grace, but in what manner do we dispose of the numerals, forty?

*A.* The singular recurrence of this number may not at first appear to the mind, unless we notice that Moses was forty days in the Mount of God, preparing the tables of stone. (Exodus xxiv: 18.) That the children of Israel were forty years in the wilderness. That our Saviour was forty days in the wilderness, tempted of the devil. That it was forty days after his crucifixion to his ascension, and that it was forty days after his ascension before the gift or baptism of the Holy Ghost.

Now, as we have shown, each dispensation had in it forty centuries—four thousand years—and this number may in all probability refer to the centuries of each of the three dispensations.

To illustrate. Moses, the law-giver, remained in the Mount of God, where he "saw the God of Israel: and there was under his feet as it were a paved work of a sapphire stone, and as it were the body of heaven in his clearness," (Ex. xxiv: 10) for forty days and nights. May not this allude to the first forty centuries, when the attributes of God rested from their labor in the bright arcana of infinite glory?

The forty days our Saviour was tempted may not inappropriately apply or allude to the typical dispensation, when, through types and shadows, through the reign of the beast, and the journeyings of the children of Israel, God had brought his redeemed and glorious Church.

And his tarrying after his decease, forty days, to the law and the prophets, which were until John, through which the "Shekinah" remained vailed in the temple, whose vail he had rent by his death; and the forty days after his ascension, before the Holy Ghost was given, may it not very appropriately refer to the dispensation of Grace or the third and last dispensation? "For yet a little while, and he that shall come will come, and will not tarry," (Heb. x: 37) and with him the glorious triumph of Grace will be accomplished.

These forty days we have used as in their relation to the days of redemption, each day being a synonym of a hundred years, instead of a thousand, as seen in Creation, or a year, as seen in the prophecy.

This number, or these numerals, may not be of any value in solving the problem of time, but taken in connection with the numerals twelve and the dispensations three, we have a very appropriate solution of the necessity that seems to fix the duration of the "rest of the attributes" while the law was being prepared; and the temptations to the typical dispensation, and also the allusion of the delay of the Holy Spirit.

*Q.* Does the change of the dispensation change the plan of redemption?

*A.* Not at all. The Jewish types pointed to the human blood of the great Messiah, and though necessary to quicken the attributes into a firm belief of the resurrection of the body of Jesus, or the relation that his blood must sustain to that action, they were not thence saved by the type. Not at all. Nothing but the archetypal blood of the Lamb, applied by the Spirit to the soul, could cleanse it and fit it for heaven; and this could be applied to Abraham, Isaac, and Jacob, to Abel, Enoch, and Noah, as well as to us.

*Q.* Why, then, was it necessary that the human blood of Jesus must be shed?

*A.* From the earth the substance part of man was made; his body, bones, and blood; hence the earth may well be called "mother earth." Job speaks of "corruption as his father, and the worm as his mother," and the decree of God was, that dust we were and to dust must we return.

Then, if there was ever a resurrection of our humanity, the element from which the man was made, and out of which he was taken, must be effected by the sacrifice.

It was thence necessary that the human blood of Jesus Christ should fall upon and connect itself with the earth; hence, he must suffer where his blood could be drank up by the earth, to fulfill the covenant plan for our resurrection, nor this even; but his dead body must be entombed, or the bars of death could not be broken.

*Q.* What are the three witnesses in earth?

*A.* The spirit, the water, and the blood. "These three agree in one." The harmony of the spirit in the combination of matter in the elements is an irrefragable argument that the mystic seven compounded them. All the seven primitive elements agree in one purpose, and that purpose is to aid man in the school of progression; hence the subtle element, electricity, has become, as it were, a post-boy, to instantly convey our wishes, hopes, or fears.

The fire, the air, the water, each and all agree in one, and as plainly unfold to us the creative power and association of the Seven Spirits of God, as substances can possibly testify. The human blood animates and vitalizes all the seven senses and seven attributes of man, and this shows the divisibility of the spirit, even in that life power of man. Hence the spirit, water, and blood, agree in one mysterious purpose, and photograph, so to speak, the power and harmony of the mystic seven upon the organism so fearfully and wonderfully made.

## CHAPTER XVIII.

CHANGE OF DISPENSATION—THE HUMAN BLOOD OF CHRIST—THE SAVING EFFECT—THE ISRAELITES—ELECTION—THE CHARACTER OF THE LAST DISPENSATION—WHAT CHRIST ASSUMED—OMNIPOTENCE OF CHRIST—THE MIND OF CHRIST—CHRIST'S HUMANITY—MARY AND THE SAINTS—THE RESURRECTION.

AS a natural result, from cause to effect, if the human blood that fell from the torn hands and feet of Jesus, or from the wound of the spear, touched the earth, then the human blood of all creatures could be aroused by the electric power of that sinless blood; and as his body had been raised from the tomb, and while therein had, by its electric power, affected all human bodies that had returned to its bosom, so he became the resurrection and the life, and all the dead that are in their graves shall hear his voice and come forth, "Some to life, and some to everlasting shame and contempt."

(250)

*Q.* How will this blood affect the Jews who do not believe that the Messiah has come?

*A.* The devout Jews believe in a Saviour, in a Messiah, as much as do Christians of orthodox schools, and the plan, as announced by the Apostle John, reads thus: "But as many as received him, to them gave he power to become the sons of God, even to them that believe on his name."—John i: 12.

If, then, a belief in his name (the Shiloh), the Messiah, could effect a salvation, we see no good reason to suppose that the devout Israelite may not be admitted to the Holiest of Holies, by the blood of Christ, although, in his zeal, he has overlooked the testimony of the prophets. But the promise is most emphatically to those who "receive him."

The earth became the great magnetic center, when God breathed into the man, whom he had fashioned from the earth, the Holy Spirit. The properties of matter were now mysteriously united to the spirit, and God's plan of Redemption, through the human nature of the Redeemer, unfolded this necessity.

*Q.* Did the ancient Israelites expect the Saviour to appear in human form?

*A.* Many of them did, but the great majority who so believed supposed his reign to be temporal; that they would become a powerful nation, and that all the nations of the earth would do them homage. Hence they were not prepared for a spiritual kingdom, based upon self-denial and faith; and rejected the Lord of life and glory, saying, "Away with him." "He came to his own, and his own received him not."

*Q.* Why were the Israelites called God's chosen people?

*A.* Because they were indeed the chosen people, who not only held the oracles of God, but the prophets of the Lord also sprung out of this nation; nor this only, but the Messiah had been promised through the lineage of Isaac; and Jacob, who was called Israel, had the promise, and bequeathed it to the twelve tribes of Israel, or his twelve sons. This is the reason why the children of Israel were called the chosen people of God. (Rom. iii: 1, 2.)

*Q.* Does the absolute sovereignty of God necessitate the doctrine of election? "Jacob have I loved, and Esau have I hated."—Rom. ix: 11, 13.

*A.* The apostle, in his allusion to this peculiar display of God's sovereignty, really explains it by referring to God's infinite foreknowledge.

*Q.* But does he not declare that this decision was made before either Jacob or Esau had done good or evil.

*A.* God's decisions were eternally made in the courts of his attributes, and infinite wisdom there can never be deceived. In these attributes all that are chosen in Christ Jesus are photographed and their names written, and this is the Lamb's Book of Life.

*Q.* Why, then, are not all photographed, as well as the limited heirs of grace?

*A.* For the very reason that they will not stand before the camera, and have their likeness taken by the operation of the Spirit.

*Q.* But could not the great God, who is infinitely powerful, make them willing?

*A.* The human *will*, springing from the judgment sense, and from thence uniting with the attributes, constitutes man a moral being, endowed with volition; take away volition, and he is a machine, actuated, like an automaton by extraneous force. Hence, if God should render volition inoperative, man would be no longer a moral actor. As well might the teamster say to the saw-log, "Well done, good and faithful saw-log; I have drawn thee here with five yoke of oxen," as for God to say, "Well done, good and faithful servant," etc., if man's volition was suspended. We are commanded to choose, hence we have the power of choice, and all heaven invites us to the camera-obscura, where our titles to heaven are photographed. But the action of a creature could not frustrate the design of the great God, for he had surveyed the plan of redemption, and to this unalterable and infinite purpose the great Messiah looked, and upon this positive result he offered himself for sinners.

*Q.* Will not and does not the doctrine of election forestall free grace?

*A.* Not in the least, because, by the grace of

God our attributes are shielded from the fiery darts of the devil, and placed under the banner of love. The Holy Spirit pleads for all, that all might be saved.

If God had not by his word placed it beyond a doubt that "whosoever will, may take of the waters of life freely," it might be objected to; but, as he has graciously invited all men, as Jesus died for all men, and as the Gospel is to be preached to all men, no man can in truth say, I am not invited; nor can the enlightened mind very easily doubt that grace, pardon, and life, is freely offered to us all.

Great sinners have hoped, deists and infidels have, when nearing the tide of death, called upon God in hope of pardon; so we see that, from every point of view, salvation is freely offered to all, on the terms of the Gospel.

*Q.* May we infer, then, that any can accept, at all times, whenever they choose?

*A.* No; God has given us no knowledge of the limit of his mercy. He may or may not offer the sinner the pearl of great price again, after he has stoutly refused the offered mercy. He ordinarily calls again and again, and his forbearance is indeed wonderful, but he has made no promise how long he will wait for us. "To-day, if ye will hear his voice, harden not your hearts."

In the questions we have already answered we have been obliged to interlink the dispensations together, so that the relations of mind to matter, of attributes to senses, would become less confused, or develop less ambiguity and incoherence, which might perplex the mind of the careful reader, and thereby the whole object of our investigation lost; still, as far as we consistently could, with this object in view, we have avoided the real investigation of the character of the Third Dispensation, to which we now invite our readers.

*Q.* What is the third and last dispensation?

*A.* The "last time," as it is called by the Apostle, we denominate the *dispensation of the triumphs of grace;* which embraces in its surroundings, and in its development, the "babe," the "child," the "man Christ Jesus;" together with the visible exhibition of the Holy Spirit (the Seven Spirits of God), their work direct, and their work or its work indirect, through the ministration of the glorious Gospel and the inspired New Testament.

*Q.* Was not the Old Testament Scriptures inspired, or written by inspiration?

*A.* Most assuredly; but the typical dispensation closed with the gift of the Holy Spirit, but not the ministration, "For the law was given by Moses, but grace and truth came by Jesus Christ."

The Old and New Testament Scriptures are alike the "record that God gave of his Son," but the one record was archetypal, and its outward types consisted in the blood of slain beasts; the other in the blood of our great Redeemer shed from the cross of Calvary—the human type of the great Archetype.

*Q.* How did the blood of Jesus, that was shed upon the earth from the cross, effect our salvation?

*A.* As a type of the glorious man, or of the man glorified, it was united in the covenant of grace to the archetype, and as many as the Father gave him, to them and to their moldering dust he became the resurrection power to eternal life.

*Q.* Then the sacrifices under the law, and the blood there offered from lambs and goats, was only a type of a type?

*A.* We should clearly understand that the body we live in is not the *we*, it is only our frail home. The immortal spirit is so superlative, that the human body is only a type, a shadow, a vapor, that passes away.

This never could have been more than a shadow or type of immortality, had not immortality been swallowed up of life, and this life proceed from God.

It would be well for us also to remember that when this mortal puts on immortality, that the entity or identity of matter will be spiritualized: *i. e.*, changed from matter or substance to a spiritual garment.

Then, if "these vile bodies" are to be changed

"into the likeness of Christ's glorious body," they can only be, while we inhabit them, types of their future advancement and glory.

So, if we look at it carefully from this standpoint, we shall readily see that the flesh our Saviour took upon him was also a type, a shadow, a veil. Hence, the blood on Jewish altars could only typify a type, and the blood of Christ was the antitype to the types of the second dispensation.

*Q.* In taking upon himself flesh, what did the Saviour assume?

*A.* He assumed our seven senses as in Adam, but not our sinful *nature*—the fallen senses.

*Q.* Why?

*A.* Because he was the "seed of the woman." The prophet had described it thus: "Behold, a virgin shall conceive, and bear a son, and shall call his name Immanuel."—Isa. vii: 14. And thus the prophecy was fulfilled.

*Q.* Was he, then, really and truly man?

*A.* As much so as was Adam, for Christ was the "second Adam."

*Q.* Did not Adam possess a sinful nature?

*A.* Not till after his transgression; for God declared that he and all his works were good. "And God blessed them."

If the works of God, which consisted in the formation and development of man, were supremely good, then the senses of Adam were supremely good also. Christ, then, taking our senses as God gave them to Adam, possessed the perfection of humanity. What some writers awkwardly call the *human soul* of Jesus, was his seven senses which he laid down for us—which soul he poured out for us. "He poured out his soul unto death." These relations to matter became "him whose descent is not counted," "him who was without beginning of days or end of life," for "it behooved him to be made like unto his brethren," in order that he might be a merciful High Priest, touched with compassion and sympathy.

*Q.* Were there not a great many types under the ceremonial law that had reference to the antitype, the blood of the cross?

*A.* They were very numerous: there was the blood of slain beasts, the blood sprinkled upon the post of the doors, or, as it was called, the passover; the book of the law and all the vessels of the sanctuary were thus set apart.

Then the blood of circumcision, shed with hands, dimly typified the circumcision without hands; the bodies of those beasts offered up on Jewish altars typified also the body of Christ; says the apostle, "For the bodies of those beasts whose blood is brought into the sanctuary by the high priest for sin, are burned without the camp. Wherefore Jesus also, that he might sanctify the people with his own blood, suffered without the gate. Let us go forth therefore unto him without the camp, bearing his reproach." Heb. xiii:

11, 12, 13. Hence they were types of his human body and human blood, which to himself were types of his archetypal self, or his humanity was the veil of Deity.

*Q.* Was Christ, then, omnipotent, all-powerful, to create or control?

*A.* Infinitely so. The seven attributes of God, like the splendor of ten thousand suns, shone upon his human senses, and through these what he chose to do he did, whether to raise the dead or still the tempest, he "spake and it was done, he commanded and it stood fast."

All the light of God, as shining through the convex lens of infinite space, illuminated the humanity of Jesus, and all power concentrated in his wonderful person.

*Q.* Would not this produce an interregnum—a time in which the throne of God in glory became vacated?

*A.* Not in the least. He is here now, "Lo, I am with you always, even unto the end;" "I will never leave thee, nor forsake thee." Hence he is here now by his Spirit—the Seven Spirits of God—and he was here then by the same Spirit. We greatly confuse ourselves when we think that the human *body* of Christ was the only Christ, for *the Christ* eternally existed.

The "Word" was made flesh. He, we may say,

"Lives through all life,
Extends through all extent;
Spreads undivided,
Operates unspent."

*Q.* But how could he condense himself, so to speak, if he filled immensity and eternity with his presence, as to, in person, occupy a human body, when, compared with a single world, it would be the minutest particle, only a speck of matter?

*A.* If we measure ourselves by the length and breadth, the height and depth of the range of our intellect, we might say of ourselves, "How can a mind that can explore the planisphere, that can trace the constellations of heaven, can scale the heights of infinite glory, or plunge beneath the shadows of eternal night, dwell in so small a body?" Nay, more, we could say, while all our thought was enlisted in casting up in mathematical figures the cubic contents of the grand luminary of day, "Was there not an interregnum, a time during this deep study, where we did not reside in this body?"

Or, we might say, in reference to the immense surroundings of reflex light: "Can there be any real sun now, as only from the moon and stars we get our light?" Certainly we can not anticipate the going out of the sun, because the light by which we see is indirectly from him, that is, from the sun to the moon, and from the moon to the earth; so we can not imagine the throne of God vacated because of the *Immanuel*, the God in man.

Our Saviour, speaking of himself, thus remarks: "And no man hath ascended up into heaven but he that came down from heaven, even the Son of man, which is in heaven."— John iii: 13.

This remark, or the idea of a *time*, in which the great archetype did not occupy the burning and eternal throne of Deity, is abundantly contradicted. Distance (for with him there can be no distance, only as he withdraws his attributes) is infinitely unknown.

"He fills, he bounds, connects, and equals all," both of time and eternity.

*Q.* Still the idea will force itself upon us, can a *one being* dwell in two places at the same time, in heaven and on earth?

*A.* Can we not direct our whole energies to the study of algebra, and not leave the body?

*Q.* But then algebra does not become a part or parcel of our organism?

*A.* In one sense, if we master the science, it does; we become algebraists.

So in the sense of the humanity of Jesus, when connected with omnipotence, it became his glorious robe, "glorious in his apparel," and as such will be the outward exhibition of his eternal attributes forever.

These conclusions also apply to the *omnipresence* of Christ. Where the world of matter exists in its life-giving relations to man the Spirit of God exists also, because it bounds, cements, and harmonizes them in all their wonderful relations, and certainly, where moral beings exist, these attributes must exist—hence the "eyes of the Lord" are over all his works, and superintend not only this *microcosm*, but worlds on worlds, and space universal.

*Q.* But is not the Spirit of God, or the Holy Spirit, sometimes called a person? "When HE is come HE will lead you into all truth." How, then, can HE be the seven attributes of God?

*A.* If the mind or attributes of man did not become his moral representative, or was not the man, we could get no direct understanding of the connection. Now if we give another instruction in any given science, we do so only by our knowledge of that science. We say, then, the teacher, when he is come, will instruct you in that science; the teacher is the embodiment of knowledge, the representative of a well-balanced mind.

This, then, represents the attributes of God. He is, it is, or they are the great teacher to *our* attributes, hence we may call them a personality if we choose, but they are no more a spiritual organization, when taken separately, than is the human sense. Who can give a form, a shape, to *sight*, to hearing, to smelling, or feeling? No one. Nor can any give shape or form to Light, Life, Mercy, or Love.

These are moral powers necessary to existences, but not persons in a physical or psychological sense.

*Q.* The Holy Spirit, then, is not a person?

*A.* No more so than the senses. We may say the spirit of Light, the spirit of Life, the spirit of Truth, and of all the seven attributes of God in their separate functions; or we may embrace them all in a general term, and call them the Spirit of God, or the Holy Spirit, and when we have thus associated them, they are no more a person than when separated. We may say the sense of sight, the sense of hearing, the sense of language, or we may unite them all in one, and call them *the sense*, and when done, we have given no idea of shape or form.

From this peculiarity of one of the three that bear record in heaven, many of the creeds read on this wise: "There is one God, everlasting, without body or parts;" but this idea loses all force when we quote the language of the Apostle: "In him (Christ) dwelleth all the fullness of the God-head bodily." If *bodily*, there must be a body of Deity, then God must have a body. But the Holy Spirit, not having a bodily form, but associated with bodily forms only, necessitated the expression before adverted to, viz.: "Without body or parts." Every orthodox Christian believes that Christ had a body before his incarnation as well as since.

This Spirit dwelt infinitely and eternally in the archetypal Saviour; and when he robed himself in humanity, they were no less the spirit or mind of Christ than before or after he suffered.

Hence, before him all intelligences must bow, and at his throne of Grace all suppliant sinners find a glorious welcome.

*Q.* Did not the Holy Spirit assume the form of a "dove" as it descended upon the great Redeemer at Jordan?

*A.* It certainly did assume that miraculous form, and it also assumed the form of "cloven tongues" on the day of Pentecost, but we do not understand from this that its real form existed, only in assumed appearance.

The fact is that the spirits of God, collectively, are the attributes of God, and are the gracious exhibit of his harmonious nature and his love. Hence we say:

> "Come, Holy Spirit, heavenly dove,
> With all thy quick'ning powers,

and, while thus praying, address the Father, the Son, and the Holy Spirit, simultaneously.

*Q.* What do we understand by God's sending "his (Seven) Spirits into the world to reprove the world," if they are only moral powers?

*A.* As we would understand, if God should remove the clouds so that the sun could shine upon us. God sent his only-begotten Son into the world to destroy the works of the devil, so that the rays of light from his throne might unfold his character as the "chief among ten thousand, and the one altogether lovely."

Thus light dissipates the darkness; life brings

immortality to view; holiness brings the sinless and spotless character of God to view; justice shows the inflexible principles of God's equity; truth reveals God's eternal purposes; mercy, his compassion and tenderness; and love, his incomprehensible desire for the eternal welfare of all sentient creatures. So the Spirit of God is sent forth to every avenue of the soul and to every power of the understanding, beseeching, persuading, reproving.

*Q.* How could our Saviour be born of the fallen and sinful Mary, and be holy, pure, undefiled?

*A.* The humanity of man, that is, our flesh, bones, and blood, are neither sinful or holy, *per se.* It is the senses that prompt us to transgression. For instance, here is a dead human body; that body is now neither guilty nor innocent, as it has no knowledge or power; in short, its senses are dead. Now, if the senses are pure, then the body is pure, and if the senses are fallen, depraved, then the body, being led by the senses, becomes sinful, and so remains as long as actuated by the fallen senses.

Our Saviour took upon him the senses of Adam in his primeval state, and in this respect only, became the second Adam. These senses were not in their traduction sinful, though the human supply to their development came from a sinful parent, no more than our songs of devotion are sinful, because coming from the lips of a believer who in this life is unholy. We might pursue this thought still farther, and remark that the relation of the holy child Jesus to Mary, did no more involve him in sin or her in a suspension of original sin, than does the growth of the hair on our heads, or the progressive development of our stature, involve sin or innocence.

Do we suppose that the babe, that only weighs ten pounds, is innocent, and that five pounds of additional flesh will make it sinful? Nay, verily; the immaculate conception of Jesus had no more to do with Mary, in reference to her original sin, than does the five added pounds of flesh to the babe, after its birth, add purity or sin to the mother. "That, that is born of the flesh is flesh, and that that is born of the Spirit is spirit." The flesh is only sinful originally by taking the fallen senses from the fallen pair by traduction; but Jesus did not thus inherit his senses, hence there need be no change in the original nature of the Virgin Mary, in order that she bear the holy child Jesus.

*Q.* It is not, then, necessary to the Holy Jesus that his mother should be holy?

*A.* Not at all, since his flesh was taken upon him through his divine nature. "The Word was made flesh," robed in flesh, veiled in flesh, not in the traduction of fallen man, but in the exalted character of Melchisedek.

*Q.* How, then, could he suffer?

*A.* He did not suffer for his own transgression,

but he placed his senses on the altar of sacrifice, an innocent, perfect offering of Divine origin, of an infinitely creative traduction; and this sinless offering, prompted by the unbounded and incomprehensible love of God, "became the end of the law for righteousness to every one that believeth."

If the human senses had been part of his Divine nature he could not have laid them down in the silence of death, and have taken the body they occupied in his resurrection; but his body, like the hand that writes this page, could be taken from the senses and be restored to its former connection again, in an undying relation; so the adorable Saviour took upon him flesh with the primeval senses, laid it down in death for us, and then awakened it and changed it to a robe of glory.

*Q.* The Virgin Mary, then, needed a Saviour as much as any other person, and was as much a subject of death as was Elizabeth?

*A.* Most assuredly. She undoubtedly believed in the great Redeemer as did Abraham, Isaac, or Jacob, and was saved through faith in his name; but the gift of a Saviour to the world, through her, did not become so much of a moral action as did the labors of Elijah, who was translated, or Moses, whose face shone so resplendent that he veiled himself before all Israel.

From all that we can learn, Mary retired to the common walks of life, not even assuming to hold any supremacy or notoriety on account of her relation to the Lord Jesus Christ.

*Q.* Why is it that so vast a host, at the present time, worship her, pray to her, and think they feel the power of her intercession?

*A.* The imagination, the marvelous chimera of the human mind, leads men to believe in things as false to science as they are false to religion. The Mohammedan believes in the ever-living Mahomet—the idolater, in the consciousness of his idol.

The children of Israel believed in the power of their golden calf, and need we wonder if idolatry should change the image from the animal to the human? "It is written, thou shalt worship the Lord thy God, and him *only* shalt thou serve." Then, if we worship any thing else than God in his triplicity, we become idolaters.

*Q.* Could not the "spirits of just men made perfect" become intercessors for us before the throne of God?

*A.* We should remember that all the human relationships that exist between us here grow out of associations and traduction. Both these cease when the senses die, and, though we may remember in glory loved ones on earth, yet knowing that the Seven Spirits of God are infinitely better intercessors than we could be, and that they, through and with the visible church, will do all that can be done, we shall necessarily sink into the divine purpose of grace.

If the same solicitude could characterize the saints there as here, heaven would not be the abode of tranquillity, but of anxiety. "If they believe not Moses and the prophets, neither would they believe though one arose from the dead."

*Q.* But did not the rich man, lifting up his eyes to Abraham, plead for a miraculous interposition in behalf of his five brethren, saying, that "if one shall rise from the dead, they will believe?"

*A.* Most truly; but did Abraham, who was a worshiper of God, and knew all the powers at work for their salvation, volunteer to act in the matter?

It is quite probable that some traces of hope linger in the memory of even the lost. Our Saviour asserts that some will knock at the door, saying, "Lord, Lord, open unto us;" and that others will say, "We have cast out devils in thy name, and in thy name have done many wonderful works;" but this even is like a spider's web.

The rich man felt the horrors of his condition, and did not wish to see his five brethren, who had, perhaps, doubted there being such a place of torment, come there; and, to make Abraham believe him to be sincerely repentant, asked this favor. But for a child of God, who knows God's love to be infinitely more active than his, and in whom all earthly ties are dissolved in death and lie unconscious in the silent slumbers of the grave, to ask infinite love to do more than it is doing, would be the height of folly.

*Q.* Then, if infinite love is now doing all that can be done for sinners, why should prayers be offered up here more than in heaven?

*A.* Our prayers here open up our minds to know the intercession of the Spirit, and through the sense of language effect the judgment sense of others; and this is the Holy Spirit's method of showing its intercession. So we pray "with the spirit and with the understanding also." All the intercession we enjoy and cherish here, is through the Spirit; and, when released from this probation, we shall, in our spiritual association, be swallowed up, so to speak, in the love of God. Hence, praying, pleading, and suffering for others will be forever banished from our minds.

*Q.* Could the Virgin Mary hear us, or could the apostles and martyrs hear us, if we should call upon them?

*A.* Not unless by divine interposition; for God knows every method that can be made available to mortals, and is prompted by the perfect fullness of his love to put all such instrumentalities into requisition. "What could have been done more to my vineyard, that I have not done in it?"—Isa. v: 4.

## CHAPTER XIX.

One Mediator—Judgment Sense and Love Attribute—Satan's Work Destroyed—Spirits Released from Prison—The Lord's Supper—Review—What is the Conscience.

THE hopes of those who die in their sins, of ever obtaining pardon, are only through their knowledge of the plan of redemption made known to them while in the flesh, and thus inscribed upon their spiritual memory; but the Christian "reads his title clear" in the Book of Life, and only remembers the human form in the promises of an increased ecstasy at the resurrection of the just.

The human, at the resurrection, will be the robe of shame and eternal disgrace, or the robe of glory and of light, just as these relations have triumphed here; if, *from* the depraved senses, and *by* the depraved senses, the attributes have been dragged down to things earthly,

(271)

"sensual, or devilish," then, when again clothed, the garment will be spotted, polluted, disgraced; but, on the contrary, if the attributes have elevated the senses to prayer and to praise, to humbly kneel and devoutly implore the pardon of sin, and the righteous robe of Jesus, so will it be in the resurrection; the natural body will clothe up the spiritual body in the emblematic habiliments of "pure linen, white and clean, which is the righteousness of the saints."

It may here be proper to again remark that the "Church of the first-born" may have been the vast host of the sons and daughters of God, the sinless children of Adam and Eve before the fall, translated. The name given would suggest that idea; and, as the posterity became innumerable during the first four thousand years, the translation of these faultless ones may have occurred at any period of time in perfect harmony with the plan of redemption. Many of them sinned by marrying the fallen of Adam's second posterity, and the one hundred and forty-four thousand were saved as salt upon the earth till near the flood; but of the hosts and myriads of this first-born church no mind can conceive, a congregation that no man could number, and heaven, undoubtedly, was filled with these to occupy the places left vacant by the revolting angels; and may be that the "man-child," Michael, who was caught up to God and his throne, was accompanied by the translated millions of the church of the first-born, and Christ alone was their Mediator as he is ours.

*Q.* Then we can have but one available Mediator?

*A.* Certainly not, for no angel could die for man, and no fallen man could offer a ransom even for his own soul. Jesus alone became the offering for sin, and most amply does that offering sustain the honor of God's law, and also declares the incomprehensible love of God to man.

Here, in his wonderful person, is all of man, for the human body, united to the sinless senses, alone reveals his creature character, while from his spiritual organism—the archetype; he applies to man this cleansing fountain, which was opened for sin and uncleanness by the power of the Holy Spirit. Love (God's love) touches the attribute of love in the mind of the believer, making him a new creature in Christ Jesus.

*Q.* How could the Holy Spirit, which is one of the three that bear record in heaven, dwell in the brain or heart of a creature of human extraction?

*A.* Just as the light is reflected by shining upon the mirror, so the character of God is reflected in the life, labors, shame, and glory of Jesus, and this light, by the Spirit, is again reflected in the heart of the believer.

Earth is said to be God's footstool; then he is as much on this earth as we would be on a footstool if our feet were resting upon it. Where our feet rests, there are we. Now, it is quite evident, that four of the senses terminate in the brain, while there are channels of sensation from every part of the body to the cerebrum.

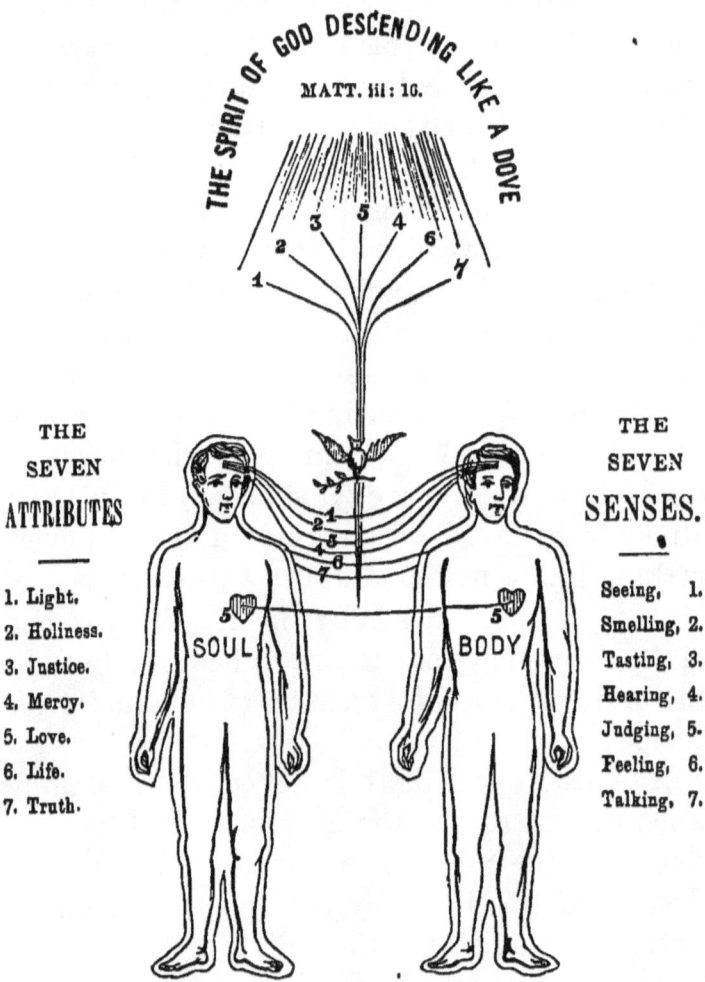

"I will praise thee; for I am fearfully and wonderfully made; marvelous are thy works; and that my soul knoweth right well." —Ps. cxxxix: 14.

Now let us suppose that seeing, tasting, hearing, and smelling are from the outer channels, conveyed direct to the brain, and that talking and feeling are as universal as the outer form of the body, and from every part connect with the brain, and that the judgment sense finds its nerve center in the human heart, which also is in harmony with the brain. Then, if the judgment sense centers in the heart of the body, and the love attribute centers in the heart of the soul, then the effect of God's love upon our attribute of love would materially effect the judgment sense, and, in truth, we might say, "Whereas I was once blind, now I see," or, "Come unto me, all ye that fear God; and I will declare what he hath done for my soul."

The love of God, or, to be more explicit, the attribute, Love, from God, harmonizes the entire affinities of our attributes, and as they form the higher power of our entire organism, it is not difficult to see that submission of the senses to the attributes would be self-evident. Therefore the indwelling of the Spirit would be as natural to the attributes as is manhood to the human organism. Hence he dwells in our hearts by the Spirit.

And still farther, many of the allusions of Scripture find their elements of development in the heart. "With the heart man believeth unto righteousness," that is, the attribute of love, from the soul, connects with the judgment sense in the heart, and when that attribute is illuminated by the love attribute of God, then our will is conquered, and, as a result, we talk of the love of God, sing of the love of God, and bow in the most humble manner before him All our senses conquered, but not regenerated, for there can be no regeneration of the senses any more than there could be of the muscles, blood, or bones. They are of earth, and totally depraved.

Then, again, we read, "From the heart proceeds evil thoughts." This, also, is true, for the judgment sense is totally depraved, and were it not for its connection with the attribute of its spiritual nature, would be more debased than the brute, because the organism has two more senses than they; but as this can not be, and man be man, we can see how sin can gain an ascendency over the will or judgment sense, and, as the attributes are disorganized in their moral relation, the depraved senses can carry even these in their rebellion against God.

*Q.* But why do some accept of salvation, if all have alike depraved senses?

*A.* The power to accept of salvation is freely given to all, but this power does not destroy human responsibility, and while we can all cheerfully say:

> "Jesus sought me when a stranger,
> Wandering from the fold of God,"

we can by no means attribute this to have been

an extraneous power that, in a mechanical way, rendered inoperative the power of choice. It is a fact that we choose Jesus when he chooses us, that is, when we ask he gives, and the *only* reason given is, "That ye *will not* come unto me that ye might have life," to all those who neglect this great salvation.

Then we must readily see that the connection of the muscles and nerves to the senses, give them the control; and that the connection of the senses to the attributes, give them the control over the senses; and when the Holy Spirit is asked for, the power to become the child of God is given.

The plan of redemption is an *eternal now*, with God, and we can not introduce the transient moments of time to, in any manner paralyze his purposes or to render ourselves irresponsible. The prize of life eternal is freely offered, and he who accepts, will find an abundant entrance into the mysteries of redeeming grace.

*Q*. What did the death of Christ accomplish?

*A*. It destroyed the works of the devil by driving him from the control of the human senses to the darkness and discord of our atmosphere; and, *secondly*, it liberated the spirits in prison, who, in the days of Noah, through the six hundred years of his life, had been in the bondage of the flesh, being Adam's prefallen race, then in disobedience and sin; yet had repented and believed in the Messiah promised to

Adam and his posterity. These, to whom no promise had been made or could be made, died in faith, not yet receiving the promise; but now they are released, their prison doors opened, and the captives set free, and with Him ascend into glory.

*Q.* What does the resurrection of Jesus teach?

*A.* It teaches us that he took upon himself humanity, that this humanity consisted in man's primeval senses, in their holy relation to the human body; that these senses and this body he could deliver up to the same power, *i. e.*, the power of death, as all the race of fallen man have inherited; and that, though dead, he could restore this body to life, and immaterialize and deify it, and in so doing become the grand human archetype of all his people; and that the home of such bodies would be the palace mansions of glory. That "when he ascended up on high he led captivity captive, and gave gifts unto men."

*Q.* Why was it that the Saviour, at the resurrection, told the weeping Mary to "Touch me not, for I am not yet ascended to my Father?"

*A.* This expression was the best manner in which to dispose of a matter which otherwise must have terrified her, for his body was now as immaterial as his spirit, and she could not have touched him if she had been allowed the opportunity

*Q.* But did not the disciples touch him after his resurrection?

*A.* We have no such record. When they knew him at the inn, as they journeyed to Emmaus, he vanished out of their sight. It is true he told Thomas to thrust his hand into his side, and the disciples to "handle him and see, for a spirit hath not flesh and bones, as ye see me have;" but this, to their affrighted natures, was only to capacitate himself to their necessities and relieve their fears. They could no more have touched him then than we can now, for he was then transcendently immaterial.

*Q.* Then how could they see him?

*A.* Just as we see a person or ourselves in a mirror. He mirrored himself to them in the glass of humanity, and they beheld him, but he could have been in their midst just as well and not have been seen by them at all.

He that could unite and harmonize spirit and matter could as easily transform that matter into a spiritual body as to, at first, fashion it.

*Q.* But does not that immateriality of the human body of Jesus inhere in, and render the bread and wine of the Lord's Supper his real presence personified?

*A.* Not in the least degree. Our Saviour explains it thus: "This do in remembrance of me." "As often as ye eat this bread, and drink this cup, ye do *show the Lord's death*, till he come."

Now, a remembrance of a person, and eating

a person, are quite distinct: to show a death by a symbol is very different from partaking of one's flesh and blood.

There are solemnities connected with this ordinance that make it one of the most soul-thrilling institutions of the Gospel; but there is nothing of a miraculous nature to a memento.

He says, "This is my body," "This is my blood;" but while he says this, is not his unbroken body before them, and does not his human blood course through his whole system as before? Did he take any of his blood and mingle it in that cup? Surely not, for he was not then even arraigned before the Sanhedrim for trial. He spoke of a remembrance of the human blood he was to shed upon the cross, and desired that the disciples should, by the use of bread and wine, continue to call this great sacrifice to remembrance. When I am gone, remember me, and I will bless this cup, and this bread, and to you it shall be for a sign of my death and of my second coming.

There may be, however, this analogy: The bread, which had no real flesh appearance, nourished the organism, and thereby became part of the organism; so his flesh should be transformed into the glorious, and thereby apply its transforming power to us; but, as this did not reach the connection between the senses and attributes, the emblem, to become complete, must embrace the wine, which, in its exciting and ethereal character, must reach the point, so to speak, of inosculation, bringing the powers of the spiritual organism to feel the great sacrifice in its connection with humanity. There may be an analogy of color between the wine and the blood, but this is not as essential as the senses receiving the emblem in their connection with the attributes. Hence, by the Lord's Supper, we derive those blessings that flow through the Divine attributes to the immortal soul. That is, the attributes of God witness with ours, that by faith we broke that bread, and by faith poured out that wine, as a remembrance of the dying Jesus, and so we partook, "discerning the Lord's body."

The ordinance of baptism beautifully shows the washing away of sin, but does not in itself wash the sin away; so we may say of the Lord's Supper, it shows the breaking of the body of Jesus, but does not in itself break that body—it shows the shedding of the blood, but does not shed the blood it represents. Hence, the idea of *transubstantiation* is as false to the character of the ordinance as it is false to science. Either our mouths must transform the morsel of bread after it is masticated, or a miracle must have preceded its reception, which would render it flesh and not bread. Then, our Saviour would himself have been inconsistent in taking bread and blessing it (the bread), and giving it to his disciples, saying, "Take, eat; this is my body."—Matt. xxvi: 26.

To be consistent with Romish ideas it should read: He took bread and transformed it into the real presence of himself, and gave it to them. And this would be no greater wonder than the priests profess to accomplish at every mass.

*Q.* But how can any person believe that one can do such a thing as to change bread into the body of Christ?

*A.* In the same manner and by the same rule as the children of Israel said to their golden calves, "These are the gods that brought us up out of the land of Egypt."

The senses are totally depraved, and when the judgment sense is educated to believe in marvelous things, spooks, hobgoblins, and witches, it will hold to these hallucinations with as great tenacity as to life itself—science, religion, and intelligence to the contrary notwithstanding. Hence, a little *holy water* touched to the forehead in presence of a picture of the Virgin Mary has a hallowed influence, and to kneel at a statue representing her would cover the deluded soul with glory.

We will now review the points already discussed in Part II.

We have by fair reasoning, we think, clearly shown that only three dispensations have as yet existed; and that the entire character of law relating to our senses has changed with the change of the dispensations. For instance, the dispensation of *purity* had a code of laws by which it was regulated. That, then, marriage was the union of attributes—infallible attributes—and that there could be no disagreement between husband and wife thus united, more than there could be between the right hand and the left; and this produced the idea that marriages are made in heaven.

Hence, the Apostle declares that "Adam was not deceived, but the woman being deceived was in the transgression."—1 Tim. ii: 14. Then, the relation of marriage made *their* action inseparable, and *his* action a necessity, though voluntary; and so, we think, God looked upon it, and immediately made corresponding provisions.

We have also shown that this dispensation must have lasted *four thousand years* to have been in harmony with divine procedure. That the seven attributes of God, after having fashioned the earth and its surroundings for man, and endowed him with power to govern it, had no other active labor to perform, for they had bound together by the laws of nature, backed up by their own incomprehensible activity, all the forces they had arranged for man, and hence had no further labor to perform in that direction. Thus they rested.

This rest did not consist in a change from creative work to some other work, as many assert, but from labor to refreshment—from toil to rest.

Thus, our minds may be very active in some

important study, and when the problem is solved the mind rests; so the attributes of God were for "six days"—six thousand years—arranging this hitherto chaotic earth for man; and when he was created, and all the machinery of this earth's concatenaceous chain of substances, both animate and inanimate, moved harmoniously on, they rested. "And God rested on the seventh day, and hallowed it." So the attributes of God rested on the seventh day.

Here, grouped together, are the three dispensations in one chain of events; and as in creation, so in redemption, each day or cycle of time is comparatively alike, making in all twelve thousand years of time from the creation or formation of Adam to the close of the present dispensation. Thus, if it should be yet two thousand years before the second coming of our Saviour, we have a period of ten thousand years for geologists to fathom before they reach the period before Adam was, and of fifteen thousand years, and more, since the earth's geological formations existed.

We also see how easy it is for persons reading the Bible to become confused on the first and second chapters of Genesis: supposing a "garden," an inclosure, to have been constructed, in which to place a being made and fashioned to govern a world. How very strange! a being who had dominion over the beasts of the whole earth, and the fishes and leviathans of the entire element of the waters, and of all the fowls that fly in the midst of heaven—to shut him up in a garden to dress it!

Absurd as such an idea would appear, we somehow have slid into it, and, because others have so interpreted it, we adopt it; when on a careful reading of the Scriptures we find for at least a certain period of Adam's existence no garden, no tree of good and evil; and that, during this period, he was to eat of every tree, without reserve. How long did this dispensation last? We have shown it to have been equal to the second dispensation, four thousand years.

We have clearly shown that Moses ends this dispensation at the third verse of the second chapter of Genesis, after which he traces the generations springing from the fallen Adam.

Our attention is then called to another race of intelligences, and not another, but the unfallen race, who had subdued the earth, and the relics of whose skill and industry have called forth the admiration and wonder of the world.

Of this branch of the human family Cain was afraid, and against any possible danger from that source God gave him a protective mark. This unfallen race were flesh and blood as much as was Adam, for they were his children; and in view of this fact he called his wife's name Eve, for she had borne until this time no other name but "woman." That with them they talked, for after Adam sinned he no longer remained in the garden, but was driven from it because the possibility of another transgression would have rendered his condition irretrievable.

That it can not be reconciled with the adopted theory that Cain could have found a wife in the land of Nod, after he had declared before God that "he had been driven out from the face of the earth," and that even in this land of banishment people lived who were under moral law, and they might slay him.—Gen. iv: 14–17.

And, again, that he builded a city as soon as his first son, Enoch, was born.

What a city this must have been, for only one man, his wife, and a babe, to build! But it was not so, a host of the unfallen lived there, and with them he married, and with them he builded a city, and there closed his brief Biblical history.

We have, then, only this reason to give in reference to the planting of the garden of Eden. For four thousand years Adam and Eve had lived in the harmonies of this new world, and, unless the plan of redemption should be laid, none of their posterity could ever die or be translated; then the earth eventually must cease to produce sufficient food for their necessities, for, place the ratio of their increase as we will, there must be a time, a period, when this earth would be positively too small for their support; and, again, four thousand years of respiration and of ceaseless activity of the functions of animal life, however gently we may suppose the elements to have dealt with them, must have worn the organism, and a retirement to a garden planted by the hand of wisdom, in which were delicacies and luxuries, not elsewhere found, would seem consistent, nay, necessary; and to dress this garden, their only work, and to enjoy all its delicious fruits, except one tree, a rich inheritance.

Thus the "Lord planted a garden eastward in Eden, and there he put the man he had formed."

Then we have a garden planted eastward of some place (say Egypt), and there the man becomes a transgressor, and there, or just outside of the garden, Cain and Abel are born, and Cain, becoming a fratricide, is driven still farther east, to the land of Nod, and there he marries a wife and builds a city.

Here we have the brief history. Now, to reconcile this with the necessity of the events, will lead us into the perplexity of a myth, or a miracle, or else we must take the broad view we have laid down as the Bible history.

We have also shown that from the laws of traduction their marriage, that is, the marriage of the sons of God with the fallen daughters of men, must be sinful.

We read "that by the transgression of one *many* became sinners;" not *all*, for ·all did not fall on account of Adam's sin, since the thousands of thousands that inhabited the earth at the time of his sin, did not sin, and, though death reigned from Adam to Moses, it did not all accrue from Adam's transgression, but the sons of God sinned by marriage and became subject to death.

We now come to the evidences of a race that have undertaken to do what nothing but superhuman beings could do, and called the attention of our readers to the *Giant's Causeway*.

We may arrive at conclusions by observing the apparent design of objects. To illustrate: if we see a vast pile of brick and dressed stone near to the foundation for a magnificent structure, we may very justly conclude that these brick and stone are evidences of the intention to erect such a mansion. Or, if we are crossing a railway track and see a passenger coach in the ditch, torn and broken, we may justly believe it to have been thrown from the track while a train was in motion.

Now, at the Giant's Causeway, we see the evidences of a gigantic undertaking no less wonderful than to bridge the North Channel to the Scotland shore, a distance of say sixty miles, and from all appearances the design was to entirely dam up this tide-rushing channel against all coming time.

To effect this object, we see the three descending pavements denominated the Giant's Causeway, each of dressed stone, the whole structure, between three and four hundred feet wide, anticipating, by the substantial manner in which the mole is arranged, to reach the opposite shore.

This would have required a vast supply of dressed rock, even to have carried this wide street across the channel, and when by the appearance it is evident that the design was to raise it several hundred feet above the waters, more rock would, of course, be needed. These rock are here; enough by every evidence we can gain to have dammed up the entire North Channel, three hundred and fifty feet wide, and three hundred feet high, and sixty miles in length. Is it, then, a wild chimera of a diseased imagination to suppose that these dressed rock were all designed for that purpose, and that, by some national calamity, the work was suspended? In fact, do we not see an evidence in this of the terrible deluge that swept away every remembrance of the nation who had thus planned and prepared to execute?

We have also noticed other works of art along the Irish coast that are equally wonderful and suggestive of human skill and mathematical precision.

The Giant's Amphitheater is among the wonders of the world, both as it relates to the object for which this vast arch was made and the means of its accomplishment.

We readily learn this one fact, that there has been a race, or races, that were more harmonious in achievements of this character than at the present time; that those operatives made astonishing preparations to carry out their designs, and were interrupted simultaneously in the grand object contemplated.

The reader's attention is then directed to the vast pile of dressed rock called the Pyramids of Egypt.

No greater wonder exists than the object for which these three four-square pyramids were erected. The fact of their having but little space within, so massive, so substantial, so grand, so high that it must have required great fortitude, great unity, and length of time to have dressed these immense piles of rock, great care in their measurement and number, and great mechanical force to have executed this design, is worthy of notice. A mountain of dressed rock, so vast; Cheops covering thirteen English acres and nearly five hundred feet in height.

Some have deciphered an inscription upon it, that it required one hundred thousand men twenty years to have erected it; but whether this inscription dates back to the time it was erected, or inscribed from some tradition of a later period, who can tell?

The best geological evidence places it as far back as one thousand years before the flood, and may have been erected, for aught we know, by Adam's prefallen race, for the burial-place of Abel; and it is our surmise that the highest pyramid once contained the earthly remains of

Adam, the second Eve, and the third Abel, but this was not the order in which they were erected.

It would be very strange reckoning to suppose that two persons, landing on Plymouth Rock, four hundred years ago, with sickness and death their inheritance, without the benefit of immigration, and after one hundred and fifty years had but two sons, to have so rapidly increased for the next two hundred and fifty years, as to have gathered an army of one hundred thousand mechanics and stone-cutters, for twenty years, in the erection of a pyramid equal to the Cheops. Would it not?

And then this is but a fragment of the history of the wonders of the Nile.

There is the Temple El Kanark and the great Hypostyle Hall, and El Uksur, and the Obelisks, Sphinxes, gigantic pillars, and massive walls, all left by the race that built them as a wonder of the courage, fortitude, and union of effort necessary to their erection.

Then, again, there are the ruins of Balbec, Heliopolis, and other magnificent ruins of destroyed cities and temples, a chapter too vast for our limited work.

Then, again, the walls of ancient cities are not confined to Egypt, but are found in the western continent, in Central America, and in other portions of the globe. All these go to show the extent of population before the flood, both in the east and west, north and south. Relics of monster men and monster animals almost startle the world in every clime and nationality.

We next come to the caves of Kentucky, and find curiosities there that too plainly tell of mechanical skill to be altogether discredited; and this, too, on a scale so far transcending any thing of the kind that could now be accomplished, that we had rather call them *natural curiosities* than to attempt any solution of the problem. See Dr. Bailey's sketch of the caves of Kentucky.

To be sufficiently credulous to believe that water, dripping from the roof, could flute a dome three hundred feet high, as well as to make it; to believe that it could fashion a magnolia flower, a cluster of grapes, or produce stalactites on the sides of the walls, or a female figure, or a Gothic arch, and a thousand other curiosities, would be no great honor to a sane man. The human race that has accomplished such wonders are extinct, and the purposes for which they were excavated will remain undoubtedly a profound mystery; still, if for four thousand years there existed a sinless race whose business it was to subdue the earth, they might have needed what to us would be useless and unmeaning.

We have also alluded to Fingal's Cave as unequaled in view of its musical charms, and shows, beside the columns that support its arch, that the design was not to have a deep cavern into the land from the sea only, but to have a perpetual organ that needed no repairs.

After showing the labor of intelligences hinted at in the Holy Scriptures, we necessarily come to the plan of redemption, which introduced the *second dispensation*, showing that the Seven Spirits of God, after their creative work, after they had rested through the first dispensation, now became intercessors for the restoration of our attributes to God and to glory.

That the peculiarities of this dispensation consisted in types of a solemn and impressive character, and in the blending of the law and the prophets together, that the way might be opened to the celestial glory. In tracing the genealogy of man through the chronological periods, we find their sins to have become so heinous in the sight of God that he determined to destroy the entire race in a flood of waters, and, to obtain a clear idea of their sin, we have applied to them the book of Revelation.

This brings out the wonder in heaven, a woman clothed with the sun, the war in heaven, the old red dragon, and all the chain of moral and demoniac evils from the fall of man to the time when the Holy City became desecrated and trodden under foot. This leads us to locate the city of Babylon. It may appear strange that any one should attempt to locate BABYLON THE GREAT, but we have two witnesses that never clash—geology and the Bible. Both these locate the great city in Egypt.

The pouring out of the vials, and all that relates to that doomed city, is not exaggerated in view of this race who inhabited the earth before the deluge, and of whom it is said that the imaginations of their heart was only evil continually.

The closing drama of this sinful race transpired with the destruction of Babylon, and the flood, for the waters had been separated by the attributes of God from the atmosphere, and so held till now, when the fountains of the great deep were broken up and chaos almost reigned supreme, the covenant only being with Noah.

We then learn of Satan's being bound till the giving of the law in Horeb, which law was a sword of defense against him to all who wielded it, and that with it our Saviour vanquished him when tempted forty days in the wilderness.

We learn, also, that the saints in glory can not be intercessors, unless by a special order from God, who has undertaken the restoration of man upon the broadest possible plenitude of mercy. We have, then, shown most conclusively, we think, that the attributes have no more form or shape than the senses, and when they are taken collectively they are called the Holy Spirit, and are also designated as the "Seven Spirits of God."—Rev. iv: 5.

We have also shown the outflowing streams

from each of these attributes, and their combination to be wisdom.

We have shown that *conscience* is the coalescence or sensitive point of inosculation between the love attribute and judgment sense, and that the judgment sense becomes irritated on account of the moral status of the attribute, which produces a sadness in this sense, which we call *conscience;* that even this gift of God may be so wantonly disregarded that the attributes will almost cease to warn the senses.

A good conscience, then, is the pleasure of the attributes flowing out through the subdued senses, and results from our self-denial, or "bearing the cross."

Hence, conscience may be either bad or good, according to the power of the attributes over the depravity of the senses; and the existence of a something we call conscience, is positive evidence of the connection of the attributes and senses. Thus we have determined the status of moral action and the reason why we are morally responsible to God.

We now invite our readers to investigate our concluding deductions from the laws of science, which we believe corroborates the facts already shown in reference to the identity of the Mystic Numbers of the Word to the mystic properties of matter.

# PART III—THE SCIENCES.

## CHAPTER XX.

THE SEVEN PRIMITIVE ELEMENTS—THE SEVEN CHEMICAL PROPERTIES OF ELECTRICITY—COHESION—THE SEVEN FORMATIONS IN CRYSTALLIZATION—SEVEN CHEMICAL METALS VOLATILE—LIGHT AN ELEMENT—ITS SEVEN NUMERICAL PROPERTIES—THE SEVEN DIVISIONS OF WATER—THE SEVEN ANCIENT METALS—UNION OF HYDROGEN AND OXYGEN IN WATER—THE SEVEN PARTS OF HYDROGEN—THE ELEMENTS WITHOUT THE ATTRIBUTES OF GOD—THE SEVEN LIBERAL ARTS AND SCIENCES—INCOHERENCE OF MATTER.

QUESTION. How many *primitive elements* do we find in the earth and its concomitants?

*Ans.* But seven.

*Q.* What are they?

*A.* We are fully aware of the sixty and more elements recorded in chemistry, but we most sincerely believe, like the primitive attributes, that we shall find but seven; but this may be a more elaborate task to clearly estab-

(297)

lish from the fact that all are blended in such a manner as to make it very difficult to find the grand central point from which they operate.

Some of them, four, viz.: Earth, Air, Fire, and Water, have been so long and familiarly recognized that we need not even question the fact of their being primitive elements.

The fifth element that we shall notice is *Electricity*.

This element seems to be in the air and in the earth, in the human body as well as in minerals, and from it springs many important properties which we shall notice. The first is *Gravity*, for electricity will draw certain substances to the earth, or from the earth, just in proportion to its volume.

The center of the earth, then, may be the great *electric battery* of this microcosm, and we favor this idea from the fact that the earth is farther through at its equator than at its poles; hence the attractive or electric power would more immediately affect the earth's outer surface at the poles than at the equator, therefore the needle would necessarily point to the north pole, for there its altitude being highest the attraction would be greatest.

If this should prove sound logic, the gravity to the earth's center is but another name for this sub-element, for it proceeds directly from electricity, and electricity overbalances gravity, or we could not telegraph by it; so may not electricity be the generic root of gravity, magnetism, and caloric?

Another proof is in the fact of the Aurora Borealis, or northern light. If, then, our hypothesis should be correct, the electricity of volcanic heat would find a nearer outlet at the north pole than at the equator, and this would cause a greater volume of electricity to gather in the polar atmosphere than elsewhere, and this would not only attract the needle to the pole, but would produce the Aurora Borealis. In support of this idea we have the names of Bailly, Franklin, Biot, Halle, and others.

Then, making electricity the elemental root, we have these seven combinations, viz.: *Gravity, Caloric, Combustion, Percussion, Friction, Animal Warmth,* and *Magnetism.* By this we find the mystical seven as much in electricity as it is in the atmosphere, which is so evidently shown in the seven tones of music.

We are aware that the idea of caloric being an exhibit of electricity, will astonish those who have so elaborately tried to prove the reverse, *i. e.,* that electricity proceeds from caloric and becomes one of its properties; but, notwithstanding all this, the fact of the existence of caloric is much less evident as a separate property than in connection with electricity; and should there be in some of the chemical affinities of substances a phenomena that would be difficult to resolve into this root, we must confess that there are also greater objections to its being rendered a primitive element.

We think, then, that electricity may be justly considered the central power from which all these proceed.

The sixth primitive element we shall notice is *Cohesion*.

*Cohesion* is that force or power that unites particles of matter, and exists in all substances, in the aëriform and in liquids. It has less strength in liquids than in solids, and in crystallization divides its substances into seven primitive formations.

We say of the whole earth that it is kept in its present shape by the force of cohesion. So with each particle of matter or metal. For instance, a bar of gold sufficiently large to suspend a weight equal to one hundred and fifty thousand pounds, would suspend, if the same sized bar was of silver, one hundred and ninety thousand pounds weight; if of platina, two hundred and sixty-two thousand; if of copper, three hundred and four thousand; if of soft iron, three hundred and sixty-two thousand; and of hard iron, five hundred and fifty-nine thousand pounds weight, and in this we see the power of cohesion.

Small particles of matter pass through the atmosphere as if there existed no power of cohesion; and so will a balloon pass with the atmosphere at a very rapid speed, and the balloonist feel no motion of the air, apparently unaffected by the force of cohesion; but it should be remembered that the whole volume of the atmosphere is bound to this planet by the laws of cohesion, and that the apparent non-existence of this force is largely dependent upon the existence of other unseen elements. *Caloric*, a property of electricity, when communicated to solid bodies, separates its particles to increased distances, as is evident from the enlargement of such substances, but this does not destroy cohesion; it only enlarges its field of operation. Suppose, for illustration, that ice is made, or water congealed by the withdrawal of caloric, this does not lessen but increases the power of cohesion. Nor does the evaporation of water destroy the force of cohesion, from the fact that the evaporation can not pass beyond the atmosphere, and will be again gathered in snow-flakes, or rain, or dew, and its properties, thus changed from a substance in which cohesion was apparent to the aëriform, do not destroy the power of cohesion, which again gathers them and by which they are reproduced, and whatever substances existed in the water, they are by evaporation reduced to crystallization.

Every substance induced by evaporation to a state of crystallization necessarily, by the laws governing cohesion, tends to one or another of the seven primitive formations of crystallography, and are thus rendered. The first is the regular *tetrahedron*, that is, a solid body comprehended under four equal triangles. Second, the *parallelopipedon*, in which the cube is included. Third, the *octohedron*, the surfaces of which are triangles, having two legs or sides only that are equal. Fourth, the *hexagonal* prism. Fifth, the *dodecahedron*, with faces unequal, two of the angles being obtuse and two of them being acute. Sixth, the *dodecahedron*, with triangular faces. And seventh, the *tetrahexahedron*, with twenty-four equal faces, four corresponding to each face of the cube.

*Q.* Can not the process of crystallization be explained in a clearer manner?

*A.* There are laws that seem inseparable to liquids, containing substances susceptible of crystallization, that tend to the shapes mentioned in the mystic seven; and when the process is regular the same shape of crystal is always formed. For illustration, sea-water, by evaporation, leaves a sediment we call salt. Each particle of this crystal has the same shape, corresponding to these forms of crystallography. By a knowledge of the regular shapes that different crystals assume, the pharmaceutist can, at a glance, tell their properties by their crystalline appearance, and he tests the qualities of different crystals by knowing the shapes they assume. The form of crystals, also, in the science of mineralogy, enables the student to easily recognize the species to which they belong.

In reference to substances that change into the

aërial, it will forever, peradventure, be shrouded in mystery. A bushel of charcoal is consumed, and nearly every particle of it is lost to observation, but not to its existence as matter; for we find that a vegetable is produced from the earth (contained in a box) of greater weight than the earth, and at the same time the earth has lost none of its matter.

Hence we learn that the plant, or root, gathered all its matter from the air and water, in neither of which is visible any substance to produce it.

Cohesion, then, affects the entire surroundings of this planet, together with each particle of matter in it or on it.

And not only do many substances connect with the atmosphere and are lost to observation from heat and combustion, but *seven* of the chemical metals also become volatile, viz.: mercury, arsenic, tellurium, cadmium, zinc, potassium, and sodium. These are all volatile below a red heat. But are these chemical metals utterly lost to cohesion because they have been rendered volatile? By no means; they still exist, though to us unseen.

Caloric can be traced in some of its operations to electricity, but cohesion does not inhere in this element, and hence it becomes a separate primitive element, and is as essential and worldwide in its operations as the entire earth we inhabit, with all its surroundings, nor can a single atom of matter dispense with its essential power.

The seventh primitive element is *Light*. Light, to those who are blessed with vision, is that power or element that renders objects visible.

To clearly illustrate the phenomena of light, when there are such a diversity of opinions, one opinion taking the precedence till refuted by some other theory, will require not only the most careful chemical analysis, but the solution of the question, Is light a fluid *per se*, or is it merely a principle, containing a sort of pression or vibration occasioned by some oscillating medium?

We have extensively remarked upon *Light* in its God-like origin, to have been an attribute, but this attribute of God created this subtile, ethereal illumination, and this omnipotent power left for our comfort this created imponderable matter.

It would not at all have been necessary to have created this aggregated volume of burning hydrogen, had it not been for the grosser essential properties of our atmosphere. Our atmosphere could not be illuminated by *moral light*, hence the spirit light of God made the temporal light to accommodate itself to our grosser needs.

Light, like all the other elements, has in its nature the mystic seven, as Prof. Newton explained by the application of the *spectrum;* if divided into three hundred and sixty equal parts the proportion of the seven prismatic colors would appear thus: of red, forty-five; of orange, twenty-seven; of yellow, forty-eight; of green, sixty; of indigo, forty; and of violet, eighty.

This element is in its operations inconceivably vast, for, throughout space, so far as any means to aid our comprehension is concerned, it is universal; nor is there, nor can there be, in the earth, or on it, so long as electricity exists in connection with our atmosphere, a place of *perfect darkness.* To our eyes there may be dark places, but other animals, by the peculiar formation of the eye, can see even better there than under a vertical sun.

We do not consider light the effulgence of the rays from the grand luminary only, but the medium of God's creative power; and through it more immediately light comes to our vision from the sun; yet our entire atmosphere, being electric, has a species of light in itself, and is in combination with other elements. Light, therefore, must be a *primitive element,* for the rays of the sun do not illuminate the dark caverns of the earth where the mole and the bat easily recognize objects.

*Q.* How is electricity affected by the rays of light falling upon it on the opposite side of the earth from us? How does that affect the dark side of the earth?

*A.* The atmosphere is a vast element, extending above the earth at all points from thirty-five to forty-five miles; beyond that point no aërial matter can reach. Then this vast volume is at all times, in one portion of the earth or another, in connection with the rays of the sun, and in that connection vitalizes the power of electricity, and through it conveys the element of light to the remotest center of the earth; and should geological discoveries go on, and unknown caverns be explored, there need be no wonder if in these, to us totally dark, recesses, living animals should be found with eyes as well as ears, having the *five senses.*

The eye of the cat, or owl, for illustration, is so formed as to catch the rays of light that pass through the channels of electricity in every conceivable portion of the earth. As the atmosphere is vitally charged with electricity, and in some portions of the earth at all times is affected by the rays of that light, there can be no total darkness so long as these connections remain, and this becomes as self-evident as the connection of the attribute, Light, with the human senses.

Electricity, when pressed by the *galvanic battery*, emits sparks of illumination from overcharged pressure, and even the northern lights are of sufficient electric power for telegraphing where no other mechanical combination exists. Hence, may not the problem be thus solved, that light is neither a fluid substance in itself, nor indeed a wave-like undulation, like the process of sound, but an element connected with electricity, and wherever the rays of the sun fall upon this electric connection light is evolved, and as much so by the explosion of a meteor or by combustion, as from the luminary of day?

By this rendering of the causes of light there can be no difficulty arising from the recent dredgings of the ocean beds. Light exists in all substances where electricity exists, and as no living animal can exist where electricity does not exist, the evidence of the truth of this theory is strengthened by this fact: that at a depth of fourteen thousand feet, or nearly three miles below the surface of the ocean, by the process of dredging, live animals have been brought up to the surface, in possession of vision. We might ask the question, Why should eyes be given to these submarine animals if no light there existed?

But we hold light to be a universal element, and to have been one of the seven *primitive elements* in the same harmony as are every-where found resulting from the mystic seven.

And why should we wonder at this, since the Seven Spirits of God fashioned the elements for man and impressed each with the mystic number of themselves, as we have shown from the entire number of primitive elements?

The earth is the grand deposit of the seven

primitive metals, viz.: gold, silver, copper, iron, mercury, lead, and tin, and all their compounds and semi-metals. Water, then, unites with earth in its variety of vegetable production.

*Q.* In how many divisions can water be associated?

*A.* In seven divisions, viz.: steam, dew, rain, frost, snow, hail, ice.

These, when gathered, are only water, but have a name in their separate appearances, and are thus distinct.

*Q.* What proportion of the air is water?

*A.* That portion called oxygen, being about one-fifth of the entire element.

*Q.* If the atmosphere should be separated in its chemical parts, how high would the water rise?

*A.* If the atmosphere is forty-five miles high, the water would rise nine miles higher than at present, and this would cover every mountain in the world more than two miles deep.

Air unites with earth also, and is the source of life to the plant and the animal.

Fire unites with earth in its coal-consuming process, whereby the rivers of oil are produced.

Electricity unites with earth and forms its battery within the molton mass of internal heat; and,

Cohesion bounds their harmony by the inexplicable force of its own power.

Thus, all in one and one in all, are these harmonies apparent, and all resolve themselves into the power and wisdom of the first seven, who, like them, can never be but an eternal and universal *one*. The geology of the earth, or the earth's strata, need not be looked to for chronological data, nor need we place layer upon layer in proof of the progress of Creation, for the Mosaic history commences with a full developed earth, and only fashions that then existing earth for man.

We thence learn that the chemical affinities of the earth's surface were arranged out of the confused and chaotic mass, when earth, and air, and water, were incoherently compounded.

*Q.* But how does hydrogen unite with oxygen in the formation of water?

*A.* Out of nine parts the analysis of chemical compounds informs us that but one part is hydrogen, and this lightest of all the substances of which we are conversant, and by which the air-balloon ascends beyond our stretch of vision, is easily divided into seven parts, viz.: chlorohydric acid, bromohydric acid, idohydric acid, sulphydric acid, selenhydric acid, and tellurhydric acid.

It became necessary that a buoyancy should exist in water as well as air, and as to the just proportions that all parts must sustain to each other, no difficulty should arise in our minds, since God, at the close of each day's labor, recognized the harmony of the parts apportioned to the labors of each day to have been arranged complete and supremely good.

*Q.* But does it not seem strange that one-ninth part of the water should be, when separated from it, the most inflammable substance known to chemistry?

*A.* That truly seems somewhat strange, and then again, is it not equally strange, on the other side, that a property of which eight-ninths of the water consists, should become about one-fifth part of the atmosphere we breathe, being that inodorous, elastic fluid, called oxygen?

*Q.* What do we learn from this union of opposites?

*A.* We learn what is meant in the Holy Bible, when it announces that the "earth was without form, and void, and darkness was upon the face of the deep," and the wonderful harmony that the Seven Spirits of God produced when the plan of redemption was uttered from the mind of the Eternal, when God said, "Let there be light."

We learn also another lesson, that these seven attributes held the parts that they had arranged in complete union by the laws of cohesion, and that, in the event of their withdrawing these powers that control the harmony of substances, they must necessarily return to incoherence.

*Q.* Have they ever withdrawn from matter?

*A.* Nearly so, at the time of the great deluge.

And in this we can see a cause for some of the marvelous discoveries of mineralogy, chemistry, and geology.

In the United States Mint, at Philadelphia, is a rock taken from a quarry in the territory of Nevada, one hundred feet below the surface, in which is a piece of an oak limb in perfect preservation. Had a volcanic eruption submerged this piece of an oak limb within this hard rock it must have been consumed in a moment of time; if it had been left to the slow process of petrifaction, which must consume a vast length of time, the oak limb would have decayed and moldered away.

*Q.* Then how could it have been accomplished?

*A.* As we have already suggested. When the formative power of the attributes withdrew from the elements, chaos must again ensue. Then all volatile substances and all evaporative substances in the atmosphere must fall to the earth in chaotic confusion.

This would again envelop the earth with water as it was "when darkness was upon the face of the deep."

The vast amount of substance in the air is only seen by the substance imparted to vegetation. All decayed substances, all evaporated substance, and the hundreds of millions of tons of wood and coal, annually consumed, is not annihilated, but passes into the aëriform. Now, should at any moment this forty-five miles height of atmosphere be rendered chaos, as are the spaces beyond it, the amount of substance within the atmosphere would be marvelously great. Like a flood, it might submerge whole provinces with coal deposit received from the craters of volcanic mountains, nor, indeed, would it be strange if huge rock were not united by this chaotic rendering, and portions of wood and stone united in the common mass.

Thus we may readily account for the multiform appearances of the earth's surface, not by the flood, but by the withdrawal of the attributes of God to the Noachian ark, thus separating all the hitherto wonderful connections of matter.

*Q.* The storm of the deluge must, then, have been overwhelmingly terrible?

*A.* Infinitely so, for the rain sprang up from the vast deeps of the ocean, as it came down from the aërial ocean above the world, commingling matter in singular incoherence.

Trees of lofty height are found in the coal beds of some portions of our earth, as well as myriads of the various fossil of animated life in the centers of rock, and at depths so wonderful that none can tell how they came there, or why they were in their flight (for the perfect shape of animals, in apparent flight, have been found in solid rock more than fifty feet below the surface) thus fettered, thus changed into coal or stone. The holding of the separate and opposite particles of matter in harmony, by the Seven Spirits of God, till near the deluge, and then suddenly withdrawing from those elements, rendering them chaotic, solves this wonderful problem in accordance with the universal law of science. "Come thou and all thy house into the ark," saith Jehovah. Not go, but "come." But the mystic number seven is also known in the seven liberal arts and sciences.

Q. What are the seven liberal arts and sciences?

A. These are grammar, rhetoric, logic, arithmetic, geometry, music, and astronomy. In all ages of the world these arts and sciences have been held in high estimation, and, as it was supposed that they held an allusion from the seven Sabbatical years, the seven years of famine, the seven years in the building of King Solomon's temple, as well as the seven golden candlesticks, the sacredness, then, of this number, could not otherwise than remain as one of the wonders of the world, pointing to and centering in the "Seven Spirits of God." Go as far back in the infancy of letters, either of sacred or profane history, as we may, these numbers meet us at every epoch of time, and point onward to the cycles of an unending eternity. These seven liberal arts and sciences embrace the root of all arts and sciences.

*Geometry*, originally and properly, embraces the earth in all its measurement and dimensions, and from it springs geography, mineralogy, geology, and all that pertains to earth or its elements.

*Astronomy:* from this science all knowledge of the celestial bodies, their motions, their magnitude and revolutions are observed. This science embraces as a cause all eclipses, as well as other various phenomena, and astrotheology.

*Grammar:* this science not only embraces all orthography, etymology, syntax, and prosody, but it embraces the art of chirography, telegraphy, typography, and hieroglyphics.

*Rhetoric:* this embraces all the art of speaking eloquently, as well as the art of so arranging sentences so as to please while it instructs the hearer.

*Logic* is both an art and a science, because, to argue logically, one must think correctly and reason forcibly. It is not mere talking, but the combining of ideas in a form conclusive and decisive.

*Arithmetic* is also one of the liberal arts, and is the science of numbers.

By it all numerical relations of man to man, together with all knowledge of distances, gravity, and ponderability, is known.

This art has been divided into addition, subtraction, multiplication, and division.

But the last and noblest of all the sciences is *Music.* By this science all harmonics of sound are learned and appreciated. This is a science as universal as it is delightful, and is associated with devotion and praise, and can never be dispensed with while man is man.

*Q.* Did the ancients have any idea of confused and incoherent matter?

*A.* Most assuredly. It has ever been known by scholars that all compounds admit of divisibility.

Paracelsus and Van Helmont pretended that they had discovered an alkahest that would decompose all substances, and by this they imposed upon the credulity of those over whom they exercised a superiority; but this pretense soon vanished, as has every other idea of such a chemical compound.

Still, that the present state of combination did not always exist, many very able scholars have ever proclaimed; and from geology and the elements outside of revelation the most conclusive proofs exist that things now, and substances now, are not combined or compounded as they once were, and this led Mr. Hugh Miller into the idea that the earth's strata afforded reliable data of man's formation and of the almost illimitable duration of time necessary to the growth of the various stratas he has so ingeniously classified. Others have also seen the evidence of confused and chaotic matter in geological research, and have tried to account for it upon scientific principles, the force of which the reader must be the judge.

ANAXAGORAS, five hundred years before Christ, in trying to solve this problem, presents it in the following poetical manner:

> " Before the seas and the terrestrial ball,
> And heaven's high canopy that covers all,
> One was the face of nature, if a face,
> Rather a rude and undigested mass,
> A lifeless lump, unfashioned and unframed,
> Of jarring seeds, and justly chaos named.
> No sun was lighted up the world to view,
> No moon did yet her blunted horns renew,
> Nor yet was earth suspended in the sky,
> Nor poised did on her own foundation lie,
> Nor seas about the shore their arms had thrown,
> But earth, and air, and water were in one.
> Then air was void, and light and earth unstable,
> And water's vast abyss unnavigable;
> No certain form on any was impressed,
> All was confused, and each disturbed the rest;
> For heat and cold were in one body fixed,
> And soft with hard, and light with heavy mixed.
> But God and nature, while they thus contend,
> To these intestine discords put an end;
> Then earth from air, and seas from earth were driven,
> And grosser air sunk from th' ethereal heaven.
> Thus disembroiled they take their proper place;
> The next of kin contiguously embrace,
> And foes are sundered by a larger space."

# CHAPTER XXI.

ANTHROPOLOGY—ALL NATIONS HAVE TRADITIONS OF A FUTURE STATE—THE WILL OF MAN—OF THE BEAST—MAN'S SENSES DIE—THE ATTRIBUTES EVER LIVE—THE RESURRECTION EFFECTS THE RIGHTEOUS—HOW—THE WICKED.

E hence learn that the laws governing the elements make their obeisance to the mystic seven, and that the primitive elements, like the primitive attributes, all proceed from the septenary number, and in some of them these seven properties inhere irrefragably.

Here, also, in the plant or the tree, we have seen the same marvelous relation to the seven. In astronomy also, and even the moon itself counts off her seven phases.

Chemistry unfolds its wonderful identity to the mystic number seven, and all nature asks the question: Has this number an allusion? We have shown that it does not allude to *time*, that it does not allude to geological strata, but to Him, who fashioned it all for man, and placed his divine impress upon it.

We have now only to examine the science of anthropology.

*Q.* What is anthropology?

*A.* The harmony of the several relations of man, physically, intellectually, and morally.

*Q.* Do the Holy Scriptures at all reveal or develop this science?

*A.* Most assuredly they do; but where words are interchangeably used to denote different properties of the organism, it may be very difficult to so explain the scriptural teachings that a clearness of perception may at all times pervade the mind.

We have endeavored throughout our entire investigation to use English terms in accordance with the meaning, as given by our ablest lexicographers.

The Greek word *pneuma,* sometimes rendered spirit, sometimes breath, we have called the *mind,* or the attributes of man. *Psuche,* from which the English term psychology finds its root, we have called the *soul immortal*—the spirit; and in this sense we shall use these terms in the future.

*Q.* What, then, is the *mind* of man?

*A.* The seven attributes connected to the seven senses.

*Q.* What, then, is the soul?

*A.* The soul of man is that immortal form resembling the body, but invisible to the fallen senses.

*Q.* How do we understand the connection between God and the soul?

*A.* The Seven Spirits of God is the author of the seven attributes of man, and by this relation originates our accountability to him. In this union is our marvelous relation perpetuated.

These wonderful powers seem to be the inmost, invisible centers of moral action, both in relation to God and to man.

*Q.* How do these associations agree with the Apostle's declaration in the seventh chapter of Romans?

*A.* We think it clearly explains the otherwise contradictory statements. "For the good," says the Apostle, "that I would, I do not, but the evil which I would not, that I do."—Rom. vii: 14. Now, if we should read this in accordance with the anthropology already adduced, it will appear thus: "For the good that I (my attributes) would do, I (my senses) do not, but the evil which I (my attributes) would not, that I (my senses) do." Now, "it is no more I (my attributes) that do it, but sin (the fallen senses) that dwelleth in me." "So, then, with the mind (the seven attributes) I myself serve the law of God, but with the flesh (the senses) the law of sin."—Rom. vii: 25.

*Q.* How is it that "they that are in the flesh can not please God?"

*A.* The *flesh*, meaning necessarily the senses that control the flesh, is fallen and under the sentence of death, and can not escape it. If, then, we discard the intercession of the Spirit, reject the offered aid of grace, we live after the flesh, and can not please God, for he must be the supreme object of our adoration. It is a natural impossibility for *total depravity* to do sinlessly right, nor does God require it, for he is infinitely just, and can exact nothing of us that we can not do. Religion, first and foremost, relates to our spiritual nature: "Seek first the kingdom of God." In our attributes, then, we can please God by accepting the intercession of his love, and be dead to the world but alive to Christ.

*Q.* Have the senses, then, no moral quality?

*A.* If separated from the attributes they would become only a beast, like any other biped, and surely then they could have no moral quality; but they can not be divested of this connection, hence they have a moral responsibility, but this accountability does not inhere, so to speak, in themselves, but in their connection with the spiritual organism.

No psychical being can be a creature only of sense, for the nation, the people, the tongue, is utterly unknown where the future state never awakens meditation. There is no such point in anthropology where the mind of man is as low as the beast; even where no law exists the Apostle declares such become a law to themselves, and must be so judged.

Then the anthropology of the Bible is corroborated by the actual exhibition of facts. Whoever saw or heard of a nation that had no traditions of a future state, that had no laws to govern moral action?

*Q.* Is it, then, man's moral nature, that inclines him to admire beauty, paintings, sculpture, or art?

*A.* No, it is his judgment sense; still, if his heart is renewed by the Spirit, he may have higher and holier reasons to admire the beauty of God's wonderful works. But admiration may spring alone from the seven senses, in which case the man is no more a Christian, by the possession of this redeemable faculty, than in his relish for food.

*Q.* If the human will is the external action of the combined senses of man, why is it that beasts have wills also?

*A.* The *will* of the beast springs from the five senses; the will of the man from his seven; hence man's will is more formidable than the beast, being in possession of two superior senses more than the animal. But the will of the beast has no moral responsibility, because he has no attributes of a spiritual nature with which he stands related to God; but man having this relation, the exercise of his will, when it contravenes the commands of God, renders him morally culpable. To deny ourselves is to conquer this will, to submit to the teachings of the Spirit, to admit God's will as revealed to us through the Spirit to be the superlative claim, to obey which should be our bounden duty, our joyful privilege.

*Q.* If the seven senses in man die, can they ever be resurrected?

*A.* Never; nor does the spiritual organism ever need their future association.

The senses have no form, no shape, no spiritual existence. Their connection, or inosculation with the attributes, obliges them to moral responsibility; when, therefore, they die, they cease to be, for the spirit form is complete without them; then death is their extinction, and hence a resurrection of any thing which has become extinct is simply ridiculous.

Not so with the human body. It has a form, does not become extinct when the senses die, hence a resurrection of that body is possible, though the matter of it may have passed even into the aëriform, because it is connected through the operation of the atonement to the deified humanity of Christ.

*Q.* What, then, is the "second death?"

"Blessed and holy is he that hath part in the first resurrection: on such the second death hath no power."—Rev. xx: 6.

"And death and hell were cast into the lake of fire. This is the second death."—Rev. xx: 14.

*A.* We can best understand the nature of this death by looking at the operation of the death of the senses, or the first death. The senses connect the body to the attributes, and in this relation we are moral and responsible creatures; death dissolves the body from the attributes by the destruction of the senses. This does not destroy the consciousness or life of the soul, because the attributes still live. By the plan of redemption and the grace of God, our attributes connect with divine mercy and hold a relation to clemency, pardon, and eternal life. When, therefore, we sin a sin unto death, then death has the power to dissolve this relation of our attributes with the attributes of God, and this is the second death; and though the death sentence is passed, and God's Spirit strives no more with the soul, yet its full realization is reserved to the day of judgment.

*Q.* We shall, then, suffer loss by death—the loss of our seven senses?

*A.* The Christian can suffer no loss by death, from the fact that his human sense of sight refused by its total depravity to allow him to behold angels or heaven. Now, released from this frail and fallen faculty, he beholds the King in his glory, the crown of life, the redeemed of earth, and all the celestial cherubim of glory.

*Q.* This, then, will be an eternal gain instead of a loss?

*A.* Truly; and of the sense of *hearing* the same. In this life, has not only his eyes been dimmed with tears often, and his soul filled with anguish at what he has seen, but he has heard much that he wishes he had never heard, and he has been deprived of hearing much that he longed to hear. No angel songs have ever saluted his ear, and even the voice of Jesus, to which his attributes have listened with rapture, his ears have never heard. Why does he longer need this sense? The language of the spirit world has only approached the senses like reflex rays of light, and then only to condemn them, and to say of them, "Oh wretched man that I am, who shall deliver me from the body of this death?" or, "I have a desire to depart and to be with Christ, which is far better." The Christian, then, no longer needs the earthly sense of hearing when the Master calls him to life and to glory.

*Q.* But will he not need the sense of feeling?

*A.* Not in the least. The present human organism is only susceptible to external things; that, then, that is spiritual we can not tangibly feel, we only hear "the joyful sound" and feel the "love of God shed abroad in our hearts" by and through the attributes, and many times we desire to feel the power of that love and the senses refuse their association, and we say, "Oh that it was as in other days, when the candle of the Lord shone upon my pillow," and we devoutly pray to feel the Spirit's power, but our fallen sense prevents.

But, after death, the soul's cup of joy will be infinitely full. Will we then ever need a sense that has baffled and trifled with joys so immeasurably vast? Surely not.

We may say the same in reference to the sense of *smell*. The odors of incense and the perfume of the flowers of the garden of the Lord, planted by the rivers of the water of life, we can not grasp with this depraved sense; but then, when the attributes are disenthralled, and the sweet odors of our spiritual Canaan fill the attribute, the joy of these higher and holier faculties will forever eclipse the human.

*Q.* Can our attributes *taste*, as does this sense in our human organism?

*A.* The *sense* of taste is prepared for substances, the attributes for the spiritual. In Scripture we read: "If ye have *tasted* that the Lord is gracious." The sense of taste accommodates itself to the pleasure of the organism in its demand for food, and at the same time the human organism is decaying and wasting away. We, then, do not need the resurrection of a sense so frail accommodated to the perishable; for we shall taste of the spiritual fountain of life, of life's ambrosial fruit, of the heavenly manna. We shall no longer need corruptible food, poisonous food, decaying food, hence the Christian loses nothing when this sense ceases to be.

*Q.* But, certainly, we shall need the judgment sense in glory?

*A.* Not at all. What value could we there place on gold, silver, jewels, apparel? What use for a sense that develops itself in the values of earth, of minerals, farms, or merchandise? No, this sense is totally depraved, and constantly undervalues pure religion.

It is even ready to barter the inheritance of heaven for sordid gold; of honor, uprightness, and virtue, to covetousness and lust. It holds us away from duty by the smallest pretext, and makes us think that "gain is godliness."

But when, liberated from this groveling sense, we look upon our heavenly mansion in glory and see the gold that cankers not, and the robes that fade not, and the glory that passes not away, we shall feel to exult in a freedom from a sense so deceptive, so false to our eternal well-being.

*Q.* But the language sense, we can not dispense with that, certainly?

*A.* "God is a Spirit and seeketh such to worship him as worship in spirit and truth." The human organs of speech are as depraved as any other sense can be. By this sense we blaspheme, by it we curse, swear, lie, tattle, slander, deceive; and still we are obliged to use this sense to express the great desire we cherish to get rid of it. It is like a fire, like a flood, like the helm to a vessel; we must control, keep it under, subdue it. "He that governs his tongue is greater than he that taketh a city."

The language sense, or power of speech, wears out. Ere we reach our three-score years and ten, our musical powers have failed, the decay of these pleasurable organs is apparent. We can *think* of singing in our attributes, and the melody we make in our hearts to the Lord is glorious; but the voice is harsh and worn, and refuses to comply with the knowledge our higher nature demands. Oh to live where we shall not be compelled to place a guard over our lips, to watch against idle words, vain words, sinful words! where we can express our triumphant joys in heaven's own language, in the song of redemption and glory! this will so delight the soul that we shall shout glory to God in the highest that we are liberated from a false tongue and from unclean lips.

Thus we shall need none of the senses that connect with sublunary things, since the undying attributes of our spirit-form, remains in all the fullness and glory of the spirit world above. This not only meets the cherished expectations of our nobler nature, but is the anthropology of the Bible, the teachings of the revealed Word.

*Q.* To what purpose, then, is the resurrection of this human body?

*A.* In order that a being, possessing the nature and form of the Divine Trinity, might exist in the love circle of incomprehensible glory, the plan of redemption is unfolded.

To this plan all the creative acts of God, as revealed in the Holy Scriptures, allude. In the creation of man the harmony of the senses and attributes constituted him in mind but one, in body but one, in soul but one; but when by sin death reigned, and the senses fell under the power of death, his nature must be dual—a twofold nature—unless the body could be resurrected and glorified. This could be done if Deity could dwell in humanity and transform its substance into ineffable light and glory.

The great archetype and antitype of man undertook this work and completed it. He changed humanity to divinity, and ascended up on high and gave gifts unto men.

If there existed a necessity of his resurrection, there must also exist a necessity of our resurrection. If his human body passed into the glorified state, ours, too, if we are like him, must pass into the glorious state.

*Q.* But what if translated?

*A.* The translation of the human body into the spiritual state necessitates the same operation. The earthly senses disappear, while the attributes of the soul vivify and immortalize the entire organism. If, as we have shown, matter can become aëriform or pass into unseen substance, surely the human form may, by the power of him who created the natural as well as the spiritual body, pass into the ethereal identity.

Nor will its decay or its change, while in the grave, render God's power more wonderful or active than it must be to resurrect the body immediately after death. This act of God is in accordance with his word and with the expectation of all the living.

That only that passes into the grave is human; the senses go not there, the attributes go not with the dead body into the grave, the soul immortal dies not nor is buried, only the human, this enters the grave, this is resurrected: "All that are in their graves shall hear his voice and come forth."

This is translation from the grave, the other a translation of the human before it reaches the chambers of the grave.

This change the Apostle calls "mortality swallowed up of life."—2 Cor. v: 4. We may not get the best idea by calling mortality a robe, yet, in a certain sense, it is like to a robe of spotless white when resurrected through the power of the Holy Spirit; it is, indeed, "mortality swallowed up of life."

It develops the organism by giving its entire nature the wonderful configuration of immortality.

*Q.* How, then, will the resurrection affect the wicked?

*A.* The same as it does the righteous. They

will be raised, and the totally depraved attributes, which they have rendered so by rejecting the Lord of life and glory, will swallow up the humanity into an eternal state of unreconciliation.

The entire plan of redemption, in its effects upon our condition, is developed only in this life. Here the Holy Spirit can harmonize the disorganized attributes. Here the soul can be washed in the fountain of grace; here the promise is made and the title given. After death, the judgment. If men refuse all the intercession of the wonderful Three, the Father, Son, and Holy Spirit, their resurrection will be the positive proof of their condition, as the character of their attributes will permeate the human development.

*Q.* What, then, is the use of raising the wicked from their graves, if they can not be better off thereby?

*A.* The resurrection power must necessarily reach the entire race if the second Adam destroyed the works of the devil and restored our fallen nature through grace to a companionship with God. The resurrection, if we accept of salvation, is the greatest gift that God could give; for all other sacrifices inhere in this triumph over the grave. Hence the resurrection is a gracious bestowment of the Spirit, and he who rejects the grace that opens into such infinite glory must abide by the consequences.

*Q.* What, then, will be the eternal condition of the wicked?

*A.* We read, in reference to the condition of the wicked, of a place called "outer darkness" (Matt. xxii: 13), and also of the fallen angels of "chains of darkness." (2 Pet. ii: 4.)

From this we may infer that a place analogous, to a realm or locality where no ray of light can penetrate, will be their final abode. The darkness, when God withdraws the attribute of light, and with it all the seven attributes of Deity in their natural and moral intercession, must be fearfully painful to a nature nurtured in light. Of the anguish of that rayless fire we know but little here, and may God grant that no eye that ever reads the lines we produce, may witness its painful hereafter!

*Q.* What, then, will be the condition of the people whose God is the Lord?

*A.* The absence of those associations, detrimental to spiritual progress, will alike be wonderful and delightful.

Here we are deprived of the fullness of the soul's capacity by many insuperable barriers. If we grasp the joys of pardon, it is only stultified by the depraved senses; for, if we attempt to express the delight of our attributes, the very language we use is so meager and indefinite that we often feel that we have spoken of it in vain. And then the outer channels through which we would desire the fountain of our love to flow is so fluctuating and unstable, that we are often led to conclude it is in vain that we labor. Depraved channels through which the pure waters of life must flow are as dissatisfying to the Christian as unpalatable food to the taste; still this necessity must go on so long as we live in the flesh, but when freed, when the channels are as pure as the fountain, the full ecstacy of our enjoyment can only then be realized.

And then, again, tracing this figure of speech on, there are so many that are always ready to choke up even these depraved channels with earthly drift-wood, and thereby hinder the good we hoped to do, originating the most discouraging results, that we become faint and our courage abates; but not so after the resurrection: every channel to the infinite fountain will be augmented as it receives the welcome of glory and of life.

The harmonies of our songs will then echo and re-echo through the realms of unbounded space, gathering harmonies and concords of correlative glory onward and onward in transcendent notes of rapture.

*Q.* Have we never in this life enjoyed the fullness of a single attribute?

*A.* Not its fullness, because it has never been entirely liberated. The attribute, Love, when touched by the love of Christ, only presses a greater desire through the senses to love him more, and the higher life that we may enjoy by the communion of the Spirit only makes us the more anxious to be wholly led by the Spirit; and in apostolic days, as well as in our own, men desire to depart and be with Christ in glory, because they can not fully drink of the fountain while in the flesh.

We may possibly catch, for a moment, the inspiration of the love of Christ, but this, at most, is only one channel to the soul, only one avenue to the fountain of infinite goodness. Let us look at the seven channels to the soul and suppose that each is full and overflowing.

First, the channel of light. God is light. This channel, filled with the light of an eternal state of glory, with the great light of God reflecting in every ray his wonderful love to man, when uninterrupted by the fallen senses, must envelop the immortal organism with incomprehensible brilliancy and glory.

## CHAPTER XXII.

THE FULLNESS OF THE ATTRIBUTES CONSIDERED—THE CHANNELS—HEAVENLY RECOGNITION—THE INHERITANCE—THE BRIDE OF CHRIST—WELCOME—MUSIC IN HEAVEN—THE BELIEVER IN DEATH GAINS GLORY—RESURRECTED BODY DOES NOT NEED HUMAN SENSES—THE MEMORY OF THE SENSES DIE—THE MEMORY OF THE ATTRIBUTES LIVE—WHY REPENT—WHAT IS FAITH—GOOD WORKS—REDEMPTION.

SOURCES of infinite delight, the realms of incomprehensible space illuminated by Him, whose "house are we," must cause the exultant soul to shout in the ecstacies of unending delight. And, again, the fullness of the attribute, Life, who has ever enjoyed in this pilgrimage?

Life, free from death; life, full of activity and delight; life, with the rainbow circles of glory surrounding it; who has ever enjoyed this side of heaven?

It is a river flowing from the throne of God to the soul through the channel of life. How glorious a life, in the company and fellowship of the great source of life eternal; fear, sorrow, grief, pain, sickness, death, darkness, gloom, and despair, unfelt and unknown, and all the channels of these forever inaccessible, either by deception or decrepitude.

And then the fullness of life, a life in glory, a life with the sanctified, whose very presence is full of joy unspeakable, must be incomprehensibly glorious.

The attributes, then, of life and light, filled with the fullness of God, must render the soul inexpressibly happy and full of the glory of God.

*Q.* Who has ever fully enjoyed all that the attribute, Holiness, might communicate? 335

*A.* It can not be enjoyed in its fullness here. Ah! to be as pure as our Author, to have no besetting sin, no unclean lips, nor deceitful heart; to abide among the sinless where every ethereal object is transcendently holy, must overwhelm the soul with ecstatic delight.

And then, in immediate proximity to this, is justice. Just in the sight of God, in the sight of angels, in the sight of the saints. No lack in the balances, complete in him, enrobed by him, justified by him, and to be forever with the Lord.

Oh what a channel to the soul is here opened into undying life, into the palace of God.

Here is the attribute, truth. Sinless, pure, perfect; no guile, no guilt, no deception, but truth, eternal truth. How beautifully it drinks into the fruition of the promise given. When in the flesh it lived by prelibation, but now by fruition. Oh the promises of God—a God of truth—not now to be disappointed, but to feel the truth, as the promise had revealed it, that no eye or ear had ever comprehended the glory of God as it is in the realms of light, laid up in store for his people!

The attribute, mercy, in us, has never yet coursed through a sinless outer channel. Obstructed by ten thousand outward influences, we can not fully realize its susceptibility to a full channel of joy. Have we been kind to the distressed, others can easily attribute it to secular motives, and the farther exercise of that pleasure seems forestalled to future action. But not so in the morn of the resurrection, for the channel of God's mercy will fill our channels of this faculty to overflow, and in the highest ecstacy of delight we can forever rejoice.

> "And when the gates of death I've passed,
> When lodged beyond the stormy blast,
> I'll shout, while endless ages last,
> Mercy's free, mercy's free."

And then the channel of love. The love of God shed abroad in the heart transcends all creature sensibility in its incomprehensible conquering power. The flame in our hearts not only illuminates the desert around us, but creates an imperishable desire for more of this illumination; and because the channel is not free outwardly we anxiously inquire:

"When shall I see my Father's face,
And in his bosom rest?"

But when we stand on Zion's bright mountain, and the love-channel is opened, and all obstructions removed, outwardly and inwardly, and a full fruition enjoyed, no language can express the capacity of this attribute to immeasurable fullness.

Then the thrill of association, as each reciprocal attribute, filled with light, life, holiness, justice, mercy, truth, and love, commingle with the attributes of Deity, will become so inconceivably great that we may ask, where, oh where, is there a word, a line, or a sentence in the entire idiom of language at all relevant to the description of the pleasures of the soul?

These are the joys of the resurrection, and not only these, but another beatitude of glory, another beam of light, will burst upon us as we catch the inspiration of a *heavenly recognition*. When in a foreign clime, to meet one we know, one a dear friend, a loved one, how great the joy and rejoicing, but how much more so when we meet those with whom we have stood side by side, shoulder to shoulder, in the battle-storm of life, now, like us, eternally free and gloriously enrolled in the ranks of the redeemed Church triumphant.

The resurrection, then, will include the whole

plan of eternal redemption, in presenting before the Father his own offspring, complete in him; and yet by the free acceptance of all the glorified.

*Q.* Will God, then, become the father of our entire natures?

*A.* Supremely so. Because, *first*, we are his offspring in our dual nature. He created the spiritual organism and the attributes from his spiritual entity, as he must have created the mighty host of angels; *secondly*, he has, by the power of his electric blood and human body, brought forth our corruptible bodies and transformed them into the likeness of his glorious body.

Hence we are joint heirs to an inheritance eternal, undefiled, and that fadeth not away. The Holy Spirit has created the new birth in our attributes, the blessed Son of God has created the new birth of our bodies by his resurrection, and God, the Father,

> "Owns me for his child;
> I can no longer fear.
> With confidence I now draw nigh
> And Father, Abba Father, cry."

Here is Deity as a trinity, and man as a trinity. Deity with seven attributes, and man also with seven attributes. Deity with the unseen Father, or soul-form, man with the same marvelously unseen soul-form. God is now seen in the person of Jesus Christ, and so, with us, we are seen in the personality of the resurrected body.

and this body is like his sinless body, pure and free.

Then our *inheritance*.

We shall inherit infallibility.

We have long mourned over our weaknesses and frailties; in fact, we have prayed to be freed from the least and last remains of sin, and in prelibation have, at times, looked over the gloomy Jordan and obtained a glimpse of the land of the blest, but no sooner awake to human consciousness, we have seen the same "thorn in flesh" over which we prayed to be delivered, and for the conformation, into the likeness of Jesus, the Spirit, bid us wait. "My grace is sufficient."

But now the long looked for and prayed for hour has come, we are "like him, because we see him as he is," and these "vile bodies are fashioned like unto his glorious body."

And not only this, but we inherit a crown.

*Q.* What have we conquered that we should inherit this badge of royalty?

*A.* We have conquered the human senses and made them bow before the throne of grace, and every one of them have we rendered passive, while we glorified God through a personal obedience to the will of his Son. We have conquered the enemy of our salvation and quenched all his fiery darts through grace, and over him been more than conquerors.

We have conquered death in this, that he had

his demand, but this was our glory and rejoicing. He took nothing from us that we longer needed, and through his death-blow we came into possession of a crown of glory triumphant.

Thus, through the Spirit, we are conquerors, and through Christ receive the crown of glory.

We inherit, also, a *mansion*.

This beautiful home has been erected through the infinite purpose of God to so charm and amaze and thrill the soul with its ethereal splendor that it might appear as a wedding gift to his bride.

All the architectural taste that infinite wisdom could bestow upon a work so significant of the combined attributes of God in their display of love to the redeemed, here find their central glory. Captivating beauty, walls radiant with light and minarets; the lofty balconies of which surrounding worlds and systems of worlds radiate in beautiful prospect, harps of sweetest tone, and vocal music of richest harmony, as well as the eternal light of the city, make it the home of the soul.

"Its glittering towers the sun outshine;
That heavenly mansion shall be mine."

And then the *welcome*.

If face greets face in rapturous smiles when loved ones meet, how will it, or can it, be expressed when intercessors meet intercessors, when God's attributes come down to welcome our attributes to his eternal mansion of light. Here the light of God greets the light in the soul with its harmonious welcome, filling every power of the immortal mind with the light of God. Then shall we see light in his light, and forever dwell where no night is known and where no gloom or darkness approaches.

The life of God hails with radiant glory the reciprocal life of the soul, which fills it to overflow with the eternal Spirit. Mortality is swallowed up of life, and the attribute of God exults in its trophies as we exult in his glorious welcome.

Now eternally beyond death by the inheritance of immortality, and our finite conceptions of this wonderful gift augmented in incomprehensible and unutterable fullness, we shall forever bask in the light of his glory and the life of his presence.

Then mercy, with its delightful welcome, joins the attribute in us in all the rapture of one who succeeded in saving a treasure so infinitely vast, which, when saved, could reciprocate the mercy that secured its pardon. Oh how vast the fountain of mercy that surrounded the soul in all its journeyings and dark forebodings, through this pilgrimage of earthly probation, now fully to be revealed. Here it disappointed our earthly hopes that, had we realized the objects we sought for, might have proved our eternal overthrow; but mercy interposed and we were saved; now, with what gratitude and joy can we recognize our great Deliverer.

The attribute, Truth, now exultant with the trophy secured in the salvation of one, nay, of millions who possessed this undying faculty, bids us a triumphant welcome to the arcana of God's imperishable glory, and then we, who had by the influence of our depraved senses almost doubted the truth of God, had a thousand times questioned the promises; we, for whom truth had by all the immutability of God pledged the soul's release from its fetters; we, now unfettered, manumitted, free, will reciprocally rejoice in the recognition of an attribute upon which we reposed when all earthly prospects failed.

Holiness and justice greet, also, our attributes of kindred assimilation, and we in response cry, Holy, holy, Lord God Almighty, thou art worthy to receive homage, for of "thy fullness have we all received, and grace for grace." And oh the transcendent fountain of God's love, how it meets us at the very threshold of our mansion in glory, and we, being knit to it by the witnessing Spirit, hail this heavenly dove, this love attribute of Jehovah, with unspeakable delight!

And now the dear person in whom these attributes dwell, even Jesus, once in the manger, once in Gethsemane, once on Calvary, once in the grave, but now in glory, in whose wonderful person all majesty, might, and dominion reside, "for it pleased the Father that in him should *all fullness* dwell;" now Jesus welcomes his bride, his redeemed, out of every kindred, language, and tongue, and, in the presence of the most august assemblage that ever convened in glory, he accepts the Church, inheriting the Spirit of Immanuel. What responsive notes of rapture burst from the sanctified lips of the Church triumphant as they "crown him Lord of all!"

Long had they sung—

> "'T is a point I long to know,
> Oft it causes anxious thought,
> Do I love the Lord or no,
> Am I his or am I not?"

But now it is changed to the new song, the song of Moses and the Lamb; they sing

> Hallelujah! hallelujah! the saints are at home,
> No longer as aliens, no longer to roam;
> The holy of holies we now can behold,
> The city celestial—the streets paved with gold.
> Our foes are all conquered, and death now must die,
> The storms have all passed from the bright azure sky,
> The hosts of destroyers to darkness have fled,
> And the saints of all ages have awaked from the dead.

The harmonies of music in heaven will be infinitely superior to those with which we are familiar on earth, and reverberations and echoes will thrill the angel hosts of heaven with unwonted rapture. Music inheres in the attributes of God, and the surroundings of his throne must constitute a polyphony overwhelmingly grand and sublime.

We have, we think, clearly shown the analogy

of Biblical anthropology to the Mystic Numbers of the Word, and our relation to those numbers to be of a divine character, and this number is so interwoven with our senses, our attributes; with matter and mind, with the elements and minerals, with geology and botany, with astronomy and anthropology as to clearly, and, we believe, unanswerably establish their allusion to the "Seven Spirits of God."

If the seven primitive attributes are not the "seven eyes of the Lord," what are they?

If the "Seven Spirits of God" are not his seven primitive attributes, what are they?

We have shown that the same Spirit is called the seven eyes of the Lord, the Seven Spirits of God, the seven golden candlesticks, the comforter, the witness, and the Holy Ghost.

All these attributes we possess, and because we possess them, and they connect with our senses, are we moral beings. Take away this connection and you take away moral responsibility.

We have shown that the immortal form is the *psyche*—the soul, and is represented in active being by the attributes, as is the human organism by the senses, and that these attributes no more die than does the soul, that when the senses die the attributes ascend to God who gave them, and must be judged by the deeds done in the body.

This, we believe, is Bible anthropology.

We have shown that the attributes have

power through grace to accept or reject the great salvation, to forever remain disorganized, and the soul over which they preside unwashed and uncleansed, notwithstanding an exhaustless fountain has been freely opened for sin and uncleanness.

We have also shown that the human body can be raised from the dead and united to its parent soul, as a living garment, like to our Divine Master; that those who die in the Lord lose nothing valuable in any regard, but gain an infinite crown of glory. That a trinity only can be the offspring of a trinity, that we are his offspring when we submit to his commandments and accept of his grace, and as such he has promised to present us before the throne of his excellence without fault and blameless.

That the resurrection will not change the character of the attributes or the soul, but will forever stereotype its condition for glory or dismay, for eternal day or eternal night, just in character as it finds the parent soul.

And that here are interests of incalculable importance, the neglect of which no future change can countervail, no ransom obviate; that if secured, a life of glory is also secured.

This, also, we believe, is the teachings of scriptural anthropology.

And now, reader, you can tell whether you are a child of God by the new birth into Christ by the application of this rule.

If you love God you will find a warfare with the senses, you will be called upon to deny them, restrain them, control them; failing to do this you will find that the way of the transgressor is hard; for you can not enjoy the senses in their worldly associations when they conflict with God's commandments, for your conscience will be wounded and pierced with many sorrows if you neglect holy living. If you love God, and are awake to self-denial, you will find his ways are pleasantness and all his paths are peace.

If you love the world the love of the Father is not in the attributes, you are under the curse of the broken law, and this condemnation is augmented by every refusal to submit to be saved by grace. The Holy Spirit alone can harmonize the discordant attributes and give to the soul a peace that is like a river, rolling on in undisturbed quietude to the pacific shores of eternal delight, while without the Spirit the soul is like the unrest of the ocean, continually halting and promising, for none but the unrenewed fully know the broken vows, the resolves, and re-resolves, unfulfilled.

*Q.* But shall we not know each other in heaven as soon as we behold the blood-washed throng?

*A.* It is a pleasing and very popular theory, that loved ones will meet us at death and accompany us home to glory, but we doubt the scriptural application to that belief. There will be neither marrying nor giving in marriage, says the Saviour, in heaven, hence the association will be of a spiritual character, like the angels of God. The human knowledge of relationship is conveyed to us through the senses. Then, if the senses die, the knowledge of the relationship, so far as they are concerned, dies also. These senses have a power that we call memory, but the attributes also have a memory as undying as the soul. It only remains for us to discover whether the attributes remember human faces as do the senses. We incline to the belief that there will be a remembrance by the attributes of actors and actions of persons and conditions; but this recognition will not enhance our love for individuals, for all will be infinitely lovely, but we think after the resurrection there may be higher delights with those we have known and loved on earth than with others, for the human form, when resurrected, will bear the perfectly developed image of our earthly organism, though infinitely spiritualized. Hence we shall then "see as we are seen, and know as we are known." It appears that Moses and Elias not only knew each other on the Mount of Transfiguration, but the Apostles knew them to be these worthies, and so remarked to the Saviour: "Let us build three tabernacles, one for thee, and one for Moses, and one for Elias." The evidence derived from this is that Moses, who died and was buried, knew Elias, or

Elijah, who was translated, and both conversed with Jesus; if so, then the memory of the attributes will be abundantly sufficient to the heavenly recognition.

That the senses have a memory, the beasts of the field, and fowls of the air witness, for even when asleep they remember and exert the muscles, as though they were awake. The horse remembers the house you stop at for years, and all the races who have no moral relations to God, no attributes, have a memory as tenacious as our own.

It will readily occur to the careful reader that we have two sources of memory; the beast has but one. We charge a *something* which is under the control of another power that we possess to remember certain events, and act toward this memory just as another would act toward us, if desirous of having us to see some object delightfully pleasing. He would point to it, tell its location, and help us to his utmost power. So we do in reference to the memory of the senses. We bring circumstances before it, we bring localities before it, and many times, after much labor, the page in the book of the senses is found where the facts we have desired to know are recorded: "Oh, yes, I now remember it plainly." Then, if we have a power over the memory, we also can direct its action. "Study grammar one hour," says the teacher, "and then study arithmetic." Can the scholar do this? Certainly. Then he has power over his *one* memory, by his other memory. And thus one is in subjection to the other. If this is true, then it is true also that we possess the attributes and they control the senses, and each have memories.

But the memory of the senses die and perish, and with the beast, as with us, there is no memory in the grave, no device, no existence of the senses. But the attributes take up the remembrances of earth and carry them past the shadow of death, as in the departed rich man, who recognized Lazarus, who once asked for crumbs at his gate.

It will greatly relieve the anxious Christian to know that he no longer retains the full senses, nor the memory attached to those senses, in two particulars:

*First*, in reference to his own transgressions; they will never come up to shame or confound him in glory, because they were of the earth, and in the acceptance of the terms of salvation they were blotted out of the book of God's remembrance; in other words, the senses and their memory have ceased to be.

*Second*, there may have been alienations of brethren here, occasioned by the same fallen senses, and though each may have designed to do right they may have widely differed, even to such an extent as to have unchurched, if not unchristianized, each other. This, too, perished when the senses died, and now they are united in heavenly triumph.

If all the relations of earthly association should come up before us in heaven, there must, of necessity, be confessions to each other there, with forgiveness, and all the chain of sorrow for sin, and mourning over imperfection there as here.

But such a state of things can not exist, and necessarily the memory of the senses must go out at death, while the memory of the attributes remain in undying idealization.

Of what benefit could it be to the soul to remember all the minor transactions of physical life? We answer, none at all, only as those acts shape our destiny in eternal things. Abraham desired the rich man to remember what a multitude of earthly blessings he had enjoyed, and for the avarice of his wicked heart he now justly suffered, while Lazarus, whose wounds attracted no notice from him, was now happy. But this irreligious transaction on his part had been the cause of his disorganized attributes, and upon whose memory these crimes had been stereotyped.

*Q.* What good, then, can come of repentance or sorrow for sin?

*A.* Repentance is the prompting of our attributes by the Holy Spirit.

In this relation it is obvious that we have no more right to restrain true repentance than we have to commit suicide; for one must result in the withdrawal of the soul's only hope, while the other is the death of the senses.

Repentance unto life is as much a gift of God as is the offering up of the bleeding Jesus, and the restraining of the first forestalls the application of the blood of the second.

*Repent* is a command of God, and not only so, but it is the urging of the Holy Ghost upon our attributes, the necessity of a compliance with the terms of the Gospel, and is prompted as much for our good as hunger prompts us for the good of the body.

We may reject either of these promptings, but must abide by the consequences; if of hunger, it will soon loose its prompting, and we shall die; if of the seven attributes of God, the like fatal consequences follow.

Hence scriptural anthropology teaches us the necessity of complying with the prompting of the Spirit, for it is sent out "into the world to reprove the world of sin, of righteousness, and a judgment."

*Q.* What, then, is faith?

*A.* Faith in God is the acceptance, by our attributes, of the intercession of the attributes of God. When we accept their teaching we will be led by them, "and as many as are led by the Spirit of God they are the sons of God."

The evidence of faith in us is the willingness we exhibit of using the means God has placed in our reach for our salvation. It would be no evidence of our belief in the power of the earth to reproduce a hundred-fold from the grain we sow, if we should sow that seed in the ocean. But if we faithfully prepare the ground, and then sow and cover the seed, the evidence of our faith is apparent. "Sow to yourselves in righteousness," or use the means that God has placed within us, and around us, and before us; and then we truly have "repentance unto life that needeth not to be repented of," and the faith that takes no denial.

*Q.* By what method of anthropology can this scriptural statement be explained, "I will dwell in them?" "Know ye not that ye are the temple of God, and that the Spirit of God dwelleth in you?"—1 Cor. iii: 16.

*A.* If our attributes connect with and govern our senses, then our attributes dwell in our senses.

If the attributes of God connect with and govern our attributes, then God dwelleth in us. This idea seems to be prominent in Scripture: that the Spirit of God, by faith, so connects itself with our spirit as to direct, guide, and lead us. The Lord's prayer supposes this power to be from God ("lead us not into temptation, but deliver us from evil"), and that by prayer in faith this divine power will prevail for us.

*Q.* But does this connection control our action without our consent?

*A.* By no means; for when God's attribute, Love, connects with ours, we are more than willing. We adore the God of grace, and only pray to be led by the Spirit continually.

*Q.* What part, then, of our salvation, is contingent upon good works?

*A.* Good works in us do not exist in a separate relation more than do the senses and attributes. God has indissolubly united the twain; we can not do an act of the senses independently of the attributes, nor can we do a good work independently of the Holy Ghost or seven attributes of God. They connect with ours when the good act is accomplished, and if they do not, the act is sinful; even prayer to God could have no effect without their intercession and assistance. "Without me," said Jesus, and he was the embodiment of the Holy Ghost, "ye can do nothing." "I in you, and you in me. As the branch can not bear fruit except it abide in the vine; no more can ye, except ye abide in me." Our works, then, are made *good works* if we are led by the Spirit, "for if any man have not the Spirit of Christ he is none of his." Good works is God working in us by not only our consent, but by our most hearty co-operation.

"We love him, because he first loved us." We receive him, and he gives us "power to become the sons of God."

We will now introduce to our readers Prof. M. Rochet, of the Paris Anthropological Society, who has brought to view *five* different characteristic and elementary principles of man:

(1.) "*Man examined externally as regards form.* There is not a single feature in the human face which, examined from an artistic stand-point, does not constitute a character of beauty and nobility foreign to the animal. Man alone has an expressive and intelligent physiognomy. This applies also to the body. The erect stature, the perfection of the hand and of the foot, are characters of the same value. The hand is especially characteristic. Man alone has a true hand, he alone uses the admirable instrument for creating the thousands of industrial and artistic masterpieces.

(2.) *"The internal, sensitive, and moral man.* Man is endowed with a moral sensibility altogether unknown to the rest of organized beings. He loves or believes in things animals have no notion of. He possesses the feeling of the beautiful, the ugly, of wrong, and right. He alone is conscious of the morality or immorality of his acts. Man alone has an idea of God, and is attached to him by feeling and intelligence. Man alone, of all animated beings, forms a complete family. The animal takes life as it finds it, without any way modifying it.

"Man, on the contrary, takes life according to his will, for all the regions of the globe form part of his domain, and he can in a thousand ways vary the mode of his existence.

(3.) *"Man considered as an active being.* Even in satisfying his lowest appetite man differs from animals. He alone prepares his food by cooking it. Man alone provides himself with clothes to protect himself from the elements. When we treat of industry, instruments, and arms, the difference is enormous. Man possesses another important character—intelligent speech.

(4.) "*Man considered as an intelligent being, or the faculty of the human mind.* Animals possess a memory, but in them it is a faculty founded only on wants, personal utility, without any true notion of the objects; while in man, who, by means of language, conveys ideas, the facts of memory acquire great value.

"The animal possesses nothing analogous to the free will of man. The animal entirely wants imagination, which for man is the charm of life, the consolation and remedy for his evils.

(5.) "*Man considered as a collective being.* The animal constantly loses territory which man gains. The day will arrive when there will be on the surface of the earth only such animals as are useful to man. Animality has no principle of cohesion in its members. Every animal lives only for itself. But men group together and combine their forces, and, although individually weak, they acquire an immense power. Man transmits his works and his conquests to his descendants. The animal perishes and leaves only his skeleton behind."

Now the reader will look at this latest notion of anthropology from a French stand-point, and involuntarily ask the question, where does moral responsibility unite with physical action, and how? But in answer he will have the extreme satisfaction of learning that it is so, because it is. Nothing more.

This Mr. M. Rochet attributes to the man on account of "his intelligent physiognomy." He, as nearly all modern anthropologists do, accounts for man's supremacy on the supposition that his brain is higher in reference to his organism than in other animals, and this makes him wiser. That his *hand* is very peculiar, and this also ranks him above other animals. But this singular formation of the hand, as a work of creation, is no more marvelous than the creation of the feathers of the peacock or bird of paradise.

We can draw no conclusions in regard to man's formation outwardly that can not conclusively be met by equally strange formations in other species; and the proneness that seems to exist in the minds of writers on the science of anthropology to either bring man up from the trilobite to his present development, or place him in a regular scale of gradation, is worthy of careful consideration. Let us take the cunning fox, for illustration, and remark in reference to his brain's location, in order to compare his sagacity or cunning with other animals, and we see the folly of this showing. The crocodile, even, has so much prescience or brain work as to completely surprise his prey, and in an instant roll his apparently lifeless form with his victim into the stream, where he devours him at once. Is it the location of the brain that gives him this pre-eminence? Surely not.

The lion, the panther, the hyena, and many of the fowls of heaven waylay their victims and spring upon them as the cat catches the unwary mouse; and is it the location of the brain or the spinal column that gives this notoriety?

Man's hand has not the sense of sight, nor can a single object be discovered by it; it has the sense of feeling, not of sight. So the beast has certain powers, and the locality of these powers have no more to do with the sovereignty or sluggishness of the animal than the sense of sight. Because it is located in the head instead of the hand, does it become nobler and thereby more God-like?

Mr. M. Rochet's second position is a simple announcement of man as a moral being. But why is he a moral being? Is this on account of his having more brains than the gorilla? No, he does not advert to brains or the spinal column, but it is so, and so it is.

"He is endowed with moral sensibility." If the formation of his hand made him physically superior to other animals, who knows but the construction of that perfect and necessary appendage to the human organism may not have been the *ne plus* of the entire phenomena? that is, man's moral sensibility arises from the construction of the hand! What an idea. And still this idea synchronizes perfectly with the other, *i. e.*, his cerebrum being higher up in the organism gives him supremacy over other animals, therefore the formation of his hand might give him a *moral* supremacy. How strange! "The animal takes life as he finds It," so we are obliged to take it. How could a cripple modify his life? How can we avoid old age, the dimness of vision, or the decrepitude of years? Man can not pass his boundary more than the animal, and shall we argue, from this, his superior nature? If man did not possess the attributes of Deity, and if those moral powers did not anastomose with his senses, he would be without moral sensibility as much as the ape or monkey. Neither his brain, or the formation of the spinal column, the hand, or the foot, could make him a moral being.

His third idea is, that man cooks his own dinner and this makes him superior to the animal. If this labor and necessity is his inheritance, does it not rather prove his inferiority? The animal kingdom content themselves, at least some varieties of animated nature are contented, with the grass, the herb, the fruit, as nature produces it; but some avail themselves of the flesh of others, and take the life even of their own species. This is the way they serve up their meals. The hawk pierces the chicken with his talons and thus takes life, then flies to a place of safety and feasts upon his forage; man cuts off the chicken's head, cooks it, and thus makes out his meal. Which has the greatest reason to glory over his condition, the hawk or the man?

"Man alone provides himself with clothes," and thereby Mr. Rochet thinks his rank superior to the beast; but let us see if this rendering is better than the other. The sheep is clothed for winter without labor or care; the man must clip the wool, card, spin, and weave it, nay, more, he must have it cut in pieces and sewed together, in order to clothe his destitute nature. What a calamity to be born without a rag of clothing, and for years unable to provide the least food or raiment, when the little quail, a week old, can fly, and is clothed against the storm and cold. What a superiority, this! Helplessness, poverty, nakedness, an evidence of superiority! This is nature's anthropology.

Mr. M. Rochet's fourth idea is that, although the beast possesses a memory, it does not subserve so good an end as the faculty of memory in man.

Let us see. The cow remembers where she hides her calf, and that, too, as tenacious and as valuable to her as it would be to us to remember the town of our nativity. The little ground-bird remembers the spot where her young fledglings are secreted, and, fearing you may find it, also, pretends that one of her wings are broken, and while you chase her as she flops along in apparent agony, you are the fool, she the bird of wisdom; she deceives the greatest deceiver, and thereby shows her superiority. Here memory, as well as wisdom, is apparent in the bird.

What an ambiguity of distinction this condition of memory affords. But man, indeed, has *two* memories, the one submissive to the other, and the higher power enables him to train all the senses; and even the memory of the senses are as a child to a teacher to him. He can say to the lower class of memory, when going to sleep, remember twelve o'clock, then wake me at that particular hour; and the lower memory (the memory of the senses) will obey the higher memory (the memory of the attributes) to the very letter; and through the lower memory bring up to his higher nature the external solution of this most complex problem. But the beast, having but one memory, can not be a mathematician or a linguist, an arithmetician or a grammarian.

"The animal possesses nothing analogous to the free will of man." Why? Mr. Rochet says "the animal entirely wants imagination."

What else than imagination prompts the muskrat to build his grassy hut? what else prompts the squirrel to fill his tree with the choice, delicious nuts he gathers during the autumnal season, sometimes even taking off the shuck and storing up the real berry? Was there no imagination, no thought, no expectation? We have shown that the animal possesses five senses, and their combination to be instinct, will, memory, sagacity. No religious meditation, no moral or scientific ideational consciousness; in short, no judgment sense. But the beast thinks, and hence dreams, and has all the associations of mental power that spring from five senses, while we posses the seven.

But Mr. Rochet finishes up his five *qualitative* characters by

(5.) *Man considered as a collective being.* "The animal constantly loses territory which man gains."

Now, is it not a fact that many animals exist because man has cleared off the forests so that they can exist? There may be some animals whose meat or skin is valuable to us, and whose species waste away before the progress of man, but innumerable other species exist, to the great annoyance of the nobler work of God.

"But men group together and combine their forces, and though individually weak, they acquire an immense power." So do sheep, so do wolves, so do many of the animal species; and as far as their senses extend are potent and powerful. Is this, then, a fair, clear, and self-evident solution of the problem of man's superiority to other animals? We think not. The dividing lines are not artistically drawn, nor is the difference between the man and the animal plainly shown.

But, taking the Biblical view of this wonderful relation, we are most happily relieved by learning that man's superiority over all animated nature consists physically in his possessing two more senses than the animal, and, connected with these earth-born powers, he intuitively inherits the seven moral faculties, the connection of which, in the inmost centers of his occult nature, place him on the scale of intelligences, corresponding to the dignity and the lofty aspirations of his progressive intellectuality.

Take away this connection, and his relation to the ape, the beast; involves confusion and ambiguity.

Then why should we attempt to develop the nobleness of the human by endeavoring to unite him to the beast in the scale of progression, and ignore the divine, the rational, the revealed?

We have now shown the symmetries and coincidences of the Mystic Numbers of the Word, and have found a remarkable identity, and, to all human appearances, a design in the frequency of the numeral seven, as above presented to the reader.

The principle is plain, simple, and easy to be comprehended; is not confused, explains the harmony of depravity with grace; shows God's love, and Christ's love, and the love of the Holy Ghost, to be co-equal and co-effective in man's salvation. No redundancy, no contradiction, no opposition to science, but harmonious as it is complete.

This number has often suggested perplexing suppositions to the minds of careful readers to observe the subtle vein of the mysterious *seven*, intercommunicating with every system of law or dispensation of grace throughout the Holy Scriptures, but why should it, if the *Seven* fashioned it all in unison with infinite and uncreated wisdom? Here, then, is the key to the Divine laboratory, and by it we are invited to enter and survey the matchless beauty of this amazing superstructure.

And now, gentle reader, we may not have asked all the questions you might have asked, but we have propounded as many as our limits would admit, and we think sufficient to establish in the mind of any unprejudiced reader the harmony of the Mystic Numbers of the Word with creation in all its geological relations, the elements in their primitive association, the creation of man, and his wonderfully and fearfully made organism, his relation to God and his accountability, his first dispensation, and the dominion he held over all animal life.

Your attention has been also directed to the great Redeemer in his archetypal and human relations, to his temptations and his victory, to the condition we occupy as sinners, so far as the senses are concerned, while through the attributes we are justified and made perfect by the operation of the Holy Spirit. We, therefore, most earnestly invite you to consider these powers in their connection, nor doubt the existence of the Seven Spirits or attributes of God, nor refuse their intercession while they stand at the door and knock.

And may this *mystic number*, the numeral seven, be like the candlestick with its seven lamps, irrepressible and unextinguishable, filling your attributes with light, life, holiness, justice, mercy, truth, and love, accomplishing in you the harmony that the blessed of God will enjoy throughout the unending cycles of eternity.

# CHAPTER XXIII.

GEOLOGICAL STRATA—OTHERS' VIEWS OF CREATION—ADAM THREE MONTHS OLD WHEN HE FELL—MAN'S MORTGAGE CLOSED BEFORE THE FIRST NOTE WAS DUE—PRESCIENCE—PREMONITION—THE ORIGIN OF LANGUAGE—MAN NOBLER THAN ANGELS—LIGHT TO THE SOUL—NEWTON'S COMET—CLARK'S IDEA OF LIGHT—THE SIDEREAL CANOPY—HEAVENLY PALACE—PORTALS OF GLORY—LIFE—MILLER'S GEOLOGY—MILLER'S MILLENNIUM—PREVIOUS ARGUMENTS CONSIDERED—CONCLUSION.

E now invite the reader to contrast with the foregoing pages some of the opinions copiously and elaborately discussed by scholars, linguists, and geologists.

The remarks of the learned Dr. Kitto, on the subject of creation, are worthy of careful perusal, as the doctor gives the opinions of many distinguished writers and scholars.

It is very singular that nearly all the writers on creation begin the investigation by taking

(365)

the earth to have been a heated mass of matter, and for a period, at least, too much heated for vegetation, and then in their conclusions stratify the earth into regular geological layers. Thus, I cast a cannon ball, I wait twenty-four hours for it to cool, and then make an incision into the ball an inch in depth, and then commence to calculate how the whole ball was made. Every little particle of metal differing from some other, I call a geological layer, and that these layers bear data as to how long they existed before the next layer was formed, forgetting that the whole ball, by my own showing, was cast at once.

It may appear a little uncouth to the reader that the world's history presents us with only three distinct periods or cycles, and upon the data of which, all that relates to time and eternity has its origin; and in reference to these *times* or dispensations we derive all our knowledge from the combined testimony of the Bible, the rocks, and the numbers. But strange as it may appear, these three beacon lights are amazingly susceptible of producing excitement, and have often startled theological divines from their beaten track to the wildest conjectures.

These three great head-lights, when taken separately or united, naturally become a polestar to all theological mariners who attempt to cross this foaming, seething ocean of formative matter, and explore the deeps of geology, theology, or science.

The first of these dispensations to which man belongs is the primitive or primeval, and suggests an investigation as to the probable duration of his innocence, his business and authority during that period, and the probability of his filling his mission.

The great and scholarly GOODRICH locates Adam in the first start in the garden of Eden. A ruler of the world, blessed of God, and commanded to multiply and replenish the earth and subdue it; in a garden, childless, and, so far as this great earth was concerned, dominionless for about three months, and then he is driven out of Eden without having even entered upon his great mission of peopling the earth with a sinless race.

This must appear a little strange, that an infinite and all-wise Creator should change his mind so quickly after he had bade them multiply and fill up the earth with sinless beings, to close the mortgage before the first note was due, and reverse the whole order in chaotic confusion.

Would it not appear inexplicable that the whole experiment, so to speak, of man's dominion, his happy relation to the pure world over which he was placed, and the posterity of pure and holy beings he might have brought into existence, and who were essential to the earth's cultivation and the Creator's glory; that then, before the first bud had blossomed, or the first fruits gathered, this lord of creation should be stricken down by the seductive serpent, and the entire dispensation reversed and destroyed in its incipiency? He who was made after the image of God blighted ere a purpose had been unfolded or a trophy gained! Impossible. Now turn from this to the great and grand purpose of eternal love, and think of the untold millions of Adam's unfallen posterity, translated through free grace by the application of the atonement, and we have an event worthy the great Jehovah.

That man was created or formed with a physical, mental, and spiritual nature, few doubt or deny; and that he was made after the "image of God" is also freely admitted; but that his physical formation had any resemblance to the shape or form of Deity, nearly all, as by common consent, doubt or oppose. They argue that his *moral nature* was thus created, and in this alone is the image of God. I should like to have some one, who is well versed in metaphysics, show the abstract, *moral image* of a being "without body or parts."

Does not this idea convey a similar impression as it would for one to tell you that the sun, moon, and stars were made after the moral image of the atmosphere? A substance, a man, made after the image of mental qualities, which have no existence in themselves, only in association with attributes and senses!

The Mosaic account expressly declares that "in the image of God created he them," and the sacred record is all that is in any manner reliable in this direction.

Having, then, the prophetic lights of four thousand years, and all the revealed light of nearly two thousand years more, we need not go astray in our conceptions of the eternal personality of Christ, after whose image God formed the man he had created, for in the triune likeness of God he is revealed. Let us make man in our image and likeness. How plain!

Now, if the revealed Saviour was the same that was "slain from the foundation of the world," the same "I am that I am" that dwelt with the eternal Father "before the world was;" if our Immanuel thus existed, is there any remarkable difficulty in our having been created in his image, in the likeness of his person, who promised to assume the humanity of man?

That the "angel Jehovah," by many and various names revealed as Lord of hosts, King of kings, as the Word, the Lamb of God, the Rock of ages, the First and the Last, the Wonderful, etc., existed from eternity, and in whose wonderful person all the divine attributes are revealed, and in whom "dwelleth all the fullness of the Godhead bodily," that he forever lives and forever hath lived, who can deny?

And, farther, that the Holy Spirit, with the Father and Son, eternally co-existed, is seen even by the commonest mind in the substances we every day handle.

What solid exists only in a triplicity, and this three in one, easily understood?

Take for illustration a pebble, or a marble: the first we see, or feel, is substance or matter; we hold it above our heads and we see in it ponderability—it falls rapidly to the floor when left in the free air; we then see that something holds it together with great tenacity; this we call cohesion. *Substance, ponderability, cohesion;* three in one and but one. Take man, created in the image of God, for an illustration: here is the human form, the senses and attributes, and the invisible spirit—three in one.

This distinguishes man from the beast, and recognizes him a triune being, body, mind, soul. Hence he is the embodiment of the mystic three, the same as his Creator, or in his "image and likeness."

But man possessed an intelligence unparalleled in all the Creator's work. This whole earth was the field of his operations; the trees of the forest were his, the fowls of the air were his, the beasts of the field and the monsters of the deep intuitively obeyed his call. He named them, and knew them, and governed them.

In order to do this he must have comparatively possessed omnipresence, together with mental power, foreknowledge, and wisdom. Even in man's present corruptible state he often has a flash of prescience, we call it *premonition,* warning him mentally of danger, and this, too, when in the stillness of repose, "warned of God in a dream." To this the original man must have possessed a perfect and complete knowledge of the arts and sciences, of architecture and music, of language and law.

He was thence protected against danger to such an extent as to render him impassive, nor could his person be harmed or deformed by any casualty or accident, for accidents, to such a being, could not occur. The reader may ask if Adam could foresee coming events and avoid them, why did he not foresee the power of the seductive serpent and avoid that also?

I answer, that being a moral evil, and he, having no knowledge of sin, being pure and holy, that evil did not exist till he sinned, therefore he could not foresee that which did not exist. The tree was there, but that tree was not a sinner; the command he knew, but the law was holy, just, and good; hence in the law there existed no moral evil.

Still, added to all this, the primitive man possessed the power to reproduce a being with all the faculties of mind and body possessed by himself, without diminishing an atom of his own glory and greatness, like his Creator; his children were his glory and his crown of rejoicing. .

How grand the conclusion! A race still higher than the angels in God's purpose, decked with the glory of dominion, possessing in their organic relations to him and in their advancement in physical and mental progress a power to reproduce for God his legitimate offspring, and before whom all animated life bowed in humble submission!

Earth, just emerged from its chaotic, incoherent state, needed the master-work of some mighty intelligence to arrange its order and subdue its irregularities; and to man God had committed this vast work, and as he had fashioned him with this end in view, he was abundantly sufficient to the responsibility.

And above and beyond all terrestrial considerations, he inherited the seven attributes of God. These faculties constituted his psychical nature, and immediately connected him with creative conceptions and a perfect knowledge of language. The Seven Spirits of God are the idioms of all language, as seen when the Holy Spirit fell upon the disciples at the day of Pentecost.

These constitute the human mind; these are light to the understanding, life to the soul, holiness to the actions, justice to another, mercy to the sufferer, love to God, and truth to the Spirit.

These the first pair inherited of God, as we inherit them of our parents; and if the absurd doctrine of man's total depravity was correct, it would be the greatest curse we could inherit; but if the position taken in this work be true, how glorious an inheritance! an open door to the realms of glory, and we invited to enter! Hence all are commanded to pray to God, and to say,

"Our Father, who art in heaven." Angels could not share in this transcendent glory, from the fact that to them the original springs were pent up and sealed. They possessed the attributes and the spiritual form, but the power of reproduction was to them a mystery, a portentious problem; they could not comprehend tenderness, compassion, forbearance, affection, hope, such as exist in human associations, for they were the servants of God while man was his affectionate child.

Invention, construction, or intellectual progression, to angels were unmeaning words, but to man this was his glory and crown of rejoicing. And then his partner became the object of his special love, his children the glory of his tenderness, the spring of affection, the hope of consolation, and the photographic resemblance of himself.

The attributes he inherited were pure and holy, nor could there be a discordant note or an unassimilating property, each being in perfect harmony with all. In the highest glory of their relationship to God, in the noblest rights of children to counsel and converse with their author, with spiritual vision to behold their archetypal Lord, and emotional natures to praise him, their glory was immeasurably complete.

It was all beautiful, glorious, and supremely good, both to man and to God. His labors, too, were in perfect accordance with the powers he possessed, for his Creator had fashioned him expressly to control and subdue the earth. Hence, in his very nature, he possessed the will and expectancy of dominion.

His first work was to name all the "cattle upon a thousand hills," and the fowls and creeping things of the earth, "and whatsoever Adam called every living creature that was the name thereof." Thus, illuminated with the light of God, and walking in this light, his glory was second to no other creature of God's sentient intelligences.

With this light man became the moral agent, or actor, under the Divine superintendence, for he walked under the all-supreme light of Jehovah and was to him accountable, because, by the laws of paternity, it was his joyful privilege to obey God. If in man there is light, in God this attribute must be incomprehensibly supreme. Just to contemplate the vast surroundings of the earth we inhabit, and then the immense distances that the rays of light must have traveled to reach the earth, and not this earth only, but other orbs and planets inconceivably far off; how overwhelmingly great, then, must the light of God appear when we realize that "he fills, he bounds," and illuminates them all by created and uncreated light!

And then to know that the center from which we draw our conclusions is only a speck in the indistinct outline of the vast center of centers, that this solar system is only one of the myriad of systems that revolve around the grand center of the Arch-architect of the universe, and we feel the nothingness of terrestrial things, and then let us remember that he who governs, controls, and illuminates them all has purposes infinitely too sublime to communicate to transient intelligences. How inexhaustive and eternal is the light of his throne, like the diamond that sparkles on for ages, yet loses nothing of its entity, so the light of God is ever progressive, incomprehensible, and glorious; and that, as he formed the earth, with all its wonderful properties, the existence of which has eluded the keenest search of mortals, and only little by little, ray after ray, has the light of science opened its treasures to the world, may we not still expect to be often astonished at developments yet concealed in the secret vault of earth's laboratory.

But there are other eyes beside the human, and other intelligences beside those, may be, that even revelation has announced; other faculties to be illuminated, which multitude can not be numbered, whose glory transcends the glory of angels as to man revealed—millions on millions, an innumerable company who derive all their light from God, and his throne is the grand repository of light unapproachable, alike to them and us, his care-worn children.

The first period of the labors of the attributes

of God began with light, "And God said, Let there be light."

The earth, as is supposed by many geologists, had just emerged, or was now emerging, from its heated chaotic state, cooling off but shrouded in vapor, when the voice of God was heard, "Let there be light."

This theory, adopted by nearly all the learned of modern ages, does not, I think, quite agree with the holy record; it says that "darkness was upon the face of the deep." It does not mention vapor, or fog, or steam—simply "deep;" the earth covered with water, a portion of it to be commingled in a substance called the firmament, and so receded and retired as to leave the dry land.

Sir Isaac Newton's comet, according to his calculation, which made its appearance in 1680, must have imbibed heat enough from the sun, if it had been iron, to have become two thousand times hotter than red-hot iron, and that our globe might once have been as hot as that, and in such a condition must have required fifty thousand years in cooling off.

I should think this condition of things would be much in the way of the six-geological-layer system, or the six days' work of creation; for neither Sir Isaac Newton nor Mr. Hugh Miller, who adopts the theory, could positively tell how deep the sub-soil plow of creation must have descended on the first day to locate the matter of the Azoic period, and where the second strata of the old red sand-stone came from; also the third Carboniferous deposit—where was this deposit while the earth was "wrapped in a mantle of steam" and cooling?

Where were the permian and triassic substances deposited while the thousands of years rolled on in the deposit of the preceding strata, and also of the Oolitic and Tertiary periods.

How strange that animal fossil should be unknown where the Azoic period is located, since it is far below the reach of vegetation; but, alas, by dredging the ocean animal life even is found upon its hidden bed, three miles below the surface, and this is a mile or so below the old red sand-stone, or even the Azoic.

But animal life could not exist without light, or, if it could, there would be no use for eyes to see by the light, and as the generally received opinion is that all light proceeds from the sun, and the sun can never shine to the bottom of the ocean, no little marvel exists in reference to these newly-discovered creeping things.

Dr. Adam Clark thinks light and heat are intimately associated, for, says he, "The original word implies caloric, by the use of which all animal life is produced," hence where light can not go caloric can not go, and hence there must be a miracle about these submarine shell fish. But, as we have shown that light is in combination with electricity, and that where electricity is seen light exists, and where these abide life may appear; we shall leave the farther investigation of this attribute and its creative combinations, only remarking that the occult seven, by which Mr. Hugh Miller hoped to satisfy the curious as to the days of Creation, is not very happily applied to the earth's strata; and of the Rev. Mr. Miller, who labored so long and arduous to apply the seven to the duration of time, and bring about a fanciful millenium into which glorious state we all should have long ago entered, was very unhappily and erroneously conceived. But, allowing this attribute to have accomplished all that relates to illumination, we have a tangible foundation on which to predicate the first day's labor.

The second day's labor, performed by the attribute, justice, was no less extensive and wonderful. The relations of the first day's work to the atmosphere and all the wonderful phenomena of its construction, its life-power, its cadences, its universality, and its properties, all declare to the exceeding grandeur and sublimity of this second day's labor.

Then, again, outside of matter and the laws of matter, this attribute guards the eternal throne and mirrors itself in the humbler walks of terrestrial life, in ten thousand kindred associations, and on, till the whole triumphant Church assemble in the palace of God to celebrate the glory and justice of him whose dominion is an everlasting dominion and whose throne is a throne of grace.

This attribute drew from the Divine commandment his burnished sword and smote the senses that dared to taste of that forbidden fruit, but sheathed it again in the bosom of the archetypal Redeemer.

How delightful to contemplate the grandeur of this second day's work, devoted, as it first appeared, in the preparation of the firmament for man, and now pleading of a sacrifice so ordered that he can be satisfied and the guilty pardoned, purified, and restored. The Scriptures assert that "the angel of the Lord encampeth round about them that fear him." This, then, is the angel Jehovah, the attribute, justice.

We also read that the angels are our ministering Spirits—"the ministration of the Spirit." These Seven Spirits of God are thus constantly engaged; not the dual spirits of created workmanship, but the Seven Spirits of God, without whose intercession and advocacy we can never "see the kingdom."

We somehow have an attractive affinity or desire to lean on some other arm than on the great God, and fancy to ourselves that some disembodied spirit watches over us and not the Spirit of God; hence we sing, and perchance believe, while we sing, that simple angels "guard us while we sleep, till morning light appears," when Jesus has said, the "I am that I am," hath declared, "I will never leave thee nor forsake thee." How much safer to trust him who has been tried in the furnace of affliction, who is touched with sympathy toward us, for "he has borne our sorrows," than to leave him, and ask an angel, a saint, or the Virgin Mary (all of whom he upholds) to watch over the interests of our immortal natures. No, indeed; the angels we need are the Seven Spirits of God. These intercessors indite our prayers, inspire our songs, and sanctify our souls; hence justice loves the acceptable offering, "a broken and contrite spirit," and encamps around that soul, illuminating the dark valley with the watch-fire and beacon-light of his glittering sword. But the angels in heaven are also in delightful harmony with the plan of redemption.

Nor of a less wonderful and glorious nature are the labors of the third day.

Holiness, next in association with the attribute whose formative power had arranged the firmament to the light, now begins his labor upon the earth in the endless variety of fruits and flowers, and herbs and grasses, of shrubs and forest trees, and this, too, with direct reference to the wants of the creature, man.

How wide the range of his operations, how wonderful the beauty, how admirable the aroma, how salutary the fruit! Shaded groves, beautiful lawns, delightful and delicious fruits, and evergreen forests, burst upon the vision from shore to shore, and from pole to pole.

Nor again was the labor of truth less wonderful—the actor of the fourth day.

He fixed the unalterable laws of attraction and repulsion; not only for our orb, but for all worlds and systems of worlds throughout the boundless canopy. He drew the plan of their motions, he weighed them and balanced them in mid-heaven, he mirrored their reflex light upon all terrestrial objects, he stretched out the heavens and bounded the orbits of the comets and constellations, he moved the pendulum of time and set its dial-plate in the purposes of the eternal procedure, and thus he performed the labors of the fourth day, majestic and sublimely grand.

Life. What is life? It is a condition, it pervades the animated clay, but seems most tenaciously located in the brain, the heart, the blood, the air. Remove from man any of the last three, and you remove his life as soon.

It seems in its spiritual associations to be a spark from the diamond of life eternal—the attribute, life.

The fifth day's labor was the work of his hand, applied to the waters and the air. How inconceivably vast, how amazingly various the formations, how perfectly adapted to the elements for which they were created.

Pope very beautifully remarks:

> "See, through this air, this ocean, and this earth,
> All matter quick, and bursting into birth;
> Above, how high progressive life may go,
> Around, how wide, how deep, extend below,
> Vast chain of being, which from God began,
> Nature, ethereal, human, angel, man,
> Beast, bird, fish, insect, what no eye can see,
> No glass can reach, from finite up to thee."

But the life attribute of God is our monitor of immortality, our earnest of that inheritance, incorruptible, and glorious, the unfolding of a life of undying ideality.

The sixth day's labor, mercy's work, was ennobled by an approach to man in the scale of being. The creeping things, and then the beasts, and then the man. How wide the domain of life in this direction, how vast this day's work! Contemplate it from whatever standpoint we choose, it is vast.

Here we have traced briefly the creative power of God, as seen in the Seven Spirits, appropriately so named, for each of them possesses alike the power of creative wisdom.

Love being the central attribute, harmonized all their work, and now all unite to crown the evening of the sixth day with the glory that only God's image can develop; a being around whose destiny, for myriad ages, Jehovah had purposed to throw his mantle, and for whose transcendent honor he constructed and fashioned a world, and then made a sacrifice of restoration alike mysterious and overwhelmingly magnanimous. Love's rest, bright morning of ineffible delight, the solace of a soul born to the royalty of heaven! What rest so sweet as thine, O holy Dove! Sweet messenger of the Father of spirits, thou ever constant intercessor of the child of God!

From the caresses of thy gentle care we have passed through the sea of troubled waters like a babe in its mother's embrace. Thou hast been a cordial to our fears, a balm to our wounded spirit, a charmer when the drear winter of life shook our whitened locks with dismay. Ah, truly, God is love.

And may you, dear reader, stranger to the writer though you may ever be on the shores of time; may you share that love and secure that passport over the billows of death, and reach that celestial metropolis, pass through the gates of the New Jerusalem, and behold the myriad faces there who bear the image of God, and may I be one of the number!

## CONCLUSION.

It has long been a question of more than ordinary perplexity to solve the relations that exist in man, when we consider the fact of his *justification* and *sanctification*.

*Q.* How can one under condemnation of death be justified?

*A.* There can be no justification of the fallen senses, consequently this act of grace does not apply to them, but as they must die, and cease to be, it matters but little; for justification relates solely and positively to the attributes. To these God applies his own, and in that inosculation, by which his Spirit intercommunicates with ours, we are justified; but this justification is alone in and through the Spirit's application of the archetypal blood of the eternal Christ to the immortal soul through the attributes. These, permeating the soul as the senses do the body, convey to its entire spiritual organism the efficacy of the atonement, and liberate it from the law of sin and death. Hence, "if any man is in Christ Jesus, he is a new creature; old things are passed away, and, behold, all things are become new."

Our attributes, then, coalesce with his, and as he liveth so shall we live, and as he hath become the end of the law to every one that believeth, so the law given to restrain our fallen senses ends in Christ, who has fulfilled the law and made it honorable.

*Q.* But does not sanctification imply the same thing as does justification?

*A.* Not the same, for sanctification is a progressive, conquering work, and is designed to enable us to lay up our treasure in heaven by "working out our own salvation" in Christ, though, it often appears to us, through "fear and trembling." Its operation, as we have shown, is by the application of the single attribute of God's love, sealing itself to ours. Sealed by the Spirit. Now, if all the divine attributes should unite with ours by positive contact, we should be infallible, which illy comports with probation or stewardship.

The Apostles received this gift on the day of Pentecost, which inspired them to preach in all languages without study; but this flood of light and knowledge could not remain; as the grand object of Christian warfare must cease to exist if the fallen senses were rendered totally inoperative; hence even this gift, or the union of all the attributes of their nature, with the Seven Spirits of God, could not be a permanent and ever-abiding monitor, because this must forestal progressive sanctification. Hence, though highly endowed, the Apostles were not infallible after this baptismal glory had passed away.

Our attributes can not regenerate the senses, they can control them when in communion with the Spirit, and are also largely aided by religious education, but at best they are frail and must die.

*Q.* What, then, is sanctification?

*A.* The term sanctification is used in Scripture to denote the *setting apart* of certain things for holy purposes, and also that of *cleansing* or *making holy*.

"For their sakes I sanctify (set apart) myself, that they also might be sanctified (made pure) through the truth."—John xvii: 19.

The truth of God, treasured up in the attributes, must, in a measure, overcome the frailty of the senses, and the more we live in the love of God the more will that love be shed abroad in our hearts.

So, then, sanctification is the putting out at usury of the one, five, or ten talents; and its progressive success over our fallen senses, the crown of glory and honor that the saints inherit, when Christ declares, "Well done, good and faithful servant; I will make thee ruler over ten cities; enter thou into the joy of thy Lord."

Justification clears the property of all debt, but sanctification improves it and beautifies it; justification "pays all the debt I owe," while sanctification makes us co-workers in the great plan of redemption; justification is the end of the law so far as our release is concerned, but sanctification honors the law already satisfied. Thus the plan of salvation is most beautifully adjusted to the happy progress of the soul in all its pilgrimage, rendering labor for God remunerative an hundred fold, both in this life and in that which is to come.

It is a cheering thought to those who believe in the Seven Spirits of God, to observe how they are mirrored in, and photographed upon, every thing we behold; as though Deity designed that mortals should search out and learn what the seven thunders uttered. "Seal up those things the seven thunders uttered, and write them not."

Here we see it in the seven conditions of this mortal body—embryo, infancy, childhood, youth, manhood, old age, the grave.

Yonder we see it in the seven prismatic colors of light; there in the seven tones of music; now again in the seven senses of man, and still nobler in the seven attributes of progressive life.

It reveals itself in the seven heads of the old red dragon, in the seven golden candlesticks, seen by the Revelator, as well as the "Seven Spirits of God."

It divides our years into fifty-two equal parts, and our weeks into seven. It enters our organism in the seven mystic properties of the air we breathe, and opens up its wonders in the seven primitive elements. It has photographed itself in the two eyes, two ears, two nostrils, and one mouth of the human head, and measures off its years by sevens. The clouds, even, are known by this rendering, and the forms assumed by the watery element inhere indeed in this septenary number.

But of the length, and breadth, and height embraced in this number, who can tell? By it we obtain the indistinct outline of God's marvelous works, but "who, by searching, can find out God?"

If we take our seven attributes, which are the seven senses to our immortal soul, and analogically associate them with the seven human senses, we can learn more of the nature of spiritual things than by any other method. Take light as an attribute and seeing as a sense, and from the latter draw out the powers of the former, and the investigation will amply reward us. The eye to us is a moral power from some cause; he, says the Saviour, "that looketh on a woman to lust after her hath already committed adultery with her in his heart." Then some power unites with our eyes that does not occupy the vision of the animal, that makes such a condition of our vision sinful. What is it, if it is not the attribute, light; given us of God, and connected with our senses and under direct responsibility to him?

Civil law can take no cognizance of such an act; in fact, to all civil jurisprudence there is no law violated by the above condition. Still our moral natures echo the sentence that thinking wrong *is* wrong, and the light that is in us tells us that the Saviour understood anthropology.

Light, then, to the eye of man, is different from any light that can fall upon the eye of the beast, hence we are forced to the conclusion that the attribute, light, fashioned the created light to the eye of the beast, but did not breathe his nature into the beast, hence the beast has no moral light; but man, inheriting this attribute, becomes morally identified with the light celestial, and his actions are amenable to that law.

It may be objected, that God's attributes could not create, govern, and control substances; but this objection can have nothing tangible, since our Saviour stilled the billowed sea by his command, and by the same voice raised to vitality the lifeless body of Lazarus. Now, there was surely something in His power of language that we do not possess, and to give to the foaming sea the sense of language and power to obey the Son of God would involve greater credulity than to suppose that the attributes of God that made the air, the sea, held those properties in their present created arrangement, and that the Son of God, through them, stilled the tempest, raised the dead, and made the blind to see. We are not in the possession of those powers that fashioned all things, but the great Redeemer held this relation to them, hence he commanded the fig-tree to die, and it died; he commanded the water to become wine, and it obeyed his voice.

Every attribute of Deity has a representative in man, for he is created after his image and must bear a relation to him.

There is something in us analogous to holiness, and as the human sense is the only outward channel to the attributes, some sense in us accords to this attribute as light does to vision. Then we ask, What is it? We say God has declared that he *smells;* then there is some attribute that unites with and governs this sense, and we have supposed it to have been holiness.

Holiness is simply a condition brought about by a perfection of moral life.

Smelling is also a condition of the sense. Now, if God smells the sweet odors of a holy assemblage, whose devotional songs and praises make his house vocal, is it not, indeed, holiness in himself that accepts this incense? and may it not accord to the sense of smell in us, whereby we are charmed by delicious odors? Thus we have rendered the connection, and have only to remark that the attribute, whatever it may be, that accords to this sense, will fill the soul with rapture when we see and enjoy the fragrance of the ambrosial trees of paradise. We can not believe that we are to be men here with seven senses, and in heaven have no faculty to correspond with faculties not only essential but universal. All of us inherit the olfactory sense.

Then, again, *taste* is a sense we all inherit, and must have an analogy in some one of the attributes.

We have associated with this sense the attribute, justice, because a just and holy law emanated from God in reference to this sense, and, as the attribute, justice, is united with and controls this sense, God could impose a law of restraint upon that sense and declare to our first parents, "Thou shalt not eat of it."

Thus to man only taste had a moral condition, and this condition existed because the attribute, justice, had power over and controlled the sense.

Hence justice we have associated as connecting with the sense of taste, and will to the soul become analogous to that human sense, and forever abide in undying life.

The sense of *hearing*, we believe, to inhere in some attribute which controls it, and is analogous to it, and makes it a moral power, and to this sense we have given the attribute, mercy.

It is so natural in figurative language to speak of the "ear of mercy," that no great difficulty will be experienced in the association. Mercy is an attribute that is always on the alert, and seems so divine in its mission that we shudder to think of a monster destitute of this faculty. But if we hear the innocent cry of distress and "shut up our bowels of compassion," why is it that the ear is guilty of a moral wrong? We answer, because the attribute, mercy, to the immortal form, occupies the same relation as does the sense of hearing to the human, and they being united, the ear is morally responsible. Hence, to the ear of one whose attributes are harmonized by the Spirit, profanity is painful, and he hastes from profane lips as from the poisonous adder. Mercy, then, inosculating with the sense of hearing, gives us power to hear the messages of mercy, and appropriate the promises to us through mercy given, and stand complete in the mercy of God. We are, therefore, commanded to "take heed how we hear," for this sense becomes responsible to God through the attribute, with which it can readily anastomose. Thus, when we are filled with the sense of God's mercy, our attribute delights in corresponding acts of philanthropy and magnanimity.

We have also proven man to possess the sense of judging—the judgment sense. If this is pedantry, we trust some other writer will give this power a better name. This power we believe to be the amazing center of all the senses, controlling, defending, and directing them in all the various uses to which the Creator intended.

That this sense should have an attribute corresponding to it that held equal synarchy over the attributes seems self-evident, and as love controls and gives force and vitality to all the others, it would seem analogous to this sense. If this sense finds its nerve center in the heart, love must also find its spiritual nerve center in the heart.

This, then, makes the will-power of the senses subservient to the love-power of the attributes; hence *believing* comes from the love center of the heart of the child of God, while unbelief and all the chain of sensuous evils spring also from the heart unrenewed.

This accounts for the idea of a "new heart," a "pure heart," to those who accept the inosculation by faith of the attribute of God's love, as well as an idea of the "deceitful heart," the "carnal heart," the "unbelieving heart," so often adverted to in the book of inspiration.

Hence the judgment sense is morally responsible, from the fact that the attribute, love, has power to control it, and when thus controlled, man is exalted to excellence and honor.

Feeling is another of the seven senses, and is, indeed, morally related to objects, for we are forbidden to cherish the feeling of covetousness. Now this sense is as universal in the system as is life itself, and with which attribute it naturally unites.

To understand life, to be a mere existence, is but a shadow compared with the substance, but a garment compared to a living man. Life as an attribute pervades the life-power of the human organism, and teaches it the grand object of its being.

The life attribute of man thrills the sense of feeling with conceptions of the great first cause and of celestial associations, and often excites to the height of ecstasy in view even of approaching dissolution, and then on in the triumph of unending life and glory. The unrenewed man at times has feelings of sadness and of uncertainty in reference to his inner life, and soliloquizes in a half prayer or sigh for the fruition of eternal life, but the Christian has a title to life eternal, and when it finds vent at all it finds it through the sense of feeling.

We thence learn that the sense of feeling unites with the attribute, life, and that life gives moral character to feeling, as seen in the decalogue, restraining the feelings from adoration to idols, or even *making them* to deceive the feelings of others. This sense is adverted to in a spiritual relation, and must coalesce or unite with the attribute life, to give it a moral type or a moral responsibility.

Language is a sense of untold value to man, for he alone has this sense. No idea of a written language is communicable to beasts. Labor is as much spent in vain in trying to learn a dog, or a cat, or any other domestic animal, to talk as it would be to try to teach the foot to see.

The language sense is morally responsible, and therefore must coalesce with some attribute. Truth is the seventh and only attribute that we have not mentioned, and language is the seventh sense. If truth, then, unites with the language sense, then it would be consistent for God to command that "thou shalt not swear," "lie," "blaspheme." That this sense has a moral identity, the associations of every-day life abundantly prove. Then is it not natural to suppose the soul to have a sense, an attribute corresponding to this faculty? Derived of God, the moral nerve center of the soul accords to the supreme lawgiver the attribute truth, and applies this alone to the language sense, and this power is exerted to so control the fallen sense as not to "sin with our lips," which is the condemnation of a false tongue.

Then, when this moral power gains supremacy over the language sense, and man is a truth-telling and a truth-loving being, he ranks with angels; nay, higher, he is one of the royalty of the King immortal.

Here, then, we can discover the whole phenomena of the moral responsibility of the seven senses, and how man is held responsible to God.

If we possess these seven attributes from God, and they have become disunited, and in this condition we can not wield them or combine them in the worship of God, and if securing a perfect release from the condemnation of death, is through the Seven Spirits of God and *these* intercessors, more willing to unite with our attributes and lead them, and guide them from things earthly to realms of glory; we say, if they are more willing to help us than we are willing to help our dependent little ones, how sublime the nature of Deity! how grand and majestic the plan of redemption! Nor is this offer of the Spirit contingent upon the possession of worldly honors, wealth or beauty; it is "let him that is athirst come, and take of the waters of life freely."

The rich, the poor, the lettered, the unlettered, the great, the small, all are invited to accept of these intercessors and become the children of God.

Then these attributes of God clothe up the soul in all the purity of heaven, and teach us the accomplishments of all the society of sanctified Spirits. What a joy to come to our Father's house, to those mansions of transcendent light, perfectly educated by the Seven Spirits of God for the triumphant welcome.

What a meeting, when the Church of the *second-born* greet in the realms of cloudless glory the Church of the "first-born." Heaven has long been filled with these trophies of sinless humanity translated through the riches of free grace to the heavenly inheritance; and long have they been preparing the mansion our Saviour mentioned, for the "Church in the wilderness," and often, looking at the dial-plate of God's purposes, have inquired: How long? Now, upon "the sea of glass, mingled with fire," they wave the conqueror's palm and hail the blood-washed throng as they near the portals of glory with rapture and unbounded delight.

Music, in unison with the attributes that have left their identity in the harmonies of sound; music of sweeter tone, and of a more captivating power than ever cheered the saints in this commingled atmosphere, will echo through heaven when the first-born Church shout, "Be opened, ye everlasting doors, and let the King of glory come in."

What harmony in us, in him; with saints, with angels, all in harmony with the Seven Spirits of God and clothed with the deified human robe of "mortality swallowed up of life." "O grave, where is thy victory? O death, where is thy sting?"

The great question is, Are these seven attributes the laborers of the six days of Creation, and the seventh of rest?

Are these identical with the Seven Spirits of God, and are they intercessors for us, and can we grieve the Holy Spirit?

If this be true, that God's Spirit cares for us and is at labor for us, then it may also be true that through the same Spirit we may reach the beatific shores of infinite glory, the Elysian fields of immortal delight.

We read that "the first man, Adam, was made a living soul; the last Adam a quickening spirit." (1 Cor. xv: 45.) Then it is obvious that there was developed in our great Redeemer an outer and inner nature, the one subservient to the other, and by the latter "he quickeneth whomsoever he will." This quickening power united with humanity and "swallowed it up," or changed it into life.

Then to us this second Adam became the end

of the law through the anointing of the Spirit. That is, his death made not only our human body susceptible to the resurrection, but it liberated the flesh of every believer from the stain of sin through the fallen senses, for he laid down his pure senses in the offering for sin, and this is all death could demand. Then, if we are in Christ we are dead to the law, for we are "not judged by the law of a carnal commandment, but by the power of an endless life."

The human body he blessed, the contaminating power of the senses he abolished.

The second Adam restored man to a spiritual trinity, which, without the plan of salvation, he never could have attained. When the human senses of Jesus saw His seven attributes retiring from them, and the full cup of sorrow overwhelming them in the agonies of death, they cried, "*Eloi, Eloi, Lama sabachthani*" to the attributes.

This was his great sacrifice for us, and opened up the way, that our human comprehension might behold his exalted mission; but had not the Seven Spirits of God thereby become our intercessors, and, like a halo of glory surrounded us, reproving, inviting, and demanding our attention, we had still refused the man Christ Jesus.

Then, when we look back in the untold eternity of his purposes and witness his archetypal sacrifice for our spiritual nature, and at the appointed cycle of time, his human sacrifice; and contemplate the rapture and glory of that innumerable "Church of the first-born, whose *names* are written in heaven," not on earth, not in sacrifice, in toil and in pain, but in heaven, and that for us they make ready a mansion and will greet us in glory, as those who have tarried at home greet the victorious warrior returning from the field of battle; and hence delight to own us as the blood-washed royalty of him whose regal power transcended the powers of darkness on the battle-field of Judea. Yea, twice washed and thrice welcome. Washed in the archetypal and human fountain opened for sin and uncleanness. What a joy to meet them, and him, and all the dual host of angels who forever await his orders, and will be the exalted servants of the Church of the Most High God.

And will this New Jerusalem descend from the arcana of incandescent light? and will this sanctified host meet us midway as we arise from the slumbers of the grave? And shall we thence be ever with the Lord?

Surely the promises are yea and amen.

Then we shall be like him, "for we shall see him as he is." No more tempest-tossed on the billows of adversity, no longer tempted by the fallen senses, no more to mourn over the losses and crosses of life, but to sing the triumphs of redemption. Lost in the first Adam, saved in the second; slain by the first, but made alive throughout the ages of eternity by the second. Then to the eternal Father be praises, and honor, and triumph, throughout eternity, and to the eternal Word, who offered up himself to honor the law, and to the Seven Spirits of God, the Holy Spirit, who shielded our attributes from the tempter's power, to the triune God, be glory, and power, and dominion forever and ever! Amen.

www.ingramcontent.com/pod-product-compliance
Lightning Source LLC
Chambersburg PA
CBHW030425300426
44112CB00009B/857